The Comic Intermezzo

Studies in Musicology, No. 9

Other Titles in This Series

The Comic Intermezzo

A Study in the History of
Eighteenth-Century
Italian Opera

by
Charles E. Troy

umi
RESEARCH PRESS

Text first published as a typescript facsimile in 1971

Produced and distributed by
University Microfilms International
Ann Arbor, Michigan 48106

Library of Congress Cataloging in Publication Data

Troy, Charles E   1936
    The comic intermezzo.

    (Studies in musicology series ; no. 9)
    Bibliography: p.
    Includes index.
    1. Opera, Italian—History and criticism.   I. Title.
II. Series.

ML1733.3.T76   782.1'0945   79-12295
ISBN 0-8357-0992-2

CONTENTS

CONTENTS

TABLES

MUSICAL EXAMPLES

Example	Source
1. Cesti, *La Dori*, I.iv	I:Vnm, MS Cl. IV, No. 410, fol. 17'.
2. *Il Giustino* (Naples, 1684), III.vii	I:Nc, MS 32.3.32, fol. 201.
3. *Il Giustino* (Naples, 1684), III.vii	I:Nc, MS 32.3.32, fol. 199.
4. *Il Giustino* (Naples, 1684), I.xiv	I:Nc, MS 32.3.32, fol. 88'.
5. A. Scarlatti, *Tito Sempronio Gracco*, comic scene No. 4	D:Dl, MS Mus. 1/F/39,1, fol. 68.
6. G. Aldrovandini, *Cesare in Alessandria*, comic scene No. 4	D:Dl, MS Mus. 1/F/39,1, foll. 185a-185b.
7. (a) *Il Giustino* (Naples, 1684), I.xiv	I:Nc, MS 32.3.32, fol. 85'.
(b) G. Bononcini, *Il trionfo di Camilla*, comic scene No. 1	D:Dl, MS Mus. 1/F/39,2, fol. 3.
8. (a) A. Scarlatti, *Odoardo*, comic scene No. 4	D:Dl, MS Mus. 1/F/39,1, fol. 34.
(b) A. Scarlatti, *L'Emireno*, comic scene no. 6	D:Dl, MS Mus. 1/F/39,2, fol. 43'.
(c) A. Scarlatti, *La caduta de Decemviri*, comic scene No. 6	D:Dl, MS Mus. 1/F/39,2, fol. 97'.
(d) A. Scarlatti, *La caduta de Decemviri*, comic scene No. 4	D:Dl, MS Mus. 1/F/39,2, foll. 91-91'.

MUSICAL EXAMPLES

Example	Source
(e) A. Scarlatti, *La caduta de Decemviri*, comic scene No. 6	D:Dl, MS Mus. 1/F/39, 2, fol. 95.
9. A. Scarlatti, *L'Emireno*, comic scene No. 3	D:Dl, MS Mus. 1/F/39,2, fol. 39b.
10. A. Scarlatti, *Odoardo*, comic scene No. 1	D:Dl, MS Mus. 1/F/39,1, foll. 16-16'.
11. Mancia, *La Partenope*, comic scene No. 4	D:Dl, MS Mus. 1/F/39,2, fol. 221.
12. Mancia, *Tito Manlio*, comic scene No. 5	D:Dl, MS Mus. 1/F/39,2, foll. 175-76.
13. A. Scarlatti, *Il prigioniero fortunato*, comic scene No. 2	D:Dl, MS Mus. 1/F/39,2, foll. 179-79'.
14. A. Scarlatti, *Il pastor di Corinto*, comic scene No. 6	D:Dl, MS Mus. 1/F/39,1, fol. 138.
15. Mancini, Intermezzi of Colombina and Pernicone, part 2	I:Nc, MS 32.2.1, fol. 131.
16. Intermezzi of Pollastrella and Parpagnacco, part 1	D:ROu, MS Mus. saec. XVIII.70²⁴ᵃ, [fol. 1].
17. Sarri, *La furba, e lo sciocco*, part 1	I:Nc, MS 31.3.10, [foll. 76-77'].
18. F. Gasparini, *Nana francese, e Armena*, part 1	D:Dl, MS Mus. 2159/F/5,I, foll. 146-47.
19. Hasse, Intermezzi of Scintilla and Don Tabarano, part 1	I:Rc, MS 2507 (0.II.105), foll. 47-47'.

MUSICAL EXAMPLES

Example	Source
20. Vinci, Intermezzi of Servilia and Flacco, part 3	I:Nc, MS 32.4.10, [foll. 225'-26].
21. Pergolesi, *La serva padrona*, part 1	I:Nc, MS 32.2.29, [foll. 8'-9'].
22. Sarri, Intermezzi of Dorina and Nibbio, part 2	I:Nc, MS 31.3.12, fol. 136'.
23. Sarri, *Arsace*, comic scene No. 1	I:Nc, MS I.6.23, [foll. 52'-53].
24. Sarri, *Arsace*, comic scene No. 1	I:Nc, MS I.6.23, [fol. 54'].
25. Sellitti, *La franchezza delle donne*, part 2	I:Nc, MS 32.4.12, [foll. 209-209'].
26. Orlandini, *Il marito giocatore*, part 3	I:Fc, MS D.239, [foll. 45-45'].
27. Hasse, Intermezzi of Larinda and Vanesio, part 3	I:Rc, MS 2507 (0.II.105), fol. 27'.
28. Caldara, Intermezzi of Pipa and Barlafuso, part 1	A:Wn, MS 17.993, I, [fol. 97].
29. Sarri, Intermezzi of Moschetta and Grullo, (a) part 1 (b) part 2	I:Nc, MS 32.2.24, [fol. 84]. [fol. 161'].
30. Hasse, Intermezzi of Scintilla and Don Tabarano, part 1	I:Rc, MS 2507 (O.II.105), fol. 49'.
31. Mancini, Intermezzi of Colombina and Pernicone, part 2	I:Nc, MS 32.2.1, foll. 127'.

MUSICAL EXAMPLES

Example	**Source**
32. A. Scarlatti, *Tigrane*, comic scene No. 1	I:Nc, MS 31.3.33, foll. 70-70′.
33. Hasse, Intermezzi of Larinda and Vanesio, part 3	I:Rc, MS 2507 (O.II.105), foll. 27′-30.
34. (a) Conti, Intermezzi of Erighetta and Don Chilone, part 1	A:Wn, MS 17.238, I, [foll. 106′-107].
(b) Vinci, Intermezzi of Erighetta and Don Chilone, part 1	I:Nc, MS 32.2.39, fol. 81′.
35. Hasse, Intermezzi of Scintilla and Don Tabarano, part 1	I:Rc, MS 2507 (O.II.105), fol. 42.
36. Orlandini, *Il marito giocatore*, part 1	I:Fc, MS D.239, [foll. 16′-18′].
37. A. Scarlatti, *Scipione nelle Spagne*, comic scene No. 5	I:Bu, MS 646 (Vol. IV), fol. 130′.
38. Hasse, *La serva scaltra overo La moglie a forza*, part 3	I:MC, MS 124-G-29, [fol. 68′].
39. Caldara, Intermezzi of Alisca and Bleso, part 1	A:Wn, MS 17.112, I, [fol. 113].
40. Hasse, *La fantesca*, part 2	I:MC, MS 124-G-28, [fol. 49′].
41. F. Gasparini, Intermezzi of Lisetta and Astrobolo, part 2	I:Rvat, Cod. Barb. lat. 4231, fol. 162.
42. A. Scarlatti, *Scipione nelle Spagne*, comic scene No. 5	I:Bu, MS 646 (Vol. IV), fol. 124.

LIBRARY SIGLA

A:Wn   Vienna, Oesterreichische Nationalbibliothek

B:Bc   Brussels, Bibliothèque du Conservatoire royal de musique

B:Br   Brussels, Bibliothèque royale de Belgique

D:Dl   Dresden, Sächsische Landesbibliothek

D:Mbs   Munich, Bayerische Staatsbibliothek

D:ROu   Rostock, Universitätsbibliothek

D:SW   Schwerin, Mecklenburgische Landesbibliothek

D:WR   Weimar, Thüringische Landesbibliothek

GB:Lbm   London, British Museum

I:Bu   Bologna, Biblioteca universitaria

I:Fc   Florence, Biblioteca del Conservatorio

I:MC   Montecassino, Biblioteca dell'Abbazia

I:Nc   Naples, Biblioteca del Conservatorio S. Pietro a Majella

I:Rc   Rome, Biblioteca Casanatense

I:Rvat   Rome, Biblioteca Apostolica Vaticana

I:Vnm   Venice, Biblioteca nazionale Marciana

PREFACE

Research for the present study was undertaken at a time when the musicological literature included not a single monograph devoted to the eighteenth-century operatic intermezzo. Since then, the genre has begun to acquire a respectable bibliography. Three important contributions need to be cited here, since exigencies of publication did not permit time for incorporating references to them in the following pages; their titles suffice to indicate their respective authors' particular emphases:

> Gordana Lazarevich, "The Role of the Neapolitan Intermezzo in the Evolution of Eighteenth-Century Musical Style: Literary, Symphonic and Dramatic Aspects, 1685-1735" (Columbia University Dissertation, 1970).

> Irène Mamczarz, *Les Intermèdes comiques italiens au XVIIIe siècle en France et en Italie* (Paris, 1972).

> Ortrun Landmann, "Quellenstudien zum *intermezzo comico per musica* und zu seiner Geschichte in Dresden" (Rostock Dissertation, 1972).

I am especially grateful to the last-named writer for her generous sharing of information in areas where our interests overlapped.

So many other individuals made important contributions that it is with a very special sense of obligation that the following few are singled out for their truly indispensable help. First thanks must go to Professor Nino Pirrotta for his invaluable advice, probing criticism, and endless encouragement; his patient guidance extended to every aspect of research and writing. Special gratitude is also due to the following European scholars and librarians whose assistance and friendliness exceeded by far their professional obligation to a visiting researcher: Dr. Anna Mondolfi and Professor Francesco Bosarelli of the Naples Conservatory Library; Dr. Wolfgang Reich of the Sächsische Landesbibliothek in Dresden; Dr. Maria Teresa Muraro of the Instituto

PREFACE

di Lettere, Musica, e Teatro of the Fondazione Giorgio Cini (Venice); and Professor Helmuth Hucke, former director of the Music Division of the German Historical Institute in Rome.

Finally, I gratefully acknowledge financial assistance from the following foundations and institutions that supported the protracted research, collation of material, and writing of the present volume:

> The Woodrow Wilson Foundation
> The Danforth Foundation
> The Italian Fulbright Foundation
> Harvard University
> The Martha Baird Rockefeller Fund for Music

Charles E. Troy
Seattle, Washington

INTRODUCTION

In the world of rapidly changing fashions that was eighteenth-century dramatic music, the *intermezzo per musica* is particularly remarkable for its evanescence. Even Pergolesi's *La serva padrona* (Naples, 1733), perhaps the only one of these little pieces that has maintained a position at least on the fringes of the repertory down to the present day, was saved from oblivion only after its performance at Paris in 1752 made it a rallying point for supporters of Italian musical style there and provoked the famous *Querelle des Bouffons*.[1] As Charles Burney observed with surprise in 1789:

> This charming Music, which all the rest of Europe so much admired, was so little noticed in Italy during its first performance, that the name of the *Serva Padrona*, as an intermezzi [*sic*] set by the celebrated Pergolesi, is not to be found in the last edition of the *Drammaturgia accresciuta e continuata fino al l'anno, 1755!*[2]

Other contemporary chronicles of the eighteenth-century theater are similarly sketchy in their treatment of intermezzi. Gian Carlo Bonlini's catalogue of opera at Venice, for example, mentions performances in that city beginning about 1706, but prefers to "pass over them in silence for the sake of greater brevity."[3] This uncharacteristic virtue on the part of Bonlini and his fellow chroniclers may well be explained in the following remarks by the anonymous eighteenth-century compiler of a two-volume manuscript repertory of Venetian theaters:

> Intermedi are incidental and uncertain adjuncts to operas. They are not printed with them, nor is their title displayed on public posters like that of the operas. They are changed at the whim of their performers, and according to the approval they encounter; therefore, to know about their changes it would be necessary to attend all of [the city's] opera houses every evening. Thus is the difficulty of knowing about them justified by the difficulty of finding them.[4]

These same difficulties seem to have deterred later historians from attempting a study devoted specifically to the operatic intermezzo. Despite its title, Jeffrey Pulver's article "The Intermezzo of the Opera" deals mainly with Renaissance intermedi.[5] When he finally reaches the eighteenth-century, Pulver can only lament that

> it is difficult to quote specimens of the Intermezzo–not because there are so few, but because it is not always easy to tell which were actually used as such. Moreover, in nine out of every ten works on

musical history the name of Pergolesi and that of his "Serva Padrona" overshadow those of all other writers of Intermezzi, so that judging by this circumstance, we might be led to the false conclusion that this composer and this composition of his were the only pertinent ones.[6]

Such is, in fact, the impression one receives from dictionary articles and general histories of music from the time of Burney onward; unfortunately, Pulver does little to correct it. Furthermore, relative neglect of the intermezzo's earlier history when compared to the considerable body of literature generated by the *Querelle des Bouffons* and its aftermath[7] might well lead one to believe that intermezzi achieved popularity only after separation from their natural environment, the entr'actes of Italian *opere serie*, and that even Pergolesi's celebrated little piece was important only as a syringe for the injection of Italian vitality into French music of the later eighteenth century.

Despite their general neglect by chroniclers and historians, however, it is clear from other sources that intermezzi enjoyed an important position in the theater of their own day and country. In the "Instructions for Impresarios" of his satirical *Il teatro alla moda* Benedetto Marcello counsels trust in the intermezzi—along with the prima donna, earthquakes, thunderbolts, and the ubiquitous bear—to overcome any possible shortcomings of the scene painters, tailors, and ballet dancers;[8] and instructs the intermezzo performers themselves to "give unending praise to the singers, the music, the libretto, the extras, the stage sets, the bear, and the earthquake, but . . . attribute the popularity of the theater exclusively to themselves."[9]

Marcello's facetious advice was prophetic; not twenty years after its publication intermezzi seem to have become so popular with the Venetian public as to be an important reason for the decline in variety and quantity of the operas themselves that was reported by the Italian actor and critic Luigi Riccoboni about this time:

> The Undertakers, not willing to run the Risk of Novelty, almost every Year react the Operas which succeeded in the preceding, nay they sometimes act the same Opera two Nights successively; a Practice which disgusts the Spectators, and not a little blemishes the Glory of the *Italian* Theatre, so fertile in Novelty.[10]

According to Antonio Groppo, the spectators, far from being disgusted, were indifferent to this sorry state of affairs. A note for the year 1740 in his manuscript catalogue explains that it is no wonder if new operas have become so rare in recent years and old ones are repeated more frequently than in the past, since at present the operas are paid the least attention. Audiences are attracted only by the ballets and intermedi, and consider the opera, which should be the principal attraction, as an interpolation and relief from the dancers and buffoons.[11]

The popularity of intermezzi in other Italian cities and important foreign centers of operatic production during the first half of the eighteenth century is attested to by the large proportion of opera libretti preserved from this period that contains either the text of an intermezzo or indications that one was to be performed. The latter may consist only of the remark "segue l'intermezzo" at the end of each act, or presence in the list of *personaggi* of two characters who do not appear in the opera itself, with or without the indication "per gli intermezzi." A patient search usually turns up texts for the latter,[12] although "the difficulty of finding them" mentioned by the anonymous Venetian chronicler quoted above is often considerable. Discovery of the libretto for an intermezzo whose performance data (city, theater, date, season, etc.)[13] match that of the opera in question is often the only means of establishing that the two were performed together—a matter of some importance, since there exists a considerable number of libretti for eighteenth-century intermezzi that were connected with theatrical genres other than opera.

Even intermezzo texts printed together with those of operas are not always easy to find. Frequently untitled, they may be inserted part by part at points in the libretto where they were to be performed—not always between the acts—and are therefore typographically indistinguishable from other scenes of the opera. Before 1722 the intermezzi of Neapolitan operas were practically always printed in this fashion, a circumstance that perhaps explains why Francesco Florimo's catalogue of opera at Naples makes no mention of them until this date.[14]

A final difficulty concerns terminology. Besides "intermezzo" and its numerous variant spellings, these pieces appear under a variety of designations, including "divertimenti musicali," "scherzo musicale," "contrascena," and "farsa in musica." Moreover, the form "intermedio," more common to the seventeenth century, is by no means unusual in libretti printed after 1700. Often used interchangeably with "intermezzo,"[15] it may be found in the libretto of a Venetian opera performed as late as 1746.[16]

More significant than the persistence of the term is the occasional appearance in the eighteenth century of the allegorical intermedio itself, containing the deities and machines usually associated with seventeenth-century Venetian opera. Such anachronisms were generally confined to provinicial theaters, presumably more conservative than those of the principal centers of operatic production,[17] or else performed with dramatic pieces in celebration of important social events for which the allegorical possibilities and scenic splendor of the seventeenth-century intermedio were probably considered more appropriate than the low buffoonery of comic intermezzi.[18]

One occasionally finds allegorical intermedi with machines in operas performed after 1700 even in the public theaters of larger Italian cities. A setting of Grazio Braccioli's *La costanza in cimento con la crudeltà* by Floriano Aresti (Venice, 1712) contains two such pieces; typically, both introduced ballets, which constituted the principal diversion of each entr'acte. The vocal portions of both intermedi consist of a recitative and aria sung by a single character (Virtue in the first and Pallas in the second) urging his followers to join in the dance. As late as 1747, similar *introduzioni ai balli* were employed between the acts of the anonymous pasticcio *Ernelinda*, performed that year in Bologna's Teatro Formagliari. Machines described in the libretto represented the descent of Venus in a car drawn by doves, and the transformation of a mountain into a garden from which dancers emerged to perform the ballet.

By the first decade of the eighteenth century, however, the new comic intermezzo had largely supplanted the older intermedio in the important operatic centers of Italy. At Naples, comic intermezzi replaced the more appropriate allegorical intermedi even in some court entertainments shortly after 1700. Between the two cantatas composed by Alessandro Scarlatti for the queen's birthday celebrations in the Royal Palace on August 28, 1709, for example, two comic servants, Violetta and Nardo, burlesqued the august occasion with slapstick jibes at the ruler herself:

> *Vio.* .... E come mai si chiama
> Questa Signora, a cui si fà tal Festa?
> *Nar.* Si chiama.... or te lo dico.... oh Dio, che testa!
> *Vio.* Come non te 'l ricordi?
> *Nar.* Si chiama.... (io lo sapevo)
> Così, come dicevo,
> Si chia.... tù non lo sai?
> *Vio.* Signor mio nò.[19]

> (*Vio.* . . . And what is the name
> of the lady who's the object of these festivities?
> *Nar.* Her name is—I'll tell you in a minute—Heavens,
> what a memory!

Vio. What? You don't remember it?
Nar. Her na—(I knew it)
Well, as I was saying.
Her na—You don't know it?
Vio. No, my lord.)

Not even the sacred operas written for Naples' conservatories around the beginning of the century were immune to the typically Neapolitan desire for a little "innocent merriment." Like many of them, Leonardo Leo's first dramatic composition, *L'infedeltà abbattuta*, performed at the Conservatorio dei Turchini in 1712, includes two characters, a page and an old woman servant, whose scenes at the end of each act functioned as comic intermezzi in an otherwise gravely pious work.

Preference for comic subjects also extended to the musical intermezzi performed in the prose theater of the eighteenth century,[20] but these pieces, although superficially similar to their operatic counterparts, differ from them in at least one important respect. Antonio Groppo calls the latter *intermezzi dramatici* because of their association with operas (*drammi* [*per musica*]), reserving the term *intermezzi comici* to denote those performed with plays (*commedie*).[21] This terminology, although somewhat confusing to readers of English, will serve to distinguish the two types while they are compared.

Venice seems to have been the center for performance of musical intermezzi between the acts of plays during the first four decades of the eighteenth century. Carlo Goldoni credits Giuseppe Imer, director of the players at the Teatro S. Samuele with their introduction there around 1734,[22] but according to Groppo's catalogue and a manuscript libretto preserved in the Biblioteca Marciana, one was sung in that theater as early as 1707 or the previous year.[23] Libretti for performances of *intermezzi comici* in Venice have also survived from the years 1711, 1722 through 1727, and 1733.[24]

Imer, then, merely continued a tradition that itself was probably derived from that of the *intermezzo dramatico*. With its simple plot, division into two or three short parts, and reliance on three singing roles at most, the early *intermezzo comico* appears to have been modelled directly on the contemporary operatic intermezzo. Goldoni, in fact, implies that Imer's wish was merely to transplant the latter from Venetian opera houses, where they had fallen into temporary disfavor, onto the stage of the city's playhouse.[25]

Whatever their original connection may have been, the later fortunes of the *intermezzo comico* and *intermezzo dramatico* were quite different; indeed, from the very beginning, their repertories were mutually exclusive. This dichotomy probably resulted from the nature of their respective performers. Imer's troupe, and most likely those of his predecessors at the Teatro S. Samuele, consisted of actors whose musical accomplishments were secondary to their dramatic abilities. According to Goldoni, the two female intermezzo singers "knew not a note of music,"[26] and Imer himself, although

> a very comic and picturesque performer in the intermezzi . . . knew nothing of music, but sang passably, . . . learned his part by ear, . . . and compensated for his shortcomings in learning and voice by personal skill, caricatures of costumes, and knowledge of the characters he played so well.[27]

The performers of the *intermezzo dramatico*, on the other hand, were professional singers. As we shall see, many of them occupied positions in the musical establishments of noble courts, and almost all had considerable operatic experience before devoting themselves to their specialty. It is hardly likely, therefore, that music composed for the *intermezzo dramatico* could have been sung by the *comici*, or that singers of the operatic intermezzo would have performed pieces composed for actors. During the period of their coexistence, *intermezzi comici* seem never to have been used in opera houses, and only exceptionally does one find pieces from the repertory of the *intermezzo dramatico* performed with plays; in all such cases, the participants were professional singers from the opera, not actors from the theater.

By about 1750, ballet interludes had almost completely supplanted performances of *intermezzi dramatici* between the acts of operas, but *intermezzi comici* continued to flourish for almost fifty more years in the playhouses of Europe. During the second half of the century they were especially popular in Rome; Ugo Sesini's catalogue alone records libretti for almost 150 examples performed there in this period.[28] After 1775 these intermezzi, or *farsette in musica*, as they were sometimes called, outnumbered full-length *opere buffe* on the Roman stage.[29]

In many respects, an *intermezzo comico* of this period can itself be considered a comic opera in miniature. After about 1760, a gradual increase in the number of characters permitted plots that were more complex—although hardly more varied—than those of earlier examples.[30] More importantly, ensembles and concerted finales with as many as seven participants became possible. It was also about this time that libretti began to indicate the participation of professional singers in intermezzi performed with plays.[31]

Except for length and function, then, these pieces differ little from contemporary *opere buffe*; many of them, in fact, were simply versions of full-length comic operas shortened to fit between the acts of a play and reduced to fit the number of available singers. *Dal finto il vero*, a *farsetta* in two parts with five characters performed in Rome's Teatro Tordinona between the acts of the second play of carnival, 1777, for example, was a reduction of Paisiello's three-act *opera buffa* of the same title originally composed for a cast of eight at Naples the previous year.[32]

Clearly, dramatic pieces called "intermezzi" or designed to serve as such comprised a wide variety of types during the eighteenth century, even if we omit from consideration the choruses, cantatas, stage battles, scenic transformations, pantomimes, *commedia dell'arte* plays, and ballets that also figured as intermezzi in operas of this period. The comic intermezzo in eighteenth-century *opera seria* is distinguished from these other types by its distinctive function, character, and repertory. It is to this repertory—its origin, diffusion, performers, composers, text, and music—that the following pages will be devoted.

ORIGIN AND EARLY STAGES

The history of orchestral music furnishes a useful analogy to illustrate the relationship between intermezzi of the eighteenth century and their seventeenth-century precursors. The Classical symphony, although it continued a tradition of independent instrumental ensemble music represented in the Baroque by the orchestral concerto, did not evolve directly from the latter; rather, it had for its chief formal and stylistic model the Italian opera *sinfonia*. Similarly, the eighteenth-century intermezzo carried on a well established operatic tradition, but its structure and content were shaped largely by comic scenes from operas of the preceding century, not their intermedi. Let us first see how the element of comedy came to be associated with the intermezzo tradition, and then consider the dramatic and musical characteristics of the scenes on which the eighteenth-century type was modelled.

The Seventeenth-Century Operatic Intermedio

It is only natural that musical intermedi, which had frequently served to articulate the acts of Renaissance plays, were adopted to fill a similar function in dramatic works written in the new *stile rappresentativo* of the early seventeenth century. The preface of Cavalieri's *Rappresentatione di anima, e di corpo* (Rome, 1600), suggests that

> when the composition is divided into three acts, which previous experience has shown to suffice, four scenic intermedi may be added, distributed so that the first is before the prologue, and each of the others comes at the end of its act, observing the following disposition: backstage a full ensemble of music and harmonious symphony of instruments should perform, to the sound of which the movements of the intermedi are coordinated, taking care that there is no need of recitation, as when, for example, the Giants are represented as wishing to do battle with Jove. And in each one of the intermedi changes of scene could be made that pertain to its occasion; it should be noted that descents of clouds are impossible, since their motion could not be coordinated with that of the music, as it would be if morescas or other dances were used.[1]

Cavalieri's rather vague instructions hardly describe a "form" in either the musical or dramatic sense of the term. Like their Renaissance predecessors, intermedi in early opera were simply entr'acte entertainments that might employ instrumental and/or vocal music either alone (*intermedi non apparenti*) or in combination with the representation of allegorical personages and deities, stage battles, scenic transformations, and ballets (*intermedi apparenti*).[2] Only the latter two elements will claim our attention here, for it was in connection with the dances and stage machines of the intermedio that comic characters from the opera first appeared at the ends of acts, preparing the way for appearance there—in quite a different context—as the intermezzo's principal attraction.

Ballets assumed an important place early in the history of the operatic intermezzo. Choral dances functioned as intermedi (although they were not so called) at the ends of acts one and three in Domenico Mazzocchi's *La catena d'Adone* (Rome, 1626),[3] while "each act" of Marco da Gagliano's *La Flora* (Florence, 1628), "concluded with a marvelous ballet performed by the most noble gentlemen of the Tuscan court."[4] And ballets figured among the "vaghissimi intermedii" praised so highly in contemporary accounts of Rospigliosi's *La vita di Santa Teodora*, performed at Rome's Teatro Barberini in 1636.[5]

Dances were also a common type of intermedio in the public opera houses of Venice, beginning in 1637 with the inaugural performance at the Teatro San Cassiano. From the preface describing the production of Francesco Manelli's *L'Andromeda* we learn that "at the end of the [first] act a madrigal was first sung backstage by several voices in concert with various instruments, and for the intermedio three very handsome youths came out dressed as Cupids to perform a most graceful dance."[6] For the second intermedio, "twelve savages emerged to do a most extravagant and savory dance of movements and gestures."[7]

Extravagance began to predominate over taste in Venetian opera ballets as the century progressed. Dancers in the second intermedio of *La finta savia*, performed at the Teatro SS. Giovanni e Paolo in 1643, represented priestesses of the god Pan; they came onstage "half naked, covered only by a large, lynxlike wolfskin, armed with a bow, wearing a headdress resembling the head of a wolf, and carrying a lighted torch . . . intertwining them in a most beautiful fashion."[8]

The presence of such fantastic creatures onstage at the end of an act was occasionally a logical outcome of the opera's plot, but more often ballets of the intermedi were unrelated to the preceding action, or even foreign to the drama as a whole. In such cases, librettists frequently attempted to justify them with quasi-dramatic introductory scenes sung by the allegorical personages or deities of the opera. The ballet concluding the first intermedio of Manelli's *L'Alcate* (1642), for example, was introduced by Jove, who sang a "canzonetta" inviting:

Soldati
Guerrieri
Che armati
Che fieri
La morte sprezzate
Hor l'armi lasciate
E festosi
E gioiosi
Danzate[9]

(Soldiers and warriors, who, armed and proud, scorn death, lay down
your weapons; dance jubilantly and joyously.)

His function fulfilled with the arrival of the dancers, the deity made his
exit on a machine, remarking:

Dei vincitori ecco leggiadro un stuolo
Già preparato al ballo, io parto à uolo.[10]

(Here's a comely troop of victors all ready to dance; I'll fly away.)

Beginning about the middle of the seventeenth century, the task
of introducing the dances of the intermedio was gradually taken over by
the opera's comic servants. Their assumption of this function may have
resulted from a lessening importance of allegorical personages and deities
in Venetian opera, an increased emphasis on comic elements, the
frequently grotesque nature of the dances themselves, or a combination
of these factors.

Whatever the reason, Jove and his mythological colleagues
gradually relinquished their duties at the ends of acts to worthies such as
Cleonte, the court jester of Daniele Castrovillari's setting of Pietro
Angelo Zaguri's *Gl'avvenimenti d'Orinda* (1659). In the penultimate scene
of act two, Cleonte calls together a group of hunchbacks, explaining that
they must practice their part in the forthcoming royal wedding. The
scene changes to a courtyard, where the jester leads his troop in a
"rehearsal" that concludes the act with a grotesque ballet:

Sù Sù Gobbi malfatti
Se la mancia bramate,
Per far proua di voi, hora danzate.
Troppo vi pesa il dorso,
E per terra tentate in van scherzare,
Perche natura vuole
Che chi nacque Delfin, viua nel Mare.
Tù con troppa lentezza il passo giri,

E tu folle non vedi,
Che troppo torci i piedi
A tè se più non sali,
Io farò far à fè salti Mortali.[11]

(Come on, misshapen hunchbacks; if you want a tip [at the wedding], try your mettle now by dancing. Your backs weigh too much, and trying to sport on land is futile because nature intends someone born a dolphin to live in the sea. You there: you're twirling too slowly—and you: lunatic, don't you see you're twisting your foot too much? And you: if you don't jump higher, I swear I'll make you do a somersault!)

Ballet introductions by the comic characters sometimes included a touch of the supernatural, perhaps to compensate for absence of the mythological beings and deities from the intermedio. At the end of act two of Cavalli's *L'Erismena* (Venice, 1655), Clerio, left alone on stage, is

drawn by curiosity to open a book given to him by a court sorcerer to take to his master, Idraspe. He has scarcely opened it when several statues in the gallery begin to move, at the sight of which he runs off terrified, and the latter join in a dance to conclude the second act.[12]

Edward Dent, quoting from the libretto for the Naples, 1686, performance of Alessandro Scarlatti's *Clearco in Negroponte*, describes the much more elaborate comic pantomime of Filocla, an old woman associated with the ballet at the end of the opera's second act:

A pavilion rises from a trap, . . . and *Filocla*, believing it to be occupied by a young man on whom she has fixed her affections, "goes to open the pavilion, from which comes forth a phantom, and *Filocla* wishing to escape from one of the wings, there appears a Moor, and the same thing follows at the others [i.e. she tries to escape at each exit in turn, and on each occasion another Moor appears]. Finally, she hides in the pavilion, whence she peeps out, while the said Moors dance with the phantom. *Filocla*, after the dance is finished, thinks they have gone away, and comes out. The phantom, who is hidden, takes hold of her by the dress; she tries to escape, leaves her dress behind, and runs away. The phantom follows her."[13]

Just as the comic servants inherited the function of introducing the entr'acte ballets from the allegorical personages and deities of seventeenth-century opera, they also sometimes took their places on the machines that effected the descents, ascents, and transformations of the intermedio. A favorite device was the *volo*, or flight, in which the comic character was lifted bodily from the stage—often unwillingly.   An example appears as early as Cavalli's *La virtù de' strali d'amore* (Venice, 1642); by the end of the century the device had been elaborated to comprise whole dramatic episodes, such as the adventures of Bleso, servant of Ulysses in Carlo Francesco Pollaroli's setting of Aurelio Aureli's *Circe abbandonata da Ulisse* (Venice, 1697).   Entering Circe's underground study in search of the sorceress at the end of act one, Bleso finds instead a magic book on a table.   "He opens the book, and in so doing, the table is transformed into a car drawn by three hellish dragons and many demons come out from the walls of the room."[14]   Seeking to escape the latter, he jumps into the car, urges the dragons upward, "flies into the air on the car, and a ballet of infernal spirits follows."[15]

In another type of association between the comic characters and intermedi, the former appear on stage at the ends of acts to witness—and be terrified—by the scenic spectacles of the latter.   During the final scene of the first act of Antonio Sartorio's *La prosperità di Elio Seiano* (Venice, 1667) the comic page and old woman view in terror what appears to be a fiery mountain.   As the flames descend toward the frightened couple, they are seen to be produced by firebrands held by eight dancers, who conclude the act with the customary ballet.[16]   Later variations on this theme expose the comic characters to all manner of spectacular transformations, sometimes themselves comic in nature.[17]

By the end of the seventeenth century, association of the comic characters with the machines and dances of the intermedi seems to have become commonplace—indeed, necessary.   Intermezzi described in the libretto for a performance of Giovanni Domenico Partenio's setting of Matteo Noris' *Il Flavio Cuniberto* at Rome in 1696 consist of "trasformationi e volo" with the participation of the opera's two comic servants, Zelta and Bleso.   At the end of the first act they appear "exhibiting several ludicrous objects from a box, including a book for finding buried treasure, and several petticoats, which turn into damsels who present Bleso with various gifts, and form a ballet."[18]   Later, at the end of the second act

> the comic charactes come with the book for finding the treasure, and discover a golden statue.   Bleso, thinking to clasp the statue and carry it away, finds himself astride a donkey, which sprouts wings and flies off with him.[19]

A mock-apologetic note addressed to the "courteous reader" of the libretto explains that "if you do not find that liveliness to which your spirit is accustomed in the *contrascene* of the comic parts, it will be easy for you to forgive, if you consider them *obligatory, and almost always dependent upon the operation of the intermedi.*"[20] (italics added)

Although the foregoing establishes a strong link between the comic characters and intermedi of seventeenth-century opera, it is still difficult to see how a piece such as Pergolesi's *La serva padrona* could have evolved from ballet introductions or scenic transformations. As has already been suggested, the eighteenth-century comic intermezzo did, in fact, draw its form from quite a different quarter. A particular type of comic scene which, although it seldom appeared between the acts of an opera in the seventeenth century, clearly furnished the musical and dramatic model for the eighteenth-century intermezzo. It is to this type of comic scene that we must now turn our attention.

The *Scena Buffa* in Seventeenth-Century Opera

Comic episodes in the midst of a serious opera were introduced by Roman composers early in the seventeenth century. One of the first examples is the drinking song of Charon in Stefano Landi's *La morte d'Orfeo* (1619); its cheerful text and tuneful melody were presumably meant to mitigate both the underworld gloom and *tedio del recitativo* of the opera's fifth act. Similarly, the antics and duet of the comic pages Martio and Curtio served to enliven both the action and music of Landi's *Sant'Alessio* (1632).[21] Comic characters also figured in early Venetian operas; Iro, the ridiculous servant of Monteverdi's *Il ritorno d'Ulisse in patria* (1641) is a familiar example.[22]

The first comic scenes definitely recognizable as forerunners of the eighteenth-century comic intermezzo, however, do not appear regularly in Venetian opera until around the middle of the century, when librettists began to provide comic relief in the form of episodes between two of the opera's stock characters, a young manservant or pageboy, and a lascivious old nurse.[23] The "plot" of these scenes invariably concerns the vigorous attempts of the old nurse to ensnare the manservant in matrimony, and his equally vigorous efforts to repulse her advances. Anna Amalie Abert has traced the stock figure of the old nurse to the Spanish theater,[24] while Hellmuth Christian Wolff claimed the *commedia dell'arte* as her source.[25] Whatever the genre of spoken drama from which this character was adapted, operatic treatment emphasized the grotesque humor already inherent in the role by assigning it to a tenor. When a pageboy (a female part) happened to be cast opposite the old nurse, the ultimate was attained in seventeenth-century operatic travesty: an old hag, played by a man, attempting to seduce a woman impersonating a boy.

An example from the Venice, 1663, version of Apolloni's *La Dori*, first performed with music of Antonio Cesti at Florence in 1661, will serve to illustrate the kind of stereotyped situation comedy that frequently formed a subplot in Venetian opera between about 1650 and 1670. In scene four of the first act, Dirce, an old nurse, attempts to force her attentions on Golo, servant of Dori's brother.[26] The whole episode is compounded of coarse humor and parody of the extravagant imagery common to Venetian libretti of the period. When Golo's rebuffs go unacknowledged, he accuses Dirce of being deaf and half blind. She replies in the operatic language of an amorous heroine:

> Son cieca è ver son cieca
> Vinta da tuoi bei lumi Idolo bello;
> E de' tuoi bacci ingorda
> Alle pene di tanti
> Miei lacrimosi Amanti, anco son sorda,...[27]

(I'm blind—it's true—I'm blind. Vanquished by the beauty of your eyes and greedy for your kisses, my handsome idol. I am also deaf to the anguish of my many tearful lovers.)

This fails to move him, and the toothless old hag becomes enraged:

> *Dir.* Voglio cauarti 'l cor
> *Gol.* Co' denti forse?[28]

(*Dir.* I'd like to tear out your heart! *Gol.* With your teeth, perhaps?)

The scene concludes with a rapid-fire exchange of insults unworthy of translation that culminates in threats of a mutual thrashing with fists and a club:

> *Gol.* Che Vecchia maledetta.
> *Dir.* Che Buffone insolente.
> *Gol.* Perfida.
> *Dir.* Dispettoso.
> *Gol.* Arrogante.
> *Dir.* Furfante.
> *Gol.* Empia.
> *Dir.* Vittuperoso.
> *Gol.* Maliarda.
> *Dir.* Spione.
> *Gol.* Adoprerò le mani.
> *Dir.* Et io 'l bastone.

A striking feature of this scene is the gradual acceleration of dialogue, ending with the rapid repartee quoted above. Placement of this realistic exchange of insults at the end of the scene foreshadows the most common climactic device of the eighteenth-century comic intermezzo: a concluding duet in which two characters express a conflict of interests—almost always of an amorous nature—in a musical quarrel.

Certain elements in Cesti's music for this scene also foreshadow the later comic intermezzo. Large portions of the text are set in closed forms, including Dirce's extravagant protestation of love quoted above, and Golo answers her with a tuneful canzonetta ("T'intendo, si t'intendo") in which are present features of a style that was to become the staple of eighteenth-century *buffo* arias: a vocal line characterized by rapid, disjunct motion, wide range, and frequent repetition of short motives (Example 1). After this, the recitative that concludes the scene is something of a musical anticlimax; it remained for operatic composers of the late seventeenth century to solve the problem of setting an argument to music.

Example 1
Cesti, *La Dori*, Act I, scene 4

Around 1670 comic scenes of the type just described began to disappear from Venetian libretti, but they continued to figure occasionally in operas performed in other Italian cities, particularly Naples, where they seem to have been especially popular. Revivals and new settings there of libretti first composed for Venice after 1670 frequently added comic scenes between the now familiar old nurse and manservant that were lacking in the Venetian originals (see Table 1).

Three comic scenes from the score of the Neapolitan version of Giovanni Legrenzi's *Giustino*[29] show that more than twenty years of operatic treatment had embroidered, but not significantly altered the kind of stereotyped situation comedy we have just observed in Cesti's *La Dori*. The old woman and manservant (here a pageboy) are called Gelidia and Brillo, but their kinship with Dirce and Golo is manifest in the coarse humor, insults, and threats of a clubbing that continue to characterize

TABLE 1

SOME REVIVALS AND NEW SETTINGS OF VENETIAN LIBRETTI AT NAPLES, *CA.* 1670-1685

Librettist	Title of Venetian Version	Performed in Venice	Naples Performance with *Scene Buffe*
Niccolò Beregani	*L'Heraclio*	1671	1673
Aurelio Aureli	*Claudio Cesare*	1672	1676
Giacomo Francesco Bussani	*Giulio Cesare in Egitto*	1672	1680
G.F. Bussani	*Massenzio*	1673	1674
Matteo Noris	*Galieno*	1676	1685
Niccolò Beregani	*Giustino*	1683	1684
Antonio Arcoleo	*Clearco in Negroponte*	1685	1686

their grotesque relationship. Even the motif of the old woman's toothlessness reappears, this time in an exchange that plumbs the lower depths of bad taste:

> *Bri.* Tanti in bocca non hai
> *Gel.* Senza scogli in un mar navigherai
>
> (*Bri.* You don't have very many [teeth] in your mouth.
> *Gel.* You'll sail in a sea without reefs!)

As might be expected from their respective dates, one of the chief differences between the *Dori* and *Giustino* comic scenes is a clearer separation of the latter's set pieces into "numbers" with well defined musical forms. Like many of the serious scenes of *Il Giustino*, the *scene buffe* consist of several such numbers separated by recitatives, as in the one that forms scene seven of the opera's third act:

Aria (Brillo)
Recitative
Aria (Gelidia)
Recitative
Aria (Gelidia)
Recitative
Duet

In contrast to most of the arias sung by the opera's serious characters, however, those of the comic servants are short and lack extended coloratura passages. All are in simple ternary form, but in only one is the repeat of the "A" section exact enough to permit the copyist use of the direction "da capo." Most fall into one of two stylistic categories that were to figure prominently in the eighteenth-century intermezzo: (1) the *buffo* type, already seen in the example quoted above from Cesti's *La Dori*, with the vocal line now supported by an active and tonally oriented bass line (Example 2); and (2) a mock-pathetic type, employed here in Gelidia's two laments, and characterized by use of the minor mode, touches of chromaticism, and expressive appoggiaturas (Example 3).

Example 2
Il Giustino (Naples, 1684), Act III, scene 7

Four of the opera's six duets occur in the comic scenes; two of the latter end in duets. Three of the comic duets are little more than arias whose melodies are either divided between the two singers or sung in parallel thirds; none of the three evidences much of an attempt by the composer to differentiate musically the usually contrasting sentiments of the texts sung by the two characters. Most disappointing in this respect

Example 3
Il Giustino (Naples, 1684), Act III, scene 7

is the duet that concludes the third-act scene, in which the comic servants never sing together, and only a shift of mode from major to minor portrays the note of unresolved conflict on which the little story ends:

> *Bri.* O vecchiarda maledetta
>   Il mio cor mai non t'amò.
> *Gel.* Fa Cupido la vendetta
>   Del crudel che m'inganno.
>
> (*Bri.* Cursed old woman, my heart
>   never belonged to you.
> *Gel.* May Cupid take vengeance on the
>   heartless one who has wronged me.)

More forward-looking is the concluding duet of the first comic scene. Gelidia has fallen to the ground in an effort to club Brillo, who rejects her pleas for help in regaining her feet. In the ensuing duet there seems to be some effort to reflect this dramatic conflict between the two characters by a thematic contrast in their opening motives; moreover, there appears a snatch of the "short vigorous phrases tossed from one voice to another," which, according to Edward Dent, characterized the comic duets of Alessandro Scarlatti after about 1693[30] (Example 4).

Such treatment also foreshadows that of duets in the eighteenth-century comic intermezzo; indeed, by around 1685 practically all of the intermezzo's formal and stylistic elements are already present in embryo. Lacking only are a change in dramatis personae to permit plots more varied than those possible with the rigidly stereotyped old nurse, and separation of the comic scenes from their connection with the opera that

Example 4
Il Giustino (Naples, 1684), Act I, scene 14

nurtured them. The first of these developments seems to have occurred at Naples around the turn of the century, the second at Venice shortly thereafter.

The Turn of the Century

Six versions of Matteo Noris' *Tito Manlio*, first performed at the Villa di Pratolino near Florence with music of Carlo Francesco Pollaroli in 1696, illustrate the fortunes of a libretto around this time. In revivals at Venice (1697), Ferrara (1698), and Verona (1699), the opera text preserved much the same form as its original version, which included only one comic servant, Lindo (called "Breno" in most subsequent libretti). For the Naples (1698) and Turin (1703) performances, however, the character of an old woman, Alcea ("Zelta" in the Neapolitan version), was added, together with the now thrice-familiar scenes between her and the comic manservant.

An anonymous note to the reader of the Turin libretto poetically explains the very practical reason for these, and other additions:

> The present drama . . . from the famous pen of Signor Noris, . . .
> always received with utmost applause in Italy's most eminent

theaters, could not help being subjected to some incidental changes each time it has been performed. A garment, no matter how excellent, or how skilled its maker, must endure some slight trimming and sewing when it has to clothe more than one person; this is not because of any shortcomings on the part of its maker, but due to the necessity of its fitting more than one figure. In this case, the parts of Fausta and Alcea have been added merely to accommodate the number of singers available.[31]

The *type* of singer available also appears to have been a consideration. Cast lists, now included regularly in libretti for the first time, show that certain singers now—if not before—had begun to specialize in comic roles. The part of Alcea in both the Naples and Turin performances of *Tito Manlio* was sung by Antonio Predieri, who seems to have made a career playing the comic old nurse in Naples' Teatro San Bartolomeo and other Italian opera houses around the turn of the century.[32]

Music for a considerable number of comic scenes from this period has been conveniently preserved in two large manuscript volumes at the Sächsische Landesbibliothek in Dresden.[33] Containing 89 complete scenes and eight individual arias from 18 operas, the collection includes music by Alessandro Scarlatti, Giuseppe Aldrovandini, Giovanni Bononcini, Francesco Gasparini, Luigi Mancia, and Severo Antonio de Luca. The importance of these manuscripts for the history of the comic intermezzo was recognized at least as early as 1867;[34] more recently they have served as the basis for an unpublished dissertation by Hanns Nietan, "Die Buffoszenen der spätvenezianischen Oper 1680-1710: Ein Beitrag zur Geschichte der komischen Oper" (Halle, 1924).

Nietan's title suggests Venice was the provenance of the operas from which the comic scenes of the Dresden collection are excerpted; the author was convinced they were that city's contribution to the history of operatic *Buffokunst*, and that the manuscripts may even have been copied there for use at the Saxon court.[35] When he attempted to trace the source of the operas themselves, however, Nietan was forced to admit that none of them received its first performance at Venice. His otherwise inexplicable persistence in assigning a Venetian origin to their comic scenes is evidently based upon an assumption that all seventeenth-century opera belonged to a "Venetian School"—superseded, of course, by a "Neapolitan School" of the eighteenth century. Unfortunately, Nietan's misapprehension has led later writers to allot Venice a role it never played in the development of comic opera.[36]

Misleading also are the title's dates, "1680-1710"; they represent merely "das spätvenezianischen Periode" of opera. According to Nietan, the comic scenes of the Dresden collection were taken from operas composed between 1696 and 1710 for Naples, Rome, and Vienna. Neapolitan libretti unknown to Nietan, however, exist for the operas he assigns to the latter two cities; all were performed at Naples between 1696 and 1702 (see Table 2). The close concordance between these Neapolitan libretti and texts of the Dresden *scene buffe* strongly suggest that if the latter were copied in any single Italian city, it was Naples. One thing is certain: these comic scenes do not reflect a Venetian usage. Many of the operas mentioned in the manuscript were never performed there, and those that were lacked comic scenes of the type it contains.[37]

The Dresden manuscript preserves examples of the *scena buffa* at a point in its evolution where it becomes appropriate to designate as intermezzi the scenes themselves, rather than the transformations and dances that occasionally continued to be associated with them. Although the term intermezzo seldom appears with this meaning in libretti and scores at the turn of the century,[38] scattered references make it plain that they were so considered, at least in retrospect. An anonymous note to the reader that prefaces the libretto for the revival of Silvio Stampiglia's *La Partenope* at Venice in 1707, for example, states that the text has been little changed from the original version first performed at Naples in 1699, except for omission of the latter's intermezzi.[39] Comparison of the two versions reveals that it is the character of the female comic servant Anfrisa and the scenes with her male counterpart Beltramme that are lacking in the Venetian print. These scenes (preserved in Vol. II of the Dresden manuscript) then, must be the intermezzi to which the Venetian libretto refers. If not among the earliest comic intermezzi, they and the other scenes of the collection at least represent a penultimate stage in the latter's development from the comic scenes of seventeenth-century opera.

The most important element in this development is a radical change in the scenes' dramatis personae. Although the lascivious old woman and her young male prey still figure in some,[40] a majority present two quite different character types: an old man and a young, beautiful girl.[41] The presence of a soubrette, of course, makes possible more varied and "realistic" plots in which it is the man who pursues the girl with amorous intent. The first substantial number of such comic scenes appears in Neapolitan libretti around the turn of the century. Naples also seems to have been the first city where women regularly sang the female comic roles in operas; the practice dates from 1699, when the name Livia Nannini "detta la Polacchina" first appears in the cast lists of libretti for operas performed at the Teatro San Bartolomeo.[42]

Another important element in the intermezzo's development from the comic scenes of seventeenth-century opera observable in *scene*

TABLE 2
CONTENTS OF DRESDEN, SACHSISCHE LANDESBIBLIOTHEK
MS 1/F/39, 1-2, VOLUME I

Comic Roles	No. of Comic Scenes	Folios	Title of Opera	Composer	Performed at Naples
Tisbe and Brenno	2[a]	1-12 '	Gl'inganni felici	Alessandro Scarlatti	1699
Lesbina and Adolfo	5	13-40	Odoardo	Alessandro Scarlatti	1700
Eurilla and Nesso	2[b]	41-46	La Semiramide	Giuseppe Aldrovandini	1702
Dorilla and Bireno	6	47-77 '	Tito Sempronio Gracco	Alessandro Scarlatti	1702
Livio and Alfeo	5	79-109	L'Eraclea	Alessandro Scarlatti	1700
Serpilla and Serpollo	6	111-146 '	Il pastor di Corinto	Alessandro Scarlatti	1701
Selvaggia and Dameta	4	147-164	Dafni	Alessandro Scarlatti	1700
Mirena and Floro	5	165-200	Cesare in Alessandria	Giuseppe Aldrovandini	1699

[a] An incomplete third scene is crossed out in the MS.

[b] The beginning of scene 2 is missing from the MS.

TABLE 2—Continued

CONTENTS OF DRESDEN, SACHSISCHE LANDESBIBLIOTHEK, MS 1/F/39, 1-2, VOLUME II

Comic Roles	No. of Comic Scenes	Folios	Title of Opera	Composer	Performed at Naples
Tullia and Linco	5	1-30	Il trionfo di Camilla	Gio[vanni] Bononcini	1696
Niceta and Morasso[a]	7[b]	30-48'	L'Emireno	Alessandro Scarlatti	1697
Lidia and Gilbo	4	49-71'	L'Aiace	Fran[ces]co Gasparini	1697
Servilia and Flacco	6	72-98	La caduta de Decemviri	Alessandro Scarlatti	1697
Lesbina and Milo	7[c]	98-122'	Il Mutio Scevola	[Giovanni?] Bononcini	1698
Filandra and Selvino	6	123-149	La donna ancora è fedele	Alessandro Scarlatti	1698
Zelta and Breno	5	149'-176	Tito Manlio	Luigi Mancia	1698
Lucilla and Delbo	7	176'-202	Il prigioniero fortunato	Alessandro Scarlatti	1698
Anfrisa and Beltramme	4	203-226'	La Partenope	Luigi Mancia	1699
Dircea and Pindoro	3	227-238'	Creonte tiranno di Tebe	Severo de Luca	1699

[a] A third character, Trasillo, sings briefly in the second complete scene.
[b] And 5 individual arias.
[c] And 3 individual arias.

buffe of the Dresden collection concerns the relationship of comic characters to the traditional intermedio ballet. The second comic scene of Scarlatti's *Odoardo*, for example, serves to introduce the ballet at the end of the opera's second act in quite a different fashion from that we have observed in seventeenth-century examples. Lesbina, a pretty, young gold digger, feigns romantic interest in Adolfo to extract as much money as possible from the old man in exchange for her favors, but a troupe of crippled beggars constantly interrupts their "love" duet. They exit, and the beggars execute a grotesque ballet, after which Lesbina returns in search of Adolfo. She sings an aria about her humble station to discourage the beggars, whereupon they resume their dance, only to be halted by the reappearance of Adolfo, who chases them away, then sings a "ciccona" to the effect that *la birba* (begging or fraud) is a game that everyone plays.

Clearly, Lesbina and Adolfo play more than an introductory role in this scene; indeed, it is the ballet that now seems incidental to their clowning, which has become the principal "business." In a reversal of seventeenth-century practice, the comic characters are now the intermezzo's chief attraction.

Even more typical of the fully developed intermezzo is the fourth comic scene of Scarlatti's *Tito Sempronio Gracco*, in which the comic characters themselves perform the ballet. When Dorilla complains that she lacks an appetite, Bireno invites her to dance with him, observing that a little exercise will bring on hunger and thirst. Begging pardon for her terpsichorean inexpertise, she accepts, and the two alternate singing strophes of a nonsense song set to the tune of the ballet music, which also serves as ritornello, then dance together to the latter "as long as they like." The naïveté of the scene's dramaturgy is matched by that of the ballet tune (Example 5).

Just as the comic characters themselves assume the function of dancing instead of merely introducing the intermedio ballet, they now make their own magic. The fourth comic scene of Aldrovandini's *Cesare in Alessandria* combines the amorous adventures of Mirena and Floro with the supernatural in much the same way as the previous example integrated the ballet with the domestic difficulties of Dorilla and Bireno. Mirena declares herself to be possessed of occult powers that will make Floro rich and enable the two to be married. She draws four circles on the ground and a golden statue is revealed, but this display of magic so terrifies Floro that he wants nothing further to do with the "sorceress" and attempts to run away, whereupon Mirena calls for infernal monsters

Example 5
A. Scarlatti, *Tito Sempronio Gracco,* comic scene No. 4

to appear and prevent him from escaping, in what surely must be one of
the last in a long line of parodies of the celebrated incantation scene
from Cavalli's *Giasone* (Example 6).[43]

Example 6
Aldrovandini, *Cesare in Alessandria,* comic scene No. 4

Other fashionable musico-dramatic stereotypes of seventeenth-century opera parodied in comic scenes of the Dresden collection include the *ombra* aria (Lidia and Gilbo, No. 3), sleep episodes (Servilia and Flacco, No. 6), dream sequences (Serpilla and Serpollo, No. 4), and the anguished farewell duet (Lucilla and Delbo, No. 1). The numerous cases of disguise and mistaken identity in these comic scenes also may have been meant as satire of a device rife in serious opera of the period; the humor in Alfeo's amorous pursuit of Livio in the *Eraclea* scenes is rendered doubly pungent by the fact that the latter is in fact a court page in woman's clothes.[44]

In their overall musical organization, the comic scenes of the Dresden collection are very similar to those we have seen in the Neapolitan version of *Giustino*. The majority consist of one or two arias for each of the two characters with intervening recitatives and a concluding duet. Such a scheme is something of an anachronism around the turn of the century, a time when the operatic *scena* had begun to assume the form of a single aria preceded by a recitative.[45] It is almost as if a scene from an opera of the 1680's had found its way into one written twenty years later. Such is, in a manner of speaking, the case. Throughout its history, the comic intermezzo retained the overall organization of the seventeenth-century *scena buffa.*

From the standpoint of musical style and form, however, the Dresden comic scenes are at least as advanced as the serious operas of which they formed a part. In respect to the recitatives of the *Giustino* comic scenes, for example, those of the Dresden collection are more "realistic," *i.e.*, they employ less complicated rhythms, more repeated tones, a greater number of notes per harmony change, and in general more closely resemble animated conversation. Two excerpts, chosen at random from among the *Giustino* comic scenes and those of the Dresden collection, illustrate the difference (Example 7).[46] This change in the style of secco recitative seems to have occurred in serious opera between about 1680 and 1700;[47] a comprehensive study of recitative in comic scenes from the latter might show that the *buffo* characters, with their traditional lively exchanges and fast-paced dialogue, led the way in this trend toward more realistic declamation.

A vocal style that may be termed "comic realism" is also prominent in the arias and duets of the collection in *buffo* style, a type that constitutes a majority of such numbers. Instances of musical

Example 7
(a) *Il Giustino* (Naples, 1684). Act I, scene 14
(b) G. Bonocini, *Il trionfo di Camilla*, comic scene No. 1

onomatopoeia abound; Examples 8a–e illustrate, respectively, vocal representations of sobbing, sighing, a stutterer's affliction, laughter, and what Edward Dent has called "a very clever study of a yawn."[48]

Another common device in *buffo* arias and duets is patter, which, contrary to later practice, occurs almost as frequently in numbers sung by the female character as those of her basso partner in these comic scenes from around the turn of the century; except for an opening and closing melodic flourish, rapid declamation on a single tone over a static bass forms the basis for every phrase of Serpilla's aria "Maledetta la mia bellezza" in the first comic scene of *Il pastor di Corinto*.[49] The typical *buffo* aria, however, combines repeated notes with several other devices,

Example 8
(a) A. Scarlatti, *Odoardo,* comic scene No. 4
(b) A. Scarlatti, *L'Emireno,* comic scene No. 6
(c) A. Scarlatti, *La caduta de Decemviri,* comic scene No. 6
(d) A. Scarlatti, *La caduta de Decemviri,* comic scene No. 4
(e) A. Scarlatti, *La caduta de Decemviri,* comic scene No. 6

including a disjunct vocal line, wide range, constant repetition of rhythmic motives and even occasional snatches of coloratura to reflect its frequently graphic text. Supporting harmony is limited to simple progressions and cadences constantly (Example 9).

Musical portrayals of the graver emotions employ quite a different style. Laments, protestations of love, and reflective texts are often set in the minor mode to a flowing *siciliano*-like 12/8 rhythm, with occasional imitation of the vocal line by accompanying instruments and bass. Suspensions and chromatic alterations, including Neapolitan sixth chords, provide welcome relief from the comparatively slight harmonic interest of the prevailing *buffo* style (Example 10).

A third aria type shows the influence of dance music in its simple, ternary rhythm, square-cut phrases, and use of binary form. Text setting is completely syllabic, with no repetition of words. Very short arias of this type may appear as melodious moments in the midst of a recitative, in connection with dance scenes, or as free-standing pieces. Example 11 reproduces one of the latter from the fourth comic scene of Luigi Mancia's *La Partenope* in its entirety.

Example 9
A. Scarlatti, *L'Emireno,* comic scene No. 3

Example 10
A. Scarlatti, *Odoardo,* comic scene No. 1

Example 11
Mancia, *La Partenope*, comic scene No. 4

Da capo form predominates in the arias and duets of the Dresden collection, but, as in their counterparts from serious opera around the turn of the century, these pieces do not yet exhibit all the traits of the fully developed "five-part" variety.[50] Many are tiny numbers of only 15 or 20 measures whose first parts are not much longer—or even less extended—than their second sections. Moreover, although first parts are usually in binary form, few of them contain the medial ritornello typical of the five-part da capo.

Ritornelli of any kind, in fact, are either short or lacking altogether in the arias and duets of the Dresden manuscripts. We shall see that short or nonexistent ritornelli were a feature that distinguished set pieces in the later intermezzo from those in contemporary *opera seria*. A limited comparison of scores from around the turn of the century suggests that, to a lesser extent, the situation was also the same at this time in regard to such numbers in comic and serious scenes.

Another feature distinguishing comic and serious treatment of the da capo form that grew more pronounced after 1700 regards the relationship of the form's two parts. Generally speaking, da capo arias in serious opera tend to avoid violent contrasts of musical style between the two sections. In the da capo arias of the Dresden collection, however, such contrasts are fairly common. The aria "Mi sento struggere," sung by Selvaggia in the third comic scene of Scarlatti's *Dafni*, furnishes an extreme example. Its first part is a flowing 12/8 adagio lament in D minor, full of expressive suspensions, appoggiaturas, and chromatic alterations; the style of the second part is that of an allegro *buffo* aria in common time, with a constantly reiterated rhythmic and melodic formula in the vocal part supported by predominantly static harmony. Rather extreme changes of style occasionally occur even within parts of da capo arias and duets of the collection. The second part of Zelta's aria "Piu bel svario" from the third comic scene of *Tito Manlio* alternates between 12/8 adagio of the type just described and presto sections composed of patter and extravagant coloratura.

Another stylistic difference distinguishes duets of the Dresden collection from those in contemporary serious opera. In comparison to such ensembles in the latter, which almost invariably take the form of an aria divided between two voices,[51] duets of the Dresden *scene buffe* show slightly more variety in the disposition of their vocal lines. The most common arrangement, employed to reflect a quarrel or conflict of interest between the two characters, consists of progressively shorter phrases tossed between the two singers, culminating in a simultaneous outburst of disagreement or mutual vituperation (Example 12). Dent has described the result in an opera of Alessandro Scarlatti from about this time as "hardly music at all, . . . [but] mere chatter emphasized by regular rhythmical movement."[52] Nonetheless, the device creates a kind of stretto effect that provides the scene with an exciting conclusion.[53]

Two other modes of disposing the voice parts portray less stressful dramatic situations. To reflect the harmonious agreement of a common text, the singers proceed in parallel thirds and sixths throughout their duet, and a type of antecedent-consequent phrase organization in which the characters never sing together is employed to set dialogues, such as the following slightly racy exchange between Selvaggia and Dameta from the third comic scene of Scarlatti's *Dafni:*

Sel.	Se vien qualche pastor quand'io son sposa?
Dam.	Digli non c'è Dameta andate via.
Sel.	E se mi richiedesse qualch cosa?
Dam.	Dagli la robba tua mà non la mia.
Sel.	Sè meco star volesse in compagnia?
Dam.	Digli che se ne vada à casa sua.
Sel.	Sè gli piacessi poi la gratia mia?
Dam.	Dagli la robba mia mà non là tua.

(*Sel.* Suppose some shepherd comes when I'm [your] wife?
Dam. Tell him to go away; Dameta isn't home.
Sel. And if he should ask me for something?
Dam. Give him your things, not mine.
Sel. If he likes my company?
Dam. Tell him to go home.
Sel. If he likes my favors?
Dam. Give him my things, not yours.)

Example 12
Mancia, *Tito Manlio,* comic scene No. 5

Example 12 (continued)

Slightly more than half of the arias and the overwhelming majority of duets in the Dresden collection are accompanied by continuo only. Unison violins furnish the accompaniment for most of the remaining numbers; the full string ensemble of the late Baroque orchestra (first and second violins, violas and continuo) appears very rarely. Soli passages for woodwinds are reserved for pastoral effects and the like, but these instruments probably also doubled the upper string parts much of the time. Orchestral instruments are occasionally employed for humorous effect, as in the slow violin and viola trill that portrays the buzzing of a hornet in Adolfo's aria "Moscone amoroso intorno ti giro" (Lesbina and Adolfo, No. 5), and the clowning bassoon that anticipates each phrase of Delbo's patter song in the second comic scene of *Il prigioniero fortunato* (Example 13).

Example 13
A. Scarlatti, *Il prigioniero fortunato,* comic scene No. 2

The First Independent Intermezzi

All the comic scenes of the Dresden collection exhibit some dramatic connection to the opera with which they were performed; typically, at least part of the opening recitative in the comic characters' first scene is given over to a discussion of the opera's tangled state of affairs.   A more fundamental connection with the serious opera characterizes the *scene buffe* of *Il pastor di Corinto* and *Dafni*, two *favole boschereccie* in which the comic servants speak with the same pastoral accents as their masters. Even the former's music sometimes reflects the opera's sylvan setting, as, for example, in the introduction to the duet of Serpillo and Serpolla that concludes their final scene together:

Example 14
A. Scarlatti, *Il pastor di Corinto,* comic scene No. 6

One might assume that the trend in following years would be away from such dramatic and musical connections and toward a reduction in the number of comic scenes, culminating in gravitation of all that were left to the ends of acts in opera libretti, where they would be labeled "intermezzi"—or even published separately for use with a number of different serious operas. Such, in fact, was the general line of development followed at Naples, but it was not until after 1725 that intermezzi reached the final stage of complete separation from the *opera seria* there. Long before that date, intermezzi dramatically independent of the operas with which they were performed had appeared elsewhere, including cities that, unlike Naples, had no continuous tradition of comic scenes in their serious operas.

We have seen that *scene buffe* of the type upon which the eighteenth-century intermezzo was modeled disappeared around 1670 from libretti for operas performed at Venice.[54] Surprisingly enough, it was here that a substantial number of separately published intermezzo libretti first appeared. No fewer than 19 such libretti have been preserved for intermezzi performed between the years 1706 and 1709, principally at the Teatro San Cassiano (see Table 3).

TABLE 3

INDEPENDENT VENETIAN INTERMEZZI, 1706-1709[a]

Title and/or Dramatis Personae[b]	Theater	Season	Year
"Frappolone e Florinetta"[c]	S. Cassiano	Carnival	1706
Nuovi intermedii per musica (Lesbina and Milo)	S. Angelo	Autumn	1706
Intermedii nell'opera di S. Angiolo (Lesba and Bleso)	S. Angelo	?	[1706][d]
"Le rovine di Troja"[ce] (Dragontana and Policrone)	S. Cassiano	?	1707
"Lisetta, e Asdrobolo"[cef]	S. Cassiano	?	1707
Melissa schernita (Melissa and Serpillo)	S. Cassiano	?	1707
Melissa vendicata (Grilletta[g] [Melissa] and Serpillo)	S. Cassiano	?	1707
Melissa contenta (Grilletta[g] [Melissa] and Serpillo)	S. Cassiano	?	1707
"Intermezzi di Erighetta e Don Chilone"[h]	[S. Cassiano	Autumn	1707][i]
Catulla and Lardone	S. Cassiano	Carnival	1708
Parpagnacco (Pollastrella and Parpagnacco)	S. Cassiano	Carnival	1708
Pimpinone (Vespetta and Pimpinone)	S. Cassiano	Autumn	1708
"Intermedio musicale di Vespetta, e Lesbo"[h]	S. Giovanni Grisostomo	?	1708
Il nuovo mondo (Bertolda and Volpone)	S. Cassiano	Carnival	1709

TABLE 3 (continued)

Title and/or Dramatis Personae[b]	Theater	Season	Year
Tulipano (Galantina and Tulipano)	S. Cassiano	Carnival	1709
Grilletta and Demo	S. Fantino	Carnival	1709
Zamberlucco (Palandrana and Zamberlucco)	S. Cassiano	Autumn	1709
Ermilla and Bato	S. Angelo	Autumn	1709
La capricciosa e il credulo (Brunetta and Burlotto)	S. Cassiano	?	[1709][j]

[a]Information from printed libretti (all in the Collezione Rossi of the Biblioteca Marciana, Venice) unless otherwise noted.

[b]For purposes of identification, dramatis personae (female role first) are added here and throughout the present study in parenthesis after those titles that do not already include them.

[c]MS libretto in the Collezione Rossi of the Biblioteca Marciana, Venice.

[d]See below, p. 38.

[e]Another MS copy in the Raccolta Correr of the Casa Goldoni, Venice.

[f]Male character named Astrobolo in the Raccolta Correr MS and all subsequent prints.

[g]See below, p. 207, note 91.

[h]MS libretto in the Collezione Rossi of the Biblioteca Marciana, Venice.

[i]See Groppo, "Catalogo purgatissimo," p. 155.

[j]See below, p. 202, note 1.

Some of these early "independent" intermezzo libretti maintain at least a tenuous connection with one of the serious operas performed at Venice during this period.[55]   The characters of *Le rovine di Troja*—Dragontana, "vecchia Trojana" and Policrone, "soldato greco"—for example, obviously belong with the cast of Antonio Lotti's *Achille placato* (Teatro San Cassiano, 1707), and both Bleso and Lesba, characters of the *Intermedii nell'opera di S. Angiolo*, are described as servants of the principals in Matteo Noris' libretto for *La regina creduta rè* (Teatro San Angelo, 1706), although Lesba never appears in the acts of the opera itself. By far the more common arrangement, however, was to maintain a complete separation between the opera's setting, subject, and dramatis personae and those of the intermezzo.

Unlike *scene buffe* of the type contained in the Dresden collection, which may number as many as seven separate episodes, *Le rovine di Troja* and *Lisetta, e Astrobolo*, the longest of these early Venetian intermezzi, consist of only four parts, an obvious maximum if they were to be fitted between the five acts of Antonio Lotti's *Achille placato* and Francesco Gasparini's *Taican rè della Cina*, the operas with which they received their respective first performances.   Even so, according to a notice in the libretto for Gasparini's opera, it was necessary to omit a considerable portion of the latter's text in order to leave time for the intermezzi and other entr'acte entertainments.[56]

The organization of individual parts in all these first independent intermezzi, however, is identical to that of comic scenes performed with operas at Naples and other Italian cities around the turn of the century. Like the latter, the majority consist of one or two arias for each character with intervening recitatives and a concluding duet.   The dramatic stereotypes are also the same: an old woman and her young male prey or a beautiful girl pursued by an older man.[57]

These similarities are hardly surprising in view of the fact that texts for at least some of the earliest Venetian intermezzi were merely adaptations of those previously performed elsewhere as comic scenes in connection with other operas. The *Nuovi intermedii per musica* (Lesbina and Milo), for example, were not new at all.[58]   Their first part is a pastiche of aria and duet texts from the second and fourth comic scenes with the same characters added to Francesco Silvani's libretto *La fede tradita e vendicata* for revivals at Florence (1705) and Lucca (1706),[59] and the arias and duet of the second of the "nuovi" intermezzi are identical to those of the second comic scene of Gellia and Zelto in Paolo Magni's setting of Matteo Noris' *Nerone fatto Cesare* (Milan, 1703).[60]   To further complicate matters, the latter also formed the first of two other Venetian intermezzi, those of Grilletta and Demo (Teatro San Fantino, 1709), the second of which is similar to the third of the Milan, 1703, comic scenes. But this is not all. The second part of the Venetian intermezzi of Lesbina and Milo turns up four years later as the first comic scene in Giacomo Facco's setting of *Le regine di Macedonia* (Messina, 1710), with the characters named Lesbina and Creperio.[61]

Quite clearly, texts of the type employed in the intermezzi performed in Venice between 1706 and 1709 were the common property of every theater poet in Italy charged with the responsibility of arranging operas to suit local tastes or accommodate the number of singers in his company. The significance of the Venetian arrangements of these texts and those written in imitation of them lies in the fact that they constitute the first sizable corpus of self-contained comic intermezzi.

The libretti printed in Venice between 1706 and 1709 are also important because included among them are texts for the first examples of what may be termed the "international"[62] intermezzo repertory. *Parpagnacco*, for example, was not only performed at Venice during the carnival of 1708 with two different operas, but in later years (doubtless in a number of musical settings) made the rounds of musical theaters in Italy and several foreign countries; it was heard as far afield as Moscow and at least as late as 1754 (see Appendix A). These pieces formed the vanguard of a repertory that spread throughout Europe in the half century following 1706, providing not only comic relief in performances of *opere serie*, but also introducing audiences at many cities to a new style in Italian dramatic music.

II

THE REPERTORY AND ITS DIFFUSION

Principal Composers

Nearly one thousand libretti for comic scenes and intermezzi performed with operas during the eighteenth century were unearthed for preparation of the present study. This number is rather small compared to that of preserved texts for contemporary *opere serie*. Moreover, to an even greater extent than is the case with the latter, surprisingly few different pieces account for a large percentage of published libretti; apparently most intermezzi sank into oblivion after only one or two performances, while relatively few enjoyed frequent revivals, presumably commensurate in number with their popularity.

Appendix A presents performance data for 22 of the most frequently revived operatic intermezzi, to judge from surviving scores, libretti, and notices of performances. Despite its many lacunae, this miniature annals of the intermezzo furnishes enough evidence regarding the dates, composers, and origins of at least some popular pieces from the repertory to permit the following generalizations: (1) the intermezzo as an "international" phenomenon flourished between the first decade of the eighteenth century and about 1750, (2) with one possible exception, the composers named most frequently in libretti and contemporary manuscript scores were also among the most popular exponents of the *opera seria* tradition, and (3) these composers belong to two generations, usually described as "Venetian" and "Neapolitan."

This is not the place to review the convincing arguments for abandoning these adjectives to denote style periods in opera; in the present study they will be used only to describe the geographical origin of pieces under discussion.[1]

As has already been noted, the seasons 1707-1709 at the Teatro S. Cassiano in Venice, which saw the production of the first sizable number of intermezzi dramatically independent of their attendant *opere serie*, also furnished the first examples of pieces that were to become part of the "international" intermezzo repertory. Although not a single composer's name is mentioned in any intermezzo libretti for these years, attributions in the few surviving scores suggest their music was by the composer of the opera with which they were first performed. Thus the score of the "Intermedij rappresentati nel teatro di S. Cassiano nell'opera d'Achille Placato"[2] (Dragontana and Policrone) bears the name of Antonio Lotti, composer of *Achille;* that of the "Intermedi dell'opera seconda di S. Casciano" (Lisetta and Astrobolo), attributed to Francesco Gasparini,[3] was performed with that composer's *Taican rè della Cina*;[4] and the three *azioni* of the intermezzo *Melissa* are the work of Lotti and Gasparini,[5] with whose operas they received their respective first performances.[6]

If these circumstances reflect the prevailing state of affairs, then Gasparini's preeminent position in the field of opera at Venice shortly after the turn of the century was matched by his standing there as a composer of intermezzi. In addition to *Lisetta, e Astrobolo* and *Melissa schernita* (Melissa and Serpillo), he would be responsible for the music of two other pieces that achieved widespread European circulation, *Parpagnacco* (Pollastrella and Parpagnacco) and *Zamberlucco* (Palandrana and Zamberlucco); he would also be the first to set the popular libretti of *La capricciosa e il credulo* (Brunetta and Burlotto) and *Intermezzi di Erighetta e Don Chilone*, all of which were first heard at Venice with one of his own operas.[7]

Although Gasparini continued to compose intermezzi for Venice until at least 1720, when his "Vecchio avaro, intermezzi alla Verita in cimento di Vivaldi" (Fiammetta and Pancrazio) was performed at the Teatro San Angelo,[8] the relatively few intermezzo libretti preserved from the decade 1710-20 at Venice suggest a decline of activity in the genre on the part of local composers during this period. *Barillotto* (Slapina and Barillotto) of 1712, the only one to mention the name of its composer, is the work of Domenico Sarri, "Maestro nella Real Cappella di Napoli," and many of the others are versions of texts previously performed elsewhere.[9]

In any case, by about 1720 leadership in the production of exportable intermezzi had definitely passed to Naples. During the preceding two decades, intermezzo-like comic scenes of the type described in Chapter I had continued to figure in almost every opera performed in that city; in the case of works first produced elsewhere, local composers added the traditional *scene buffe*. To judge from notices in surviving libretti, the composers most frequently called upon to furnish this additional music were the same ones who also regularly supplied the Neapolitan stage with their own complete operas during the same period, including Giuseppe Vignola,[10] Francesco Mancini,[11] Francesco Feo,[12] and Leonardo Leo.[13]

Texts of comic scenes from Neapolitan operas occasionally appear as intermezzi in operas performed at other cities, but not enough scores or composer attributions in libretti have come to light to determine when the music as well was first regularly so employed. The first two intermezzi of Vespetta and Milo in Antonio Lotti's *Giove in*

Argo (Dresden, 1717), attributed to Alessandro Scarlatti, may be an early example, if, as is possible, they consist of comic episodes composed at Naples for an as-yet-undiscovered opera by that composer.[14]   Sarri's *Barillotto* (Slapina and Barillotto), performed at Venice in 1712, would furnish an even earlier instance, if a libretto for a Neapolitan opera with these comic roles should be found.

Naples' first major contribution to the "international" repertory, however, seems to have been Domenico Sarri's intermezzi of Brunetta and Burlotto, performed with his *Ginevra principessa di Scozia* during the carnival of 1720 at the Teatro San Bartolomeo. They reached Rome in 1724 and Venice the following year, when they were heard as intermezzi in Tomaso Albinoni's *Didone abbandonata* under the title *La capricciosa e il credulo*.   Performed with the same opera was another of Sarri's Neapolitan intermezzi, *L'impresario delle Canarie* (Dorina and Nibbio).[15] Sarri also appears to have been the first to set the popular intermezzi of Moschetta and Grullo, a two-part version of which was performed between the acts of his *Siroe rè di Persia* at Naples in 1727.

The most prolific of the Naples-based intermezzo composers seems to have been the Italianized German, Johann Adolph Hasse. Before his departure for Dresden in 1731, Hasse set at least seven intermezzi for the Neapolitan stage, the number and subsequent popularity of which show him to have been as facile and successful in works of this genre as in the *opere serie* for which he is now much better known.[16] The confusion of this composer's most popular intermezzo, *La contadina* (Scintilla and Tabarano) with Pergolesi's *La contadina astuta* (Livietta and Tracollo) by theatrical chroniclers and the editor of Pergolesi's complete works may help to account for Hasse's present lack of recognition in the field of intermezzo composition.[17] The fact that his name appears more often in the libretti listed in Appendix A than that of any other composer suggests that during his lifetime Hasse was acknowledged as much for his comic pieces as for his serious works.

The intermezzi of Giovanni Battista Pergolesi belong to the final years of their cultivation at Naples, a time during which libretti from performances at the Teatro San Bartolomeo were not preserved with the same regularity as previously.[18] It is for this reason, together with the composer's early death and posthumous fame, that a number of dramatic works were falsely attributed to this composer. Recent scholarship has stripped Pergolesi of all but three of the half dozen or more intermezzi that have at one time or another been ascribed to him; the spurious works include *Il maestro di musica* (a condensed version of the pasticcio *Orazio*) and *Il geloso schernito* (Dorina and Masacco), *La contadina* (Scintilla and Don Tabarano), and *La vedova ingenosa* (Drusilla and

Strambone), now attributed respectively to Pietro Chiarini, Johann Adolph Hasse, and Ignazio Prota or Giuseppe Sellitti.[19]

Besides *La contadina astuta* (Livietta and Tracollo) and *La serva padrona* (Serpina and Uberto), only an untitled work with characters Nerina and Nibbio is now considered genuine. It should be noted, however, that Pergolesi's name does not appear in the libretto for the latter, which was printed together with that of his opera *La Salustia* (Teatro San Bartolomeo, 1731). And as Frank Walker has pointed out, Pergolesi may only have arranged another composer's music and set new recitatives for this intermezzo.[20] In any case, it appears not to have enjoyed much success; the only indication of a revival seems to be a notice for an intermezzo with the characters Nerina and Nibbio in the libretto for the premiere of Niccolo Jommelli's *Ricemero re de' Goti* at Rome's Teatro Argentina during the carnival of 1740.

This leaves *La contadina astuta* and *La serva padrona*. No evidence has come to light suggesting that the music used at any of the numerous revivals of the latter was not at least mostly by Pergolesi. *La contadina astuta*, however, is a different matter. Many revivals of this piece were given under the titles *Il finto pazzo* and *Amor fà l'uomo cieco*.[21] The change of title in this case is significant, since, as Frank Walker has convincingly demonstrated:

> 'Il finto pazzo' of 1741 was a *rifacimento*, almost certainly by [Carlo] Goldoni and [the Brescian composer Pietro] Chiarini of [Tomaso] Mariani and Pergolesi's 'La contadina astuta'. 'Amor fa l'uomo cieco' of 1742 was quite certainly a *rifacimento*, by Goldoni and Chiarini, of 'Il finto pazzo'. . . . Its musical content consisted of three numbers by Pergolesi, one by Latilla and (probably) four by Chiarini. New recitatives must have been provided by Chiarini.[22]

The inescapable conclusion is that one of the two pieces on which Pergolesi's reputation as a composer of intermezzi rests gained its popularity in a pasticcio version to which Pergolesi himself contributed less than half the music.

If the importance of Pergolesi in the history of the intermezzo has been exaggerated, that of Giuseppe Maria Orlandini (1688-1760) has been all but ignored.[23] To judge from surviving libretti, Orlandini's intermezzi received their premieres between about 1712 and 1742 in cities scattered throughout Italy, suggesting that his reputation was both long lasting and widespread. Testimonies by the Bolognese composer's contemporaries and immediate successors, moreover, leave no doubt as to his predilection for the genre. According to Francesco Quadrio he was "singular for his time in setting music to comic subjects";[24] Charles

Burney brackets his name with that of Pergolesi as the only two masters who "understood" the intermezzo,[25] and LaBorde agreed that he "excelled" in their composition.[26]

Even more significant evidence of Orlandini's success as an intermezzo composer is the presence of his name in at least one libretto for no fewer than six of the pieces listed in Appendix A.[27] The lengthy column of revivals recorded there for *Il marito giocatore* (Serpilla and Bacocco) not only ranks this work as one of the most popular examples of the genre, but places it among the most successful and durable pieces of Italian dramatic music produced during the whole of the eighteenth century.[28] It is therefore of some importance to determine whether Orlandini, whose name is mentioned in the libretto of only one, relatively late revival (London, 1737), was, in fact, the first to set this popular text, and whether a majority of later performances may have employed his music.

These questions, which have been argued inconclusively by musicologists for almost three quarters of a century,[29] may now be definitely answered in the affirmative.

As Oscar Sonneck has pointed out, the text of the London libretto is virtually identical to that of the premiere at Venice in 1719, a circumstance which in view of the eighteenth-century penchant for pasticcio and textual alterations for every new setting argues strongly for Orlandini having been the first to set *Il marito giocatore*.[30] A score unknown to Sonneck in the library of the Florence Conservatory (MS D. 239) substantiates his view and furnishes additional evidence regarding subsequent revivals of this intermezzo. The Florentine score includes both Orlandini's name as composer and the complete text of the Venetian libretto; moreover, its two vocal parts are notated for soprano and tenor, the ranges of Rosa Ungarelli and Antonio Ristorini,[31] who created the roles of Serpilla and Bacocco at the Teatro San Angelo in 1719, and featured the intermezzo until at least 1730 in their tours through Italy, Germany, the Austrian Netherlands, and France (see below, Table 4). The fact that Ristorini was one of the very few tenors who specialized in the singing of intermezzi during the first third of the eighteenth century leaves little doubt that the Florentine score preserves the version of Orlandini's music for this intermezzo that furnished a mainstay of his and Ungarelli's repertory, making it possible to attribute the music of the premiere and at least eight revivals of *Il marito giocatore* to the Bolognese composer.[32]

The question of whether later performances of the work, particularly those outside of Italy, employed Orlandini's music may also be answered affirmatively, although with less substantiating evidence from libretti and contemporary scores. Antonio Groppo credits

Orlandini with authorship of *Il marito giocatore* at both its 1741 and 1742 Venetian revivals;[33] the *Mercure de France* attributes to him all the recitatives, two duets, and at least two arias of the pasticcio version performed by the *Bouffons* at Paris in 1752,[34] and Ernst Gerber states that as late as 1792 his name was known in Germany as composer of this intermezzo.[35]

Other intermezzi by Orlandini enjoyed similar widespread popularity and longevity. His setting of *La preziosa ridicola* (Madama Dulcinea and il cuoco del Marchese del Bosco), probably premiered at Rome in 1712,[36] was performed as late as 1746 in Hamburg; even later productions in Russia, Denmark, and Spain may have employed his music. Orlandini, then, must be considered the most "international" of intermezzo composers; his works belonged to no particular local tradition in Italy, and seem to have enjoyed universal success beyond their native country.

Composers in at least two cities outside of Italy during the first half of the eighteenth century were active in the composition of intermezzi, but their contributions to the repertory appear to have met with only a local success. During his tenure as court composer at Vienna, Francesco Conti set at least five intermezzi for that city, including the first one dramatically independent of its attendant *opera seria*. An untitled piece with the characters Dorimena and Tuberone, it was performed in 1714 with *L'Atenaide*, a hybrid work to which Marc' Antonio Ziani, Antonio Negri, and Antonio Caldara each contributed one act. Conti's name also appears as composer in Viennese libretti for the following intermezzi, all of which received their premieres with one of that composer's own operas:

Year	Characters of the intermezzo	Opera
1715	Bagatella, Mamalucca and Pattatocco	Ciro
1715	Galantina and Pampalugo	Teseo in Creta
1717	Grilletta [Vespetta] and Pimpinone	Sesostri re di Egitto
1718	Farfalletta, Lirone and Terremoto	Astarto

In spite of Conti's considerable gift for the comic style, a talent cited by Johann Mattheson,[37] and exemplified in the composer's *tragicommedie* and the comic scenes that figured in many of his serious works,[38] as well as these intermezzi, the latter seem to have enjoyed only a few revivals at minor German courts in following years;[39] none seems ever to have been performed in Italy or at important musical theaters in other European countries, with the possible exception of those of

Dorimena and Tuberone.   It may have been Conti's setting of these intermezzi that inaugurated presentations of the genre at the Hamburg opera in 1719.[40]

As was the case with that city's serious opera repertory, however, Hamburg generally maintained a measure of local autonomy in the production of intermezzi until the collapse of the German musical establishment there in 1738.   Between 1725 and 1731 Georg Philipp Telemann, the last important indigenous German composer active at Hamburg, set at least three intermezzi for the city's theater, all of them composed to libretti previously employed by Venetian composers in the first decade of the eighteenth century.[41]

His *Die ungleiche Heyrath zwischen Vespetta und Pimpinone* of 1725 represents an early attempt to create a German intermezzo on Italian lines;[42] all the recitatives of Pariati's text were sung in a German translation by Johann Philipp Praetorius, who also added an aria and two duet texts in German to the original libretto.[43]   It is pointless to speculate, however, whether Telemann's German intermezzi might have led to a "naturalization" of the genre, or provided the impetus for a new type of national German comic opera, paralleling the type developed in France after 1752 under the influence of Italian models.   The termination of German opera at Hamburg in 1738 put an end to all such possibilities, and opened the way to an invasion of Italian composers and travelling opera companies, including troupes of singers that previously had propagated the Italian intermezzo repertory in nearly every other European city.   It is to the activities of these singers that we must now turn our attention.

Singers and Travelling Troupes

Naples was the only major operatic center in which nearly every serious opera presented between 1700 and 1735 was accompanied by comic scenes or intermezzi.   It was also the only city whose principal musical theater maintained a pair of singers on a permanent basis for their performance during this period.   Thus for 25 years (except for a short absence from the autumn of 1713 until the spring of 1714) the basso Gioacchino Corrado, "virtuoso della Real Cappella di Napoli," played the male comic roles at the Teatro San Bartolomeo opposite a succession of female partners that included Santa Marchesini (1711-16 and 1719-24), Rosa Petrignani "detta la Portughesina" (1717-19), Celeste Resse (1725-31), Maria Natalizia Bisagi (1732), and Laura Monti (1733-35).[44]

Elsewhere, performances of intermezzi depended upon the availability of specialized singers who travelled from place to place, spreading the repertory from its centers of origin to provincial theaters—first in Italy, and later throughout all of Europe. They must have made a colorful spectacle arriving in town with their luggage of "big mustaches, whistles, and drums, along with all kinds of other gadgets necessary to their profession," that Benedetto Marcello advised "they should supply so that they will not burden the impresario with expenses other than their generous salary."[45]

One of the earliest and most important of these specialists in the singing of intermezzi was a Mantuan basso, Giovanni Battista Cavana, whom the librettist Paolo Rolli singled out in the preface to his opera *Teti e Peleo* as "perhaps the first and last who knew how to portray with decorous wit all the emotions of those characters with an inexpressible liveliness through singing and acting."[46] Cavana's name first appears as interpreter of *buffo* parts in libretti for operas performed at Rome, Naples, and other Italian cities around the turn of the century.[47] In 1706 he joined with the Bolognese alto Santa Marchesini to perform the comic parts in Antonio Lotti's *Sidonio* at Venice's Teatro San Cassiano; during the following two years at the same theater they created the roles in many of the earliest independent comic intermezzi,[48] two of which the pair repeated during the spring of 1708 in Bologna at that city's Teatro Malvezzi.[49] Continuing on to Naples, they introduced in the fall and winter of 1709 at least three pieces from their Venetian repertory, *Melissa schernita* (Melissa and Serpillo), intermezzi of Vespetta and Pimpinone, and those of Lisetta and Astrobolo.[50]

Except for two further tours with Cavana during 1712 and 1716-18, Marchesini remained in Naples as resident intermezzo singer at the Teatro San Bartolomeo until 1724.[51] Cavana, however, continued to circulate around the opera houses of Italy repeating pieces from his repertory and accumulating new roles in pieces written for him by local composers. In 1711 he introduced the Roman public to *Astrobolo, e Lisetta* and the intermezzi of Vespetta and Pimpinone at the Teatro Cerveteri,[52] and during the carnival season of 1712 at the Teatro Capranica created the male role in the popular intermezzi of Madama Dulcinea and il cuoco del Marchese del Bosco, in which he appeared later at Reggio (1715) and Modena (1717).[53]

Other Italian cities at which Cavana performed in the following years include Vicenza (1712), Naples (1713), Parma (1714), Ferrara (1715), Milan and Brescia (1716), Genoa (1717), and Pesaro (1722).[54] The singer's activities continued until at least 1727, when his name appears in the cast list of an unnamed intermezzo performed with a revival of Domenico Sarri's *Didone abbandonata* at the Teatro Regio in Turin.

The temporary associations of Cavana with Santa Marchesini typify a pattern of similar partnerships formed by pairs of intermezzo singers during the first half of the eighteenth century. One of the longest lasting and most influential of these associations was that of Rosa Ungarelli and Antonio Ristorini, the first interpreters of the fantastically successful *Il marito giocatore* (Serpilla and Bacocco) and performers of the first Italian intermezzi ever heard in Munich, Brussels, and Paris.

The soprano[55] Rosa Ungarelli (her name is also spelled "Ungherelli," "Ungharelli," and "Ongarelli" in libretti) seems to have begun her career as intermezzo singer in her native city of Bologna, where she performed the female comic role of Giuseppe Aldrovandini's *Li trè rivali al soglio* in 1711. At Ferrara the same year she sang *Pimpinone, e Vespetta* opposite Giovanni Battista Cavana, from whom she may have acquired the repertory of intermezzi which she performed with several partners at various Italian cities between 1712 and 1714.[56]

The Florentine tenor[57] Antonio Maria Ristorini (or "Restorini") appeared in minor roles in operas during the 1701 and 1703-1705 seasons at Venice's Teatro San Cassiano; in a libretto for 1703 he is described as "virtuoso del ser[enissimo] gran pren[cipe] di Toscana."[58] After an engagement at the Teatro Fiorentini in Naples,[59] Ristorini returned in 1708 to the Teatro San Cassiano, where he sang serious parts in Gasparini's *Engelberta*, Pollaroli's *Il falso Tiberino*, and Albinoni's *Astarto*,[60] the three operas in which Santa Marchesini and Giovanni Battista Cavana performed comic intermezzi that year.

Ristorini seems not to have begun his career as a specialist in the singing of intermezzi until about 1716. In that year or before he and Ungarelli joined in a partnership that lasted at least 17 years; during this period engagements took them to practically every city in northern Italy that supported an opera house and also three foreign countries.[61] Table 4, although by no means a complete record of the pair's activities, will give some idea of their peregrinations and repertory. It also demonstrates they heeded Marcello's satirical advice that *parti buffe* "should play the same old intermezzi in every town."[62]

The Pistoiese diarist Giovanni Cosimo Rossi-Melocchi has left a vivid record of the pair's performance of *Il marito giocatore* with a spoken drama on the occasion of their visit to his city in 1725. Rossi-Melocchi's account includes interesting sidelights on the private lives of these intermezzo singers as well as the impression they created on stage:[63]

> July 15, 1725. This evening at 8:30 p.m. they began the [first of the] three plays [*Ciro*] . . . and the work wasn't well received because of the cuts made to shorten it, and there was nothing in its favor except for two doctor parts played by Vivarelli and Batachio, who

TABLE 4

INTERMEZZO PERFORMANCES BY ROSA UNGARELLI AND ANTONIO RISTORINI BETWEEN 1716 AND 1732[a]

Year	Season	City	Theater	Title and/or Dramatis Personae
1716	Carnival	Turin	Carignano	Vespetta and Pimpinone
1717	Spring	Bologna	Formagliari	*La serva astuta* (Vespetta and Pimpinone)
1717	Autumn	Bologna	Formagliari	Palandrana and Zamberlucco
[1718	Summer-Autumn	Florence	Pergola][b]	Vespetta and Pimpinone
[1718	Summer-Autumn	Florence	Pergola][b]	[*Intermezzo di Erighetta e D. Chilone*][c]
1718	Autumn	Venice	S. Angelo	*Lisetta, e Delfo*
1719	Carnival	Venice	S. Angelo	*La preziosa ridicola* (Madama Dulcinea and il cuoco del Marchese del Bosco)
1719	Carnival	Venice	S. Angelo	*Il marito giogatore, e la moglie bacchettona* (Serpilla and Bacocco)
[1719	Summer-Autumn	Florence	Pergola	?][d]
1720	Carnival	Turin	Carignano	Flora and D. Giroldo
1720	Summer	Livorno	S. Sebastiano	?
1720	Autumn	Venice	S. Angelo	*L'avaro* (Fiammetta and Pancrazio)
1721	Carnival	Venice	S. Angelo	*Melinda, e Tiburzio*
1721	Carnival	Venice	S. Angelo	[*Il marito giuocatore, e la moglie bacchettona*][e]
1721	Autumn	Venice	S. Angelo	*Scannacapone ammalato imaginario e Vespetta vedova*
1722	Carnival	Milan	Regio Ducal	?
1722	Autumn	Munich	Hofoper	*Serpilla, e Bacocco*
1722	Autumn	Munich	Hofoper	*Vespetta, e Pimpinone*
1723	Carnival	Milan	Regio Ducal	?
1723	Spring	Genoa	Falcone	*Serpilla è Bacoco*
[1724	Carnival	Genoa	Falcone	?][f]
1724	Spring	Parma	Corte	?
[1725	Carnival	Florence	Pergola][g]	[*Un vecchio innamorato* (= ?)][h]
[1725	Carnival	Florence	Pergola][i]	[*L'ammalato immaginario*
[1725	Carnival	Florence	Pergola	*Le bourgeois gentil-homme*][j] (Larinda and Vanesio)
[1725	Summer	Pistoia	Risvegliati	*Il marito giocatore e la moglie bacchettona*
1725	Summer	Pistoia	Risvegliati	*Il capitano Don Micco e Lesbina*

TABLE 4 (continued)

Year	Season	City	Theater	Title and/or Dramatis Personae
1725	Summer	Pistoia	Risvegliati	*L'ammalato imaginario* (Erighetta and D. Chilone)][k]
1726	Carnival	Turin	Regio	?
1727	Carnival	Milan	Regio Ducal	*Monsieur di Porsugnacchi* (Grilletta and Porsugnacco)
[1727	Carnival	Florence	Pergola	?][l]
1727	Ascension	Venice	S. Samuele	*Monsieur di Porsugnacco*
1727	Summer	Florence	Cocomero	*Monsieur di Porsugnacco*
1727	Autumn	Venice	S. Angelo	*Il marito giocatore, e la moglie bacchettona*[m]
[1728	Spring	Genoa	Falcone	?][n]
1728	Summer	Faenza	Accademia de' Remoti	*Monsieur di Porsugnacco*
1728	[Autumn	Brussels	de la Monnaie	Vespetta and Pimpinone][o]
1728	Autumn	Brussels	de la Monnaie	*Don Micco e Lesbina*
1728	Autumn	Brussels	de la Monnaie	*Serpilla e Baiocco, o vero il marito giocatore e la moglie bacchettona*
1728	Winter	Brussels	de la Monnaie	*Il malato immaginario* (Erighetta and D. Chilone)
1729	Carnival	Brussels	de la Monnaie	*La trufaldina* (Moschetta and Grullo)
[1729	Summer	Paris	Académie Royale de Musique	*Serpilla e Baiocco, o vero Il marito giocatore e la moglie bacchetona*
1729	Summer	Paris	Académie Royale de Musique	*Don Micco e Lesbina*][p]
1730	Carnival	Milan	Regio Ducal	?
1730	Spring	Venice	S. Samuele	*Serpilla, e Bacocco*
1732	Carnival	Florence	Pergola	*L'ammalato immaginario*
1732	Carnival	Florence	Pergola	*Le bourgeois gentilhomme* (Larinda and Vanesio)

[a]Information other than that contained in libretti is enclosed in brackets and its source identified.

[b]Palmieri Pandolfini, "Notizia di tutte l'opere che si sono recitate in Firenze nel teatro di via della Pergola dall'anno 1718 in poi," Florence, Biblioteca Nazionale Centrale, MS II-97, No. 3, [fol. 181'].

[c]Pietro Toldo, *L'OEuvre de Molière et sa fortune en Italie* (Turin, 1910), p. 431.

TABLE 4 (continued)

[d]Pandolfini, [fol. 182].

[e]Groppo, p. 191.

[f]*Tavola cronologica di tutti li drammi o sia opere in musica recitate alli teatri detti del Falcone, e da S. Agostino da cento anni in addietro,...* (Genoa, 1771), p. 20.

[g]Pandolfini, [foll. 183-183$'$].

[h]Ugo Morini, *La R. Accademia degli Immobili ed il suo teatro "La Pergola" (1649-1925)* (Pisa, 1926), p. 41.

[i]Pandolfini, [foll. 183-183$'$].

[j]Morini, p. 41.

[k]Alberto Chiappelli, *Storia del teatro in Pistoia dalle origini alla fine del sec.* XVIII (Pistoia, 1913), pp. 119-20.

[l]Pandolfini, [fol. 184].

[m]The singers, not identified in the libretto, are named by Groppo, p. 212.

[n]*Tavola cronologica,* p. 21.

[o]See Alfred Wotquenne's MS catalogue of libretti in the Brussels Conservatory Library, No. 22.259; the libretto itself is no longer to be found in the collection of this library.

[p]*Mercure de France,* June, 1729, pp. 1222-1230, 1401-1403; and [Louis César de La Beaume Le Blanc La Vallière], *Ballets, opera, et autres ouvrages lyriques, par ordre chronologique depuis leur origine. ...* (Paris, 1760), p. 176.

were the troupe's best performers. . . . The intermezzo singers, however, succeeded like a wonder of nature unrivaled since the foundation of Pistoia, and never to be equaled. They are Signora Rosa Ungherelli from Bologna and Signor Antonio Ristorini, a Florentine, who were paid 150 scudi in salary and 50 scudi for travel and food along the way, including their return trip. Eighty scudi were spent alone for the two singers' costumes, which, to tell the truth, were enchanting. One was a hypocrite's and the other that of a pilgrim—all of silk; they really were beautiful. For Signor Antonio they made a gambler's suit, also well fashioned.

The intermezzo concerned the fate of a gambler who lost everything at basset, and whose wife scolded him for having lost all his money, and found cards in his possession. After scolding some more, she went to do worse—to call him before a judge, and thus ended the first act. In the second intermezzo he appeared dressed as a judge sitting as a court, and she came out and prosecuted her husband to send him to jail, making gestures that would have moved a boulder, and he said he would do as she wished if she were his mistress. After many entreaties she resolved to be his mistress, and gave him her hand. After she did it, he pulled off his beard, took off his disguise, and she recognized him as her husband. She begged his pardon, but he only replied, "what a hypocrite you are, my fine, fine, fine, fine lady," and there it ended.

At the end of the third act she appeared dressed in a beautiful costume, as a pilgrim, driven out by her husband and begging alms—dressed, as I said, as a pilgrim with a bundle, and her husband drew his sword as if to kill her, took the bundle, and sent her away. All the while, she implored him, saying, "kill me, [but] remember our earlier love" in words that would have liquified bronze. In the end he took her back and said that what is past is past.

The actions, the fine manners that she showed her husband can't be described; I'll say only that her gestures and manner on the stage are something that can't be believed by one who hasn't seen them. For this reason I gave her the name "man-killer," because if one had a wife who behaved as she does on the stage, every man would be worn down, and couldn't resist—or if he did, would die, and for this reason I call her the "man-killer." And she really isn't pretty; God help us if she were.

Apparently, Signora Rosa was, in fact, as winning off the stage as on it. In his account of the troupe's departure from Pistoia, Rossi-Morlacchi tells of the fringe benefits accorded this personable intermezzo singer:[64]

August 29, 1725. Today at 2:15 p.m. Signora Rosa Ungherelli left this city with Signor Antonio Ristorini. They went to Florence on their way to Bologna, where they will stay until it comes time for them to go to Turin, where they are going to perform for the fifth time. Many gentlemen went to visit them. Certainly she is a shrewd woman; it's enough to say she's a singer, and there are no fools in that profession. This woman has done well in Pistoia, and so has Signor Antonio. But it's no wonder, because during my time here in Pistoia there have never been women as shrewd as this one—there have, but they weren't like this one. It's enough to say that she brought to her feet people whose names you would never believe. But with presents of food, because in our time there is little money, and only a few who can give it. And the woman was ugly; God help us if she had been beautiful, because she had an inimitable manner, and a way of showing affection that is more than could be described in words. Most favored by her was Doctor Giuseppe Biagio Desideri, who was one of the impresarios. Even so, he gave her many substantial gifts, escorted her as far as Florence, and entertained her; and this gentlemen is a miser, but for this woman he would have gone broke.

Ristorini and Ungarelli were only one of several pairs of traveling singers who introduced Italian intermezzi at foreign courts during the second and third decades of the eighteenth century. Intermezzo performances by itinerant troupes are recorded as early as 1716 in Wolfenbüttel, 1717 in Brunswick and Dresden, 1724 in Prague, 1726 in Mannheim, and 1727 in Breslau.[65] After 1725 the Saxon court at Dresden maintained a pair of intermezzo singers on a permanent basis; they were the husband and wife team of Cosimo and Margherita Ermini,[66] who had previously appeared in intermezzi at Modena, Recanati, Padua, Faenza, and Verona between 1719 and 1724.[67] These two singers were among the troupe of actors and musicians brought from the Saxon court to Moscow by the czarina Anna Ionova in 1731; the intermezzi they performed there between the acts of *commedia dell'arte* plays were the first examples of Italian dramatic music ever heard in Russia.[68]

Intermezzi also figured among the earliest Italian dramatic music heard in Spain; Johann Adolph Hasse's *Don Tabarano* (Scintilla and Tabarano) accompanied the performance of that composer's *Il Demetrio*, which inaugurated presentations of Italian opera at Madrid's Teatro de los Caños de Peral in 1738. The part of Scintilla was played by Santa Marchesini, whom we have already encountered as intermezzo singer in Venice, Naples, and other Italian cities; she seems to have remained in Madrid until her death or retirement sometime before 1748.[69]

Italian intermezzi reached London rather late, considering that this city's close musical connection with Italy dated from the first decade of the eighteenth century. An English "intermede" was performed between the acts of an opera at the Queen's Theater, Haymarket, as early as 1709,[70] but no intermezzi in English, or any other language, appeared in subsequent operas performed at the Haymarket Theater until the season of 1736-37, when a pair of Italian intermezzo singers, Anna Faini and Antonio Lottini, were imported to serve as a weapon in the Opera of Nobility's war against Handel's operatic enterprise at the Covent Garden Theater.[71] Although the pair's repertory consisted of five of the most popular pieces from the Continent,[72] their intermezzo performances seem to have been ineffectual in increasing admissions at the Haymarket Theater, for Burney remarks that "even with that additional lure, according to Colley Cibber, it was at this time that Farinelli sometimes sung [sic] to an audience of five and thirty pounds."[73] Burney records no further performances of intermezzi in London operas until 1750, when Pergolesi's La serva padrona was given as an afterpiece to Vincenzo Ciampi's Adriano in Siria.[74]

Travelling opera companies active on the Continent after 1730 completed the process of spreading the intermezzo repertory into nearly every corner of Europe, as well as continuing local traditions of intermezzo performances already established in some cities. Members of the Pietro and Angelo Mingotti opera companies on tour in Austria, Germany, and Denmark, for example, presented intermezzi with opere serie in Bruenn (1734), Graz (1736-39), Linz (1743), Hamburg (1743-48, 1751-53), Prague (1744), Leipzig (1744, 1751), Dresden (1746-47), Copenhagen (1748-50, 1752-53), and Luebeck (1753).[75] Among the singers most frequently named in intermezzo libretti preserved from the troupes' performances in these cities are Cecilia Monti, Anna Isola, Ginevra Magagnoli, Giovanni Michelli, and Pelegrino Gaggiotti,[76] all of whom had appeared previously at Venice and other Italian cities.[77]

It was probably during their travels in Italy that these singers collected the repertory of their foreign tours; although a few pieces, such as Filippo Finazzi's Il matrimonio sconcertato, dalla forza di Bacco (Rosetta and Policardo), first performed at Prague in 1744, were written especially for them by composers associated with the Mingotti troupes, the repertories of the companies' intermezzo singers seem to have consisted mainly of "old favorites," including Hasse's La finta tedesca (Sciarlotta [Carlotta] and Pantaleone) and Il Tabarano (Scintilla and Tabarano), Pergolesi's La serva padrona (Serpina and Uberto), and Orlandini's La preziosa ridicola (Madama Dulcinea and il cuoco del Marchese del Bosco).[78]

On the departure of his company from Copenhagen following its 1749-50 season there, Pietro Mingotti left behind four members in the Danish capital. The group consisted of Pelegrino Gaggiotti and Grazia

Melini Scalabrini, two specialists in the singing of intermezzi; the composer, Paolo Scalabrini, husband of the latter; and Francesco Darbés, violinist, composer, and librettist.[79] Between 1754 and 1758 this little troupe presented no fewer than 171 performances of at least 19 different Italian intermezzi with spoken dramas; according to contemporary records, the most popular with the Danish audiences were Domenico Paradies' setting of the intermezzi of Moschetta and Grullo and Pergolesi's _La serva padrona_, with a respective total of 19 and 18 performances each.[80]

Another troupe active around the middle of the century in the performance of intermezzi from the operatic repertory outside their original context was that of the impresario Nicolini. Italian intermezzi seem to have been a regular adjunct to the pantomimes presented by his troupe of _Piccoli Holandesi_ (Dutch children) in Germany, Austria, and Bohemia between about 1745 and 1750.[81] Nicolini's company appeared at Frankfurt am Main in 1745 for the festivities celebrating the coronation of Franz I;[82] in following years they visited Munich (1746), Vienna (1746-47), Prague (1747-48), Leipzig, Hamburg, and Dresden (1748-49).[83] Sometime during 1749 Nicolini arrived in Brunswick, where he remained until 1771 as "Directeur des Spectacles" and impresario of the court opera.[84]

One of the last—and certainly the most spectacular—of the intermezzo's extraterritorial conquests was that of Paris during the years 1752-54. We have already noted that the travelling team of Rosa Ungarelli and Antonio Ristorini had introduced Italian intermezzi in that city as early as 1729; according to the _Mercure de France_, their first offering, _Il marito giocatore_ (Serpilla and Bacocco), premiered on June seventh of that year, "was much applauded by reason of a precise and lively performance, in spite of its slight similarity to our customary operas."[85] But a heat wave cut short Ungarelli and Ristorini's activities in Paris;[86] they returned to Italy, and no more Italian intermezzi were heard in the French capital until October 4, 1746, when Pergolesi's _La serva padrona_ was performed there for the first time. On this occasion, it seems to have met with less than complete success; although the _Mercure_ found its music "excellente," popular favor seems to have been reserved for an Italian comedy, _Le Prince de Salerne_, which opened a few nights later.[87]

The 1752-54 seasons, then, furnished the Parisian public's third exposure to Italian intermezzi. This time the singers were members of a troupe brought from Strasbourg by Eustache Bambini, who, since 1749, had been producer of the Italian opera there.[88] His company's repertory included several full-length _opere buffe_ and four intermezzi: Pergolesi's

La serva padrona and *Tracollo, medico ignorante* (Livietta and Tracollo), the pasticcio *Il maestro di musica* (Lauretta, Lamberto and Colagianni), and *Il giocatore* (Serpilla and Bacocco), with music by Giuseppe Maria Orlandini and other composers.[89]

The French reaction to this Italian "new music" was the celebrated *Querelle des Bouffons*, a pointless controversy in which gallons of ink were wasted in a vain effort to compare the Italian *buffo* style with that of the traditional French *tragédie lyrique*. The *Querelle des Bouffons*, however, not only generated an enormous quantity of literary polemic, but also inspired a rash of musical parodies and imitations that opened a whole new chapter in the history of French opera.[90] As such, it represents a significant climax to a half century of activity by travelling Italian singers engaged in propagating the intermezzo repertory.

The *Raccolta copiosa d'intermedj*

A literary counterpart to the activities of travelling singers just discussed was the appearance in 1723 of a two-volume collection entitled *Raccolta copiosa d'intermedj, parte da rappresentarsi col canto, alcuni senza musica, con altri in fine in lingua milanese* ("Copious collection of intermezzi, part of which are to be performed with singing, some without music, with others at the end in Milanese dialect"). The title pages of the volumes cite Amsterdam as the place of publication, but according to Allacci and other eighteenth-century sources, the collection was printed at Milan.[91] It contains texts for 54 musical intermezzi, each consisting of from one to four parts (see Table 5).

A preface by the anonymous compiler explains the raison d'être of the volumes:

> Great care is often taken in the selection of intermezzi that are inserted during performances of operas for the necessary relief from the excessive gravity of the subjects presented on the stage. Therefore, in order to facilitate their use, I have thought it well to make a very copious collection of them, having to that end gathered together a great number of manuscripts, including foreign ones, and having obtained the remainder [from among those] that are reported to have acquired the greatest renown in the principal cities of Italy, in whose theaters they were performed with universal applause.[92]

The preface fails to point out that several of the texts included in the collection were not originally written for performance as intermezzi in *opere serie*. The episodes of Povertà and Apparenza and Sincerità and Providenza, for example, served as intermezzi in the comic play *Il barone di birbanza* by the Milanese poet Carlo Maria Maggi (1630-1699), while those of Poeta and Verità and Avarizia and Imeneo figured in another comedy of the same writer, *Il manco male*.[93] Moreover, the "intermedio" of Lesbo and Cocca is actually an abbreviated version of a prologue for a spoken drama by Maggi,[94] who was also the author of at least one other intermezzo included in the *Raccolta, Il consulto de' medici*.[95] There is no evidence to indicate that these and several other texts contained in the collection were ever employed as operatic intermezzi.[96]

Also somewhat misleading is the emphasis the preface places on "foreign manuscripts" as a source of the collection's contents. As may be seen even from a comparison of the titles and dramatis personae in Table 5 with the comparatively few listed in Appendix A and Table 3 (Chapter I), a large percentage—if not a majority—of the texts contained in the *Raccolta* that actually served as operatic intermezzi first appeared in Italian prints.[97] The pasticcio practice, already noted in connection with the earliest independent Venetian intermezzi, and well advanced by 1723, makes it possible to identify with some certainty the exact editions of the texts reprinted by the editor in his *Raccolta* by a comparison of their respective aria incipits (see Table 6).

If, as its preface suggests, the purpose of the collection was to offer impresarios and potential composers a wider variety of texts, the *Raccolta* must be counted largely a failure. As we have seen, travelling singers tended to restrict their repertories to "the same old intermezzi" that found favor in town after town; moreover, nearly all the international successes composed after 1723 were settings of libretti not contained in the collection. Nor did reprinting in the *Raccolta* of some operatic comic scenes that had not previously been employed as independent intermezzi seem to have facilitated their use as such. The comic scenes of Tullia and Linco, which accompanied many revivals of Bononcini's setting of Silvio Stampiglia's *Il trionfo di Camilla regina de Volsci* (Naples, 1696),[98] for example, seem never to have been employed as intermezzi in any other opera either before or after 1723.

Nonetheless, publication of the *Raccolta copiosa d'intermedj* may have stimulated new settings of at least some forgotten intermezzo texts from the first decade of the eighteenth century. For instance, there seem to have been very few performances of *L'ammalato immaginario* (Erighetta and D. Chilone) between 1707, the date of its first setting, and 1723, after which a rash of revivals is recorded.[99] Only one of the libretti for these revivals bears the name of a composer (Vinci's version for Naples in 1726), but it seems unlikely that all the other revivals employed the music of Gasparini's original setting of this text after so long a period of disuse. Unfortunately, not enough composer attributions are recorded to determine how many other intermezzi were given

TABLE 5

CONTENTS OF THE *RACCOLTA COPIOSA D'INTERMEDJ*
VOLUME I

Title	Dramatis Personae In Order of Appearance	Number of Intermezzi	Pages
Il consulto de' medici	Infermo, Chimico, Primo Medico, Secondo Medico, Paggio	1	1-7
L'ammalato immaginario	Erighetta, D. Chilone	3	8-22
	Carissimo, Dirindina, Liscione	2	23-36
	Lisa, Luzio	2	37-44
	Tifo, Grifina	3	45-53
	Lucrina, Lesbo	4	54-64
	Birena, Niso	2	65-69
Il matrimonio per forza	Gerondo, Rosmene	3	70-85
	Tiburzio, Melinda	3	86-102
Cola mal maritato	Cola, Drusilla	2	103-111
Melissa vendicata	Griletta, Serpillo	3	112-25
	Mirena, Floro	3	126-36
Ircano innamorato	Lidia, Ircano	3	137-49
Il marito giocatore, e la moglie bacchettona	Bacocco, Serpilla	3	150-63
	Catulla, Lardone	3	164-74
Il mondo nuovo	Bertolda, Volpone	2	175-83
L'avaro	Pancrazio, Fiammetta	3	184-203
	Batto, Lisetta	2	204-210
	Lisa, Bleso	2	211-16
	Linco, Tullia	2	217-21
	Dorisbe, Lido	2	222-29
Zamberlucco	Palandrana, Zamberlucco	3	230-44
	Povertà, Apparenza	1	245-46
	Sincerità, Providenza	1	247-48
	Poeta, Verità	1	249-50
	Avarizia, Imeneo	1	251-52
	Sciabla, Lindoro	3	253-61
	Memmio, Attilia	3	262-69
	Dalisa, Breno	3	270-82
	Lesbina, Milo	2	283-88
	Grilletta, Demo	2	289-92
	Quinzio, Sestilia	1	293-98

TABLE 5 (continued)

Title	Dramatis Personae In Order of Appearance	Number of Intermezzi	Pages
	Armilla, Rafo	2	299-307
	Corrado, Lauretta	2	308-315
	Rosinda, Nesso	3	316-329
	Daliso, Piccariglio, Climene	1	330-36
	Paride, Dottore, Soldato, Poeta	1	337-39
	Lesbo, Cocca	1	340-45
	Giunone, Momo, Eolo	1	346-50
	Momo, Dori, Nettuno	1	351-55
Il baurgois genthilomes	Larinda, Vanesio	3	356-71
	Grilla, Maffeo	2	372-83
	Donna Speranza, Don Pronto	2	384-91
	Burlotto, Brunetta	3	392-409
	Vespetta, Pimpinone	3	410-21

VOLUME II

("Parte da rappresentarsi col canto" only)

Title	Dramatis Personae In Order of Appearance	Number of Intermezzi	Pages
	Lisetta, Astrobolo	4	1-13
	Polastrella, Parpagnaco	3	14-28
	Lisetta, Creperio	3	29-38
	Flacco, Servilia	3	39-46
La preziosa ridicola	Madama Dulcinea, il cuoco del Marchese del Bosco	3	47-63
	Spiletta, Batto	3	64-72
Il bravo poltrone	Fiammetta, Grillone	3	73-88
La gallina perduta	Pandora, Betta, Lisetta, Caja, Califronia, Doralice, Procuratore, Dottore primo, Dottore secondo	2	89-102
Giudizio di Paride su le tre Dee	Saturno, Momo, Vulcano, Marte, Giunone, Venere, Pallade, Giove, Mercurio	2	103-114

TABLE 6

SOME SOURCES OF THE *RACCOLTA COPIOSA D'INTERMEDJ*

Title and/or Dramatis Personae	Textual Concordances
Batto, Lisetta	*Batto, e Lisetta* (Venice, 1713)
Il mondo nuovo (Bertolda, Volpone)	*Il nuovo mondo* (Venice, 1709)
Catulla, Lardone	Untitled *Intermezzi* (Venice, 1708)
Cola mal maritato (Cola, Drusilla)	*Cola mal maritato* (Venice, 1721)
Corrado, Lauretta	Comic scenes 1 and 4 in [Francesco Silvani], *Il duello d'amore e di vendetta* (Naples, 1715)
Dorisbe, Lido	Comic scenes in [Apostolo Zeno and Pietro Pariati], *L'Engelberta* (Milan, 1708)
Grilletta, Demo	Untitled *Intermedii* ([Venice, 1709])
L'avaro (Pancrazio, Fiammetta)	*L'avaro* (Venice, 1720)
Quinzio, Sestilia	Comic Scene 3 in [Apostolo Zeno], *Lucio Vero* (Naples, 1722)
Rosinda, Nesso	Comic scenes in [Apostolo Zeno], *L'Eumene* (Naples, 1715)
Tiburzio, Melinda	*Melinda, e Tiburzio* (Venice, 1721)

such a new lease on life by their publication in the *Raccolta*. In any case, the collection's actual utility seems to have fallen considerably short of hopes the compiler expressed for it in his preface; indeed, the nature of its contents leads one to suspect that the *Raccolta copiosa* may have been the work of a dilettante designed for consumption by literati rather than a practical handbook compiled by a professional man of the theater.

THE LIBRETTO

Intermezzo and *Opera Seria*

It is difficult to establish a purely functional raison d'être for eighteenth-century intermezzi. Occasional references in libretti suggest they sometimes served a useful purpose in the staging of an opera; the notice to the reader of an anonymous *Il Seleuco* (Messina, 1711), for example, states that the comic scenes printed at the end of the book for insertion at various points during the performance were added to allow time for the operation and changing of the sets.[1] In this connection, it is perhaps significant that when an intermezzo appears in the midst of an act (usually the last) of an *opera seria*, it almost invariably is placed before a change of scenery. And Henry Carey, author and composer of *Nancy: or, the Parting Lovers*, an English interlude, justifies the existence of such entr'acte pieces with the observation that "these little starts of fancy, . . . afford a pleasant diversion, and supply a vacancy on the stage, while other entertainments are getting ready. . . ."[2]

As was the case with the seventeenth-century intermedi they replaced, comic intermezzi performed during the course of an opera also served to articulate the drama and provide the illusion of a time lapse before resumption of the principal action. The edition of Domenico Lalli's *Il pentimento generoso* printed at Venice in 1719 specifies the necessity for such an interruption after the crucial twelfth scene of act three, during which Aldrico, brother-in-law of the queen of Sparta, repents of his disloyalty to the latter and resolves that instead of assisting the villainous Almanzorre in the murder of the queen's son, he will make peace with her ally and defend the royal family. Immediately following this scene, a note in the libretto informs the reader that "here the third intermezzo must be performed to allow time for Aldrico's deed."[3]

Such isolated notices may reflect more widespread theatrical conventions than their frequency of occurrence would suggest, but it is more likely that the intermezzo's most important function was simply to provide the humor that had been supplied as an integral part of the text in seventeenth-century operas. Although the Arcadian reform had largely eliminated the indiscriminate mixing of clowns and kings—not to mention the clowning kings—that had figured in the latter, avoiding unalloyed tragedy was still a major concern of eighteenth-century librettists; the preface to the Neapolitan edition of Antonio Salvi's *Arsace* exemplifies a poet's vacillation between fidelity to an original subject (Thomas Corneille's *Le Comte d'Essex*) and the demands of Italian musical theater of his time:

> The purpose of the author was to create a musical tragedy with a really tragic ending (a novelty no longer seen, at least on Italian stages) and to gain the reputation of being the first to have you leave the theater in tears. . . .

But—

> the ending has been somewhat altered in another theater in order not to render it completely funereal, as has been done again here by its director with no little difficulty; . . . likewise it was necessary to add the comic parts, but in a manner so as not to interrupt the drama, but merely lessen the melancholy with a little gaiety.[4]

The consideration, then, seems not to have been *whether* to allow the comic element a place in musical tragedy, but *how*. The manner in which a comic intermezzo was dramatically related to an *opera seria* may be characterized "somewhat fancifully" with the terminology employed by Willi Apel in quite a different context as "connected," "unconnected," or "disconnected."[5]

Audiences at Naples during the first quarter of the eighteenth century seem to have preferred intermezzi dramatically related to the operas with which they were performed. A note in the libretto for Alessandro Scarlatti's setting of Agostino Piovene's *La principessa fedele*, presented at the Teatro San Bartolomeo in 1710, four years after appearance of the first substantial number of dramatically "unconnected" intermezzi at Venice, cautions the reader that

> if you find the present drama altered in some respects from its original form, performed last Autumn in Venice [with music by Francesco Gasparini], do not attribute it to the presumption of he who was in charge of its adaptation, but only to the taste of the city in which it is performed, it being necessary to interweave the comic roles and render them in some measure necessary to the plot of the drama, . . . in order to adapt it to the usage of this city.[6]

"Interweaving the comic roles" generally took the form of making the latter servants of the opera's principals, and allowing them to appear in scenes with their masters, where they usually conducted themselves in a decorous manner, giving advice, carrying messages, imparting gossip, and generally rendering themselves useful, if not essential to the unfolding of the drama. In their own scenes, the comic characters often discussed affairs of their royal masters as a preliminary to their clowning, further strengthening their relationship to the opera's principal action.

As has already been noted, the form and content of these comic scenes is similar—indeed, sometimes identical—to those of dramatically independent intermezzi performed at Venice and elsewhere during the same period. Except for their relationship to the drama, Neapolitan *scene buffe* during the first quarter of the eighteenth century differed only in number and placement within the opera from contemporary unconnected intermezzi, and even in these respects they began to resemble the latter as the century progressed. Before 1715, *opere serie* performed at Naples contain up to seven comic scenes, with an average of four per opera. Between 1715 and 1730 the average falls to three; after 1730 two are standard. Shortly after the turn of the century *scene buffe* in Neapolitan operas began to gravitate—"sink like sediment" in the words of Edward Dent—to the ends of acts.[7] Before 1710, fewer than half the preserved libretti have comic scenes at the ends of both acts one and two; after 1710 the proportion is reversed, and by 1720 it had become the invariable arrangement to end the first two acts with comic scenes. It was not until 1722, however, that the term "intermezzo" began to be applied to these scenes,[8] and comic characters continued to make sporadic appearances with their royal masters during the acts of Neapolitan *opere serie* at least until 1726.[9]

Although such connected intermezzi occasionally figured in operas performed outside of Naples even after this date,[10] by far the more usual custom was to maintain complete separation between the cast, setting, and plot of the intermezzo and opera with which it was presented. The practical advantages of this scheme are obvious; any "unconnected" intermezzo may be performed with equal propriety—or lack thereof—with any opera. The disadvantage is equally obvious. With no relation between the intermezzo and opera, their performance together creates an operatic sandwich of two totally unrelated plots and dramatis personae presented in alternation. We have seen that this arrangement first became popular beginning in 1706 at Venice; twenty-five years later, Gian Carlo Bonlini was able to report with almost complete accuracy that intermezzi performed there "never had any connection with the drama to which they were coupled, it being possible to use or omit them at will . . . all the more so since they are always printed separately [from the opera libretto] and are capable of being adapted to any [dramatic] theme."[11]

The practice Bonlini describes seems to have resulted from a typically Italian compromise between literary idealism and practical necessity. As Robert Freeman suggested in his dissertation "Opera without Drama: Currents of Change in Italian Opera, 1675 to 1725, and the Roles Played Therein by Zeno, Caldara, and Others," libretti written for Venice seem to have led the way in musico-dramatic changes that culminated in Zeno's celebrated reform of seventeenth-century opera, one important element of which was the elimination of comic subplots from the principal story line.[12] As early as 1675 the preface of a libretto published at Venice by Francesco Frugoni had inveighed against the indiscriminate admixture of heroes, royalty, and buffoons.[13] Librettists active primarily at Venice after this date seem to have pioneered in eliminating the combination of serious and comic elements in opera; Giovanni Maria Crescimbeni calls special attention to the disuse of comic characters in Venetian libretti around 1700, crediting Domenico David and Apostolo Zeno with this innovation.[14] It may be safely assumed, however, that audiences at Venice were no less desirous than their cousins in other Italian cities for comic diversion in their serious operas. Relegating the comic element to the ends of acts seems to have been a successful compromise that satisfied both the idealism of librettists and practical demands of the theater.

Poets and impresarios in most centers of operatic production outside of Naples were quick to see the advantages of "unconnected" intermezzi. Comic scenes dramatically independent of the *opere serie* with which they were performed and labeled "intermezzi" were published (either separately or at the ends of acts in the opera libretto) at least as early as 1708 in Milan and Bologna, and 1711 at Ferrara and Rome.[15] That this practice originated (or at least first gained currency) at Venice and was reasonably widespread by the beginning of the second decade of the eighteenth century is apparent from remarks that preface Girolamo Gigli's adaptation of his *La fede nei tradimenti* published at Rome in 1711 under the title *L'Anagilda*. This preface is also noteworthy for continuing to reserve the term "intermezzo" for the dances and scenic display that accompanied the comic characters' clowning, rather than the scenes themselves:

> This opera, which has appeared so many times in various Italian theaters, is now seen in Rome with a few small changes and the addition of arias with which it was decided to revive and better adapt it to present-day usage by its own original author. The latter, by command of the generous individual under whose patronage the work is performed [Francesco Maria Ruspoli], . . . has inserted two comic roles, completely separate from the knot of the drama (as is done nowadays on the stages of Venice and elsewhere) with which are interwoven the intermezzi, consisting of amusing contrivances of dance and supernumeraries, composed for your greater pleasure.[16]

It is only natural that a majority of the most popular intermezzo texts of the eighteenth century were written expressly to be "completely separate from the knot" of a particular musical drama; such texts required no alterations to allow their performance with any number of different operas, and were thus perfectly suited for use by the itinerant troupes that spread them across the face of Europe beginning about 1710. A few pieces, however, originated as comic scenes in one opera and were later detached and modified for more universal application. The number of such intermezzi seems to have been comparatively small; only one, in fact, appears among the popular texts listed in Appendix A of the present study. Known variously as *Lidia, e Ircano, Ircano innamorato*, and *Li amori d'Ircano e Lidia*, its history will serve to exemplify the vicissitudes of a "disconnected" intermezzo libretto.

The comic scenes of Lidia and Ircano originally appeared as an integral part of Silvio Stampiglia's *L'Abdolomino*, premiered with music of Giovanni Maria Bononcini at Vienna during the carnival of 1709. Stampiglia's drama is based very loosely upon an episode from the fourth book of Quintus Curius' *Historiae Alexandri Magni* which recounts Alexander's bestowal of the kingdom of Sidon on one Abdalonymus after a pair of young Sidonian gentlemen (named Eldiro and Rosmeno in the opera) had themselves refused the crown. Most of Stampiglia's added *accidenti verissimi*, including a pair of amorous triangles formed by the cast's four noblemen and two ladies of Sidon need not detain us here; more important for our purpose is the subplot involving Lidia, a gardener in the service of Abdolomino, and Ircano, a Sidonian bourgeois. The following outline will indicate the character of their scenes together and general relationship to the opera's principal action:

I.i   Ircano wonders aloud when Lidia will marry him. She tells him to be silent; her master is sleeping.

I.vi   Ircano presses his suit again; Lidia promises she will be his bride after he helps her water the garden and orchard.

I.xii   The arrival of a crowd proclaiming Abdolomino king prevents the pair from announcing their engagement.

II.ii   Lidia once again puts Ircano off; she must inquire if her newly crowned master needs anything from his garden or orchard.

II.v   Ircano attempts to claim his promised bride, but Lidia will have nothing to do with him. Abdolomino has given her the orchard and garden; she is now a "padrona."

III.ii   Lidia brings Abdolomino a basket of apples from the orchard, but he is preoccupied with affairs of the heart and sends her away. Ircano petitions the king to make him a page; Abdolomino ignores him. "Silence gives consent," reasons Ircano.

III.vi   Ircano informs Lidia of his "appointment" as page in the royal court; she is unimpressed and rejects his suit again.

III.x   Resplendent in his new page's outfit, Ircano visits Lidia; she remains implacable.

III.xi   The opera's principals straighten out their amorous entanglements; Lidia finally agrees to marry Ircano.

In 1711, two years after its premiere at Vienna, Bononcini's setting of Stampiglia's drama, including these *scene buffe*, was revised at Naples with some new music by Francesco Mancini; the opera itself seems then to have dropped from sight, but the comic scenes of Lidia and Ircano maintained an independent existence in one form or another until at least 1747. Their first appearance as a disconnected intermezzo seems to have been in conjunction with an anonymous setting of Zeno and Pariati's *Astarto* performed at the Teatro Capranica in Rome during carnival of 1715.[17] This version of the intermezzo retains only two of Stampiglia's *scene buffe* in somewhat altered form; part one is roughly similar to Act I, scene vi of *Abdolomino* except for the substitution of a new terminal duet, while the intermezzo's second part preserves most of the dialogue and the two aria texts contained in Act II, scene v of Stampiglia's opera. A new duet was necessary to end the little drama on a note of reconciliation. Eliminated, of course, is all connection with the principal action of *Abdolomino* except for the garden locale, now property of "la regina."

The same year of their performance in Rome, these intermezzi were published in a three-part version at Ferrara, probably for use with Fortunato Chelleri's setting of Belisario Valeriani's pastoral drama *La caccia in Etolia*, performed sometime during the summer of 1715 at the Teatro S. Stefano.[18] Despite a prefatory note in this edition informing the reader that "these three intermezzi were extracted from several scenes of the [musical] drama *Abdolomino*, performed in Naples,"[19] Allacci attributes authorship of the text to Valeriani.[20] Obviously, the latter's connection with this piece (if any) could have been only that of arranger. Part one of the intermezzo is a much expanded and altered version of *Abdolomino* I.i; while part two is similar to I.vi, with two additional aria texts, one of them drawn from II.vi of the model. The intermezzo's third part is based very freely upon I.xii, and ends with a duet whose first half derives from one in III.vi. Once more changes were necessary to effect a happy ending. Needless to say, the redactor deleted all references to Stampiglia's drama in his arrangement of the intermezzo text. Substituted for the original opening dialogue in which Lidia cautions Ircano not to awaken the sleeping Abdolomino is a warning not to disturb "povera Aminta"; otherwise the text is also dramatically independent of the opera with which it was performed. The same was doubtless true of the at least ten other versions of the text performed with as many different operas between 1716 and 1747 in various Italian cities.[21] In view of this intermezzo's rustic setting, it is interesting to note that at least some of these operas were pastoral in character (see Table 7). The majority, however, were *drammi per musica* in which Lidia's agricultural activities must have interjected an incongruous element, to say the least. It seems likely, however, that such incongruities troubled eighteenth-century audiences very little; once one accepts the convention of alternating musical tragedy and comedy with no dramatic connection, the character of the comedy itself becomes a relatively insignificant consideration.[22]

Structure and Verse

As a point of departure for our survey of the intermezzo's organization, language, and poetry, we may take the brief comments of Francesco Quadrio, apparently the only contemporary Italian writer who addressed himself to these subjects:

> Now, since the manner in which musical intermezzi are written is the same as that customary in the composition and performance of operas, we would waste our energy if we were to expend more words about it. It will be enough to note here that in regard to their style and verse the same rules apply as in other types of musical poetry.

> As for the division of these intermezzi in acts, or in parts and scenes, until now each has capriciously done as he wished. It would be praiseworthy indeed if some attempt were made to give them, too, proportionate and correct form.[23]

TABLE 7

OPERAS PERFORMED WITH INTERMEZZI OF LIDIA AND IRCANO

Date	City	Author	Title	Genre
1715	Rome	[Apostolo Zeno and Pietro Pariati][a]	Astarto	Drama per musica
1715	Ferrara	[Belisario Valeriani	La caccia in Etolia][b]	Pastorale per musica
1716	Bologna	[Francesco Antonio Novi	Il Diomede][c]	Drama per musica
1719	Modena	[Francesco Silvani and Domenico Lalli	Li veri amici][d]	Drama per musica
1722	Venice	[Niccolò Minato	L'Iffide greca][e]	Drama per musica
[1726	Venice	Giovanni Battista Neri	Amor indovino][f]	Favola pastorale in musica
1729	Venice	[Pietro d'Averara	La Dori][g]	Pastorale eroica per musica
[1730	Venice	Antonio Maria Lucchini	Selin gran signor de' Turchi][h]	Drama per musica
[1730	Bologna	Guiseppe Maria Buini	La maschera levata al vizio][i]	Divertimento comico per musica
[1730	Venice	Francesco de Lemene	L'inganno felice][j]	Pastorale
[1731	Venice	Giovanni Palazzi	Armida al campo d'Egitto][k]	Drama per musica
1747	Bologna	?	Aleria	Drama per musica

TABLE 7 (continued)

[a]Allacci, *Drammaturgia,* col. 123.

[b]*Ibid.*, coll. 151, 470.

[c]*Ibid.*, col. 470; [Alessandro Macchiavelli], *Serie cronologica dei drammi recitati sù de' pubblici teatri di Bologna* (Bologna, 1737), p. 69.

[d]Alessandro Gandini *et al.*, *Cronistoria dei teatri di Modena dal 1539 al 1871* (Modena, 1873), I, 55-56.

[e]Groppo, "Catalogo purgatissimo," p. 193.

[f]*Ibid.*, p. 208.

[g]*Ibid.*, p. 219.

[h]*Ibid.*, p. 221.

[i]Macchiavelli, p. 77; *cf.* Allacci, coll. 513-14.

[j]Groppo, p. 224.

[k]*Idem,* p. 225.

The apparent capriciousness of which Quadrio complains in regard to the number of parts into which intermezzi were divided seems to have resulted from a number of factors, including length of the *opere serie* with which they were originally performed, changing taste, and the personal preference of the singers themselves.

All of the relatively few preserved intermezzi in four parts seem to have been premiered with five-act operas, but the reverse was by no means always the case. Francesco Gasparini's setting of the four-part *Lisetta e Astrobolo*, for example, was first presented between the five acts of his *Taican rè della Cina* at Venice's Teatro S. Cassiano in 1707; yet another of Gasparini's five-act operas, *Engelberta*, performed at that same theater one year later was accompanied by *Parpagnacco* (Pollastrella and Parpagnacco), an intermezzo of only three parts.[24] And it was customary at Vienna after 1714 to fill only the first and third intervals of five-act operas with musical intermezzi, while devoting the periods after acts two and four to the performance of ballets.[25]

Despite such variations in local custom, audiences in most cities seem to have preferred their intermezzi divided into three parts during the first three decades of the eighteenth century. In the *Raccolta copiosa d'intermedj* of 1723, which advertises itself as a catholic collection of the most popular pieces produced to that date, three-part intermezzi account for a substantial majority of those of the operatic type represented.[26] We have already noted that after 1730 the number of intermezzi performed in conjunction with *opere serie* at Naples dropped to two. Other Italian cities soon followed Naples' lead in this respect, if for no other reason than that intermezzi of Neapolitan origin dominated their stages by this time. Three-part intermezzi written before 1730 were sometimes even truncated to suit the new fashion; Antonio Salvi's popular text, *L'artigiano gentiluomo* (Larinda and Vanesio), for example, was cut from its original three to two parts for revivals at Dresden (1734), London (1737), Cortona (1738), and Venice (1739).[27]

Finally, as an example of the pure whimsy that apparently sometimes determined how many parts of an intermezzo were actually presented, we may record Groppo's statement that during a revival of *Monsieur de Porsugnac* (Grilletta and Porsugnacco) at Venice's Teatro S. Angelo in conjunction with the premiere of Ignazio Fiorillo's *Il vincitor de se stesso* during the autumn of 1741, the singers, Catterina Brogi and Pietro Pertici, initially performed only the first two of the intermezzo's original three parts, then after several evenings added the third, which was not even printed in the libretto used at the performance. Groppo notes further that just one year later at the same theater Brogi and Pertici repeated the intermezzo with Pietro Pellegrini's *Cirene*, this time performing only its first and third parts.[28]

In regard to the internal organization of their individual parts, we have already observed that intermezzi closely followed the model of the seventeenth-century comic scenes from which they evolved: a series of arias separated by recitatives and terminating in a duet. Librettists generally allowed each of the intermezzo's two singing roles one aria per part; the organization of the popular *Zamberlucco* (Venice, 1709) is typical in this respect of hundreds of intermezzo texts written during the first half of the eighteenth century:

> Part 1   Aria (Palandrana)
> Recitative
> Aria (Zamberlucco)
> Recitative
> Duet

Part 2   Recitative
          Aria (Zamberlucco)
          Recitative
          Aria (Palandrana)
          Recitative
          Duet

Part 3   Aria (Zamberlucco)
          Recitative
          Aria (Palandrana)
          Recitative
          Duet

Minor variations on this scheme include the addition or subtraction of an aria text for one or another of the characters and the occasional substitution of a duet for an initial or medial aria, but in general the sequence of numbers in the individual parts of intermezzi is just as immutable as the chain of recitative and aria texts found in the acts of contemporary *opere serie.*

Like the latter, and in contrast to *opere buffe* during the first half of the eighteenth century, which, particularly at Naples, frequently employed regional dialects, intermezzi generally are written entirely in the literary Italian of Tuscany. In the few exceptions, snatches of dialect are confined to the portrayal of character and local color—the latter usually not that of the intermezzo's place of origin. Thus Aurilla and Cola, protagonists of the intermezzi premiered with the opera *Il pescatore fortunato principe d'Ischia* by the Neapolitan composer and librettist Francesco Antonio Novi at Bologna's Teatro Formagliari during the carnival of 1716, sometimes speak in the dialect of Naples, but the intermezzi seem never to have been performed in that city, although they were later revived in Modena (October, 1716) and Venice (autumn, 1720).[29] Similarly, the male character of *Petronio, e Dorise,* an intermezzo performed at Venice in 1721, expresses himself in the argot of Bologna, but there is no record of the piece ever being heard there. And *La franchezza delle donne* (Lesbina and Sempronio), an intermezzo set in Venice and employing snatches of that city's dialect, is the work of a Roman poet, Tomaso Mariani, and received its premiere at Naples.[30]

As one might expect, librettists employed dialectical expressions rather sparingly even in these examples so as to permit their comprehension by audiences in all regions of Italy. Surely no audience anywhere in the peninsula would fail to comprehend the words, much less the humor, of arias such as the following, in which a henpecked Neapolitan husband expresses his woe in typically watered-down dialect:

> Uh managgia la fortuna,
> Che Moliera m'ave dato,
> Che me fruscia de notte, e de journo.
> Mo me dole assae lo capo,
> Ca se dura, aggio paura
> Priesto priesto 'n ce nasca no cuorno.[31]

> (Oh damn the luck my wife has brought me;
> It torments me night and day.
> Right now my head is killing me;
> From its hardness I'm afraid that soon a horn will sprout from it.)

Similar to the treatment of dialect is that of classical and foreign languages, short passages of which, frequently diluted by Italian words for easier comprehension, sometimes appear in intermezzi to establish character or local color. Thus Carlotta, female protagonist of an intermezzo frequently performed under the title *La finta tedesca,* mouths ersatz German to help create her disguise; in the third comic scene of Alessandro Scarlatti's *Tigrane,* Orcone appears dressed as Doctor Gratiano spouting nonsense in Latin; and French idioms frequently figure in intermezzi set in that country or modeled on plays of its dramatists.[32]

Librettists also occasionally employed foreign languages in intermezzi for comic effect. As an example let us take a dialogue between Pericca and Varrone, characters in the anonymous comic scenes added to Zeno's *Scipione nelle Spagne* for its performance at Naples in 1714 with music of Alessandro Scarlatti. In the fifth episode Pericca appears disguised as a Spanish lady; her ventures into that language and their misinterpretations by Varrone must have been a source of considerable amusement to the Neapolitan audience:

> *Per.* Digame Cavallero
>   Tan bizarro, su nombre?
> *Var.* Signora, non son ombra,
>   Ma son uomo davvero.
>   . . . .
> *Per.* Digame, que ora es?
> *Var.* Che oras? Or la servos;
>   Ecco l'orloggio, veggas.
> *Per.* Siette, ocho, nueve, dies, y onze . . .
> *Var.* Pesa altro, che dieci oncie.

(*Per.*   Tell me your name [*nombre*], most gallant sir.
Var.   My lady, I'm no shadow [*ombra*], but a real man.
. . . .
Per.   Tell me, what time is it?
Var.   What time? Let me serve you;
        Here is my watch, you may see.
Per.   Seven, eight, nine, ten, and eleven [*dies, y onze*] –
Var.   It weighs more than ten ounces [*dieci oncie*].)

As in other types of Italian dramatic poetry produced during the eighteenth century, the recitatives of intermezzi consist of freely alternating lines of seven and eleven syllables. Unlike the recitatives of contemporary *opere serie*, however, where blank verse predominates, those of intermezzi are generally rhymed throughout. A succession of couplets is a common verse type, as in the following discourse between Lauretta and Corrado:

Lau.   Ecco il luogo opportuno,
        Ove non verrà alcuno
        A disturbare il nostro gran duello.
Cor.   (Corrado abbi cervello.)
        E che è venuto a far quell'uomo là?
Lau.   Adesso partirà.
        Prendi tu quella spada, e quel pugnale,
        Che teco esser degg'io ne l'armi equale.
Cor.   Bene, bene: obbligato del favore.
        (O che gran batticore!)[33]

But many other rhyme schemes appear, including lengthy monorhymes, such as found in a speech of the male protagonist of the intermezzi *Despina, e Niso*:

Sì, io qui bugie non sforno.
Anzi allor, ch'io volea far quì ritorno
Mi si son posti tutti quanti intorno,
Che volean, che facess' ivi soggiorno.
E vè s'è ver, che in abbracciarmi un orno.
Osserva ben m'à quasi rotto un ciglio.[34]

Aria texts in intermezzi are also similar in form to those of contemporary *opere serie*, but differ from them in matters of style. A sampling of arias from popular intermezzi represented in the *Raccolta copiosa d'intermedj* of 1723 reveals a decided preference for verses of eight-syllable lines, the same length favored by librettists of *opere serie* around the second decade of the eighteenth century, according to the poet and critic Pier Jacopo Martello.[35] Nor is there any difference between the basic construction of aria texts in *opere serie* and intermezzi during their period of coexistence. In both genres an aria text typically consists of two stanzas containing three or more lines apiece, the rhyme schemes of which are variable except for a customary consonance between the final line of each stanza. In short, the typical intermezzo aria text, no less than its counterpart in *opera seria*, was designed for treatment in da capo form. We shall see that they were almost invariably so treated.

Only the greater length of aria texts in intermezzi, in fact, distinguishes them formally from those of contemporary *opere serie*. The latter almost always confine themselves to eight lines arranged in a pair of quatrains, while aria texts in a given intermezzo may average as many as 14 lines each, and may number up to 31 verses.[36] A comparison of the arias in Metastasio's only contribution to the genre, *L'impresario delle Canarie* with those of his *Didone abbandonata*, the opera with which it was premiered at Naples in 1724, reveals that only three of the opera's 24 arias are longer than eight lines; yet three of the intermezzo's four arias exceed this length,[37] and one of them, "Recitar è una miseria," runs to 18 lines.

The comparatively greater length of aria texts in intermezzi is easily explained by the type of musical treatment for which they were destined. Clearly, the extensive coloratura customary in arias of *opera seria* precluded lengthy texts, while the more syllabic settings of the intermezzo permitted more verses, even when one makes allowance for the constant repetition of short phrases characteristic of the *buffo* musical style.

A more fundamental difference between the verse of *opera seria* and that of the intermezzo is the latter's natural, fast-moving, almost improvisatory quality, which contrasts sharply with the stilted speech of contemporary serious opera. The impromptu character of dialogue in the intermezzo is seen best in the arguments and amorous exchanges that account for a large portion of their recitatives. Passages such as the following from the intermezzi of Moschetta and Grullo are strongly reminiscent of models for improved dialogue in *commedia dell'arte* plays:[38]

> *Gru.*   Tu?
> *Mos.*   Mi.
> *Gru.*   Amante?
> *Mos.*   Amante.
> *Gru.*   Di Grullo.
> *Mos.*   Sì di Grullo.
> *Gru.*   Ed il tuo cuore?

Mos.	Sì ed il mio cuore.
Gru.	Da me vorrebbe amor?
Mos.	Vorrebbe amore.

(*Gru.*	What you?
Mos.	Yes, I—
Gru.	In love?—
Mos.	In love—
Gru.	With Grullo?
Mos.	Ay—with Grullo!
Gru.	And can your heart?—
Mos.	Yes, yes, my heart—
Gru.	Have any love for me?
Mos.	Has love for none but thee!)[39]

Despite the prevailing realistic quality of their dialogue, characters in intermezzi are not above philosophizing aloud in arias that constitute a comic counterpart to the sententious verses of the wooden figures in a Metastasian *opera seria*. Larinda's monologue near the beginning of *Le Bourgeois gentil-homme* (Larinda and Vanesio) provides a sample of such "moralizing in reverse":

Le moneta è un certo che,
Che oggi giorno tutto può
Tutto spunta e tutto fa.
Piace agli altri, e piace a me
E perche
Io son povera, e non l'ò
Vado intorno ad un che l'à.

(For far and near say all you can,
'Tis money! money makes the man.
The ready is a certain spell,
That even makes the worst go well!
    With those that can but ra[i]se it!
Since all adore it, why may'nt I?
I have it not, and therefore try,
    To catch the fool that has it.)[40]

More usually, the theme of arias in intermezzi is the same as that of their counterparts in serious opera—love. Yet even this favorite topic is treated far more realistically in intermezzi than was customary in the libretti of *opere serie*. It is hard to imagine, for example, a Metastasian hero ruminating on marriage to his beloved in the following manner:

Consiglio a noi consiglio,
   La piglio o non la piglio,
   E Signor sì, pigliarlà,
   E Signor nó, lasciarla,
   Pigliarla, è un gran periglio,
   Lasciarla, è come resto;
   Sì nò, nò sì, sì nò, nò sì;
   Impiccio come questo
   Non ò provato più.
Veder la successione,
   Ma in casa aver la guerra,
   Io son come un pallone,
   Che'ora è sbattuto in terra,
   Ora è sbalsato in sù.

(Consider well! consider
   shall I take her,
   Or forsake her?
Pursue her, or forbid her?
O, sir! by all means take her!—
By no means, no! forsake her!
To wed may raise the devil about her!
And 'tis the devil to live without her!
'Tis so—no, no—yes 'tis—no, no—'tis so!
   And yet while the matter stands thus!
   My heart's in a horrible fuss!
But must I never have an heir?
No—man and wife's a civil war.
   How, like a footbal[l], I,
   By love and fear
   Kick'd here and there,
Am sometimes high, and sometimes low,
While I'm in doubt of ay, or no!)[41]

We have seen that Quadrio's assertion to the effect that intermezzi were merely an offshoot of the *opera seria* is correct only as regards formal features of their respective libretti. In subject matter and its treatment, the intermezzo more closely resembles the dramatic types from which it sprang, and to which we may now turn our attention.

Sources and Themes

The intermezzo's literary roots lie hidden forever beneath the tangle of written and improvised comedy, non-theatrical burlesque poetry, and dramatic verse that luxuriated and intertwined in Italy and other European countries between the beginnings of the Renaissance and eighteenth century. Nevertheless, it is possible to find proximate, if not ultimate, sources in the dramatic literature and traditions of France and Italy for the libretti of at least a few intermezzi, and to trace some of their common themes and dramatic devices back to the *scene buffe* of *seicento* opera.

The intermezzo texts most clearly related to the prose theater of the seventeenth century are those based upon comedies of Molière, an Italian edition of which was published at Leipzig between 1696 and 1698.[42] No fewer than six of the pieces included among the most popular libretti of the eighteenth century listed in Appendix A have antecedents in the works of the French playwright; their original or subsequent titles are often literal translations of the prose comedies upon which they were modeled:

L'ammalato immaginario (Erighetta and Don Chilone)	*Le malade imaginaire*
L'artigiano gentiluomo (Larinda and Vanesio)	*Le Bourgeois gentilhomme*
L'avaro (Fiammetta and Pancrazio)	*L'Avare*
Il matrimonio per forza (Rosmene and Gerondo)	*Le Mariage forcé*
Monsieur di Porsugnacco (Grilletta and Porsugnacco)	*Monsieur de Pourceaugnac*
La preziosa ridicola (Madama Dulcinea and il cuoco del Marchese del Bosco)	*Les Précieuses ridicules*

The adaptors of these intermezzi retained much of the flavor and even some of the language of the French originals in the musical versions of these comedies. Thus Madama Dulcinea of *La preziosa ridicola* closely paraphrases the extravagant speech of Molière's *précieuse* Cathos in offering her guest a seat ("Mais de grâce, monsieur, ne soyez inexorable à ce fauteuil qui vous tend les bras il y a un quart d'heure; contentez un peu l'envic qu'il a dc vous cmbrasser."):[43]

> In grazia onori
> Questa mia sedia, che con braccia aperte
> Quivi la sta attendendo.

And Aragon's computation of his pharmacist's bill ("Trois et deux font cinq, et cinq font dix, et dix font vingt; trois et deux font cinq."), in the first scene of *Le Malade imaginaire* appears only slightly altered as an aria text at the beginning of the Italian musical adaptation:

> Uno, due, tre, e quattro,
> Quattro, e quattro, che fan otto,
> Otto, e diece fan diciotto,
> E poi sei fan venti quattro.

It was obviously impossible, however, for the Italian arranger to preserve any more than the barest outlines of Molière's plots and characterizations in the reduced format dictated by the intermezzo's traditional two roles and two or three short episodes. Antonio Salvi's *L'artigiano gentiluomo*, adapted from the familiar *Bourgeois gentilhomme*, will serve as an example of the extreme condensation necessary to reduce a full-length play to an entr'acte musical entertainment.

Salvi retains the character of the vainglorious, social climbing, and credulous M. Jourdain in his hero Vanesio, but unlike the protagonist of Molière's comedy, he is unmarried (thus eliminating one role), and in search of a bride rather than a mistress. Larinda, heroine of the intermezzo, portrays nearly all the other principal characters of the French model. She first appears in male dress impersonating a combination fencing teacher and ballet master, in whose double capacity she gains Vanesio's confidence and proposes a suitable noble match for him, just as Count Dorante pretends to furnish M. Jourdain a mistress in the French original. Larinda's candidate for Vanesio's wife is no other than herself in yet another disguise, that of the Baroness d'Arbelle, a fictitious noble lady modeled on Molière's Marquise Dorimène. The ruse succeeds. Vanesio, eager to style himself a "baron," marries the disguised Larinda, who then reveals herself to be a simple commoner like her new husband. The latter eventually resigns himself to both his old social status and new wife, just as Molière's *bourgeois gentilhomme* finally accepts the marriage of his daughter to Cléonte by similar trickery.

Molière himself, of course, borrowed many such dramatic tricks (*lazzi* or *burle*, to give them their Italian names) from the *commedia dell'arte*,[44] a source from which librettists of intermezzi also drew freely. One traditional *burla*, involving a kind of peep-show, furnished the subject and title of one of the earliest independent intermezzi, *Il nuovo mondo* (Venice, 1709).[45] Indeed, the loose, almost plotless story line characteristic of nearly all intermezzi is reminiscent of a *commedia dell'arte* scenario. And we have already noted the resemblance between the intermezzo's quasi-impromptu dialogue and preserved specimens of speeches from improvised Italian comedy.

Still more striking is the appearance in intermezzi of stock character types from the *comedia dell'arte*. The reader no doubt has already recognized some of the latter's traditional masks among the dramatis personae of intermezzi mentioned so far in the present study; they include Pantaleone and his close relative Pandolfo, the Bolognese pedant Balanzone, Colombina, the Neapolitan Cola, and the braggart Captain, all of whom retain personalities from improvised comedy in their musical incarnations. In the second part of *La fantesca*, for example, Capitan Don Galoppo tries to disguise his cowardice in a show of verbal belligerence directed at his servant Vespa, then shrinks in terror at the sight of his adversary, a maid in the costume of a Spanish captain:

> *Gal.* Levamiti d'avanti.
> Vuoi ch'io mi batta con un vil Spagnuolo!
> Vilissimo che sei!
> Allor combatterei
> Quando vi fosse de' Spagnuoli un stuolo.
> E pure.... adesso è troppo.
> Che timor! Che timore!
>
> *Mer.* (Ecco Galoppo!
> Con questo mostaccino
> Non mi conoscerà. Finger mi voglio
> Quel Capitan Spagnuolo,
> Ch'ei di sfidar paventa.)
>
> *Gal.* Se l'incontro....
>
> *Mer.* (Vediam se si sgomenta.)
>
> *Gal.* Con un soffio l'atterro.... Vespa, Vespa.
> Fosse costui? (*avvicinandosi a Vespa intimorito,...*)[46]
>
> (*Gal.* Get out of my way! So you want me to fight a vile
> Spaniard! Vile as you are! Well, I'd fight a whole
> troop of them. Yet—not right now. What fear!
> What fear!
>
> *Mer.* (Here's Galoppo! With this moustache he won't
> recognize me. I want him to think I'm that
> Spanish Captain he's afraid of challenging.)
>
> *Gal.* If I meet him—
>
> *Mer.* (Let's see if he's frightened.)
>
> *Gal.* I'll blow him down with a single breath—Vespa,
> Vespa! Was it this one? (runs terrified to Vespa, . . .)

By far the most common stock type in the intermezzo is the cunning servant girl, widow, or shepherdess who, despite her humble station, through feminine wiles plays a *burla* on her male partner or (more usually) ensnares him in matrimony. Often the soubrette's name indicates her sharp cunning, as for example, Serpina (little snake) of Gennaro Antonio Federico's *La serva padrona* or Vespetta (little wasp) in Pietro Pariati's popular libretto *Pimpinone*. *La serva padrona* is the most familiar of intermezzi whose titles suggest their denouements; others include *La serva scaltra ovvero La moglie a forza* (Dorilla and Balanzone), *Il matrimonio per forza* (Rosmene and Gerondo), and *Monsieur de Porsugnacco ingannato da Grilletta*.

In addition to this stereotyped plot, which furnishes the subject for perhaps half or more of the preserved libretti, a number of themes and dramatic devices familiar from the *scene buffe* of seventeenth-century opera also figure prominently in the intermezzo.

The supernatural element probably derives from the close connection between the comic characters and transformations of the intermedi in *seicento* opera. We have seen that around the turn of the century the *parti buffe* began to create their own magic; in later intermezzi the female protagonist may use her occult powers to trap a husband, as in Francesco Antonio Novi's intermezzi of Aurilla and Cola,[47] or entice her partners with the promise of a lost treasure her magic art alone can recover (see Rinaldi Francesco Cantù's *Barlafuso, e Pipa* [Vienna, 1716]).[48]

A satirical theme is joined with that of the supernatural in the comic scenes of Ermosilla and Bacocco added by Bernardo Saddumene to the libretto of an anonymous *Publio Cornelio Scipione* published at Naples in 1722. According to a prefatory note in this edition, Saddumene's *scene buffe* were intended to burlesque the mistaken faith the ancients placed in oracles; the third, set in a deep subterranean vault decorated by a statue of Bacchus astride a wine cask, is also a self-burlesque. Ermosilla evokes a descent of Venus on a shining machine, and Bacocco rushes to embrace the goddess, but his partner conjures up a vision of the children that would result from such a union. Three figures issue in succession from the cask: first an extremely short, fat woman, then a man in heroic costume, and finally an invalid. Ermosilla explains the meaning of each apparition to Bacocco:

Erm.	.... questa
	Sarà un vaga, e snella ballerina.
Bac.	Veramente ne hà il garbo, e la vitina
	E chi sarà quest'altro?
Erm.	Sarà un valente Musicon da scene,
	Da combatter con l'Orso, e col Leone.
Bac.	Onesta professione.

Erm.	Questo sarà un Poeta
	Lirico, Eroico, Comico, e Satirico.
Bac.	Lodato il Ciel, che al fine,
	Doppo tante baruffe,
	Faran gli eredi miei le Scene Buffe.

(*Erm.*	. . . this one will be a beautiful and graceful ballerina.
Bac.	She really has the elegance and figure for it. And what about this other one?
Erm.	He will be a valiant castrato and fight on stage with bear and lion.
Bac.	An honest profession.
Erm.	This one will be a writer of lyric, heroic, comic, and satiric verse.
Bac.	Thank heaven that after so much imbroglio my heirs will participate in comic scenes.)

Parody of the opera seria as an ingredient of the intermezzo may also be traced back to the comic scenes of seventeenth-century opera. During one of the *scene buffe* added to Aureli's *Il Claudio Cesare* for its performance at Naples in 1675, Drusa, an old nurse, attempts to convince the servant Niso that her merits as wife include ability as a singer. Asked for a demonstration of her musical talent, she begs off, claiming a touch of catarrh. "The usual excuse of virtuosi for not singing," rejoins Niso, echoed by generations of conductors. A number of eighteenth-century intermezzi were devoted entirely to satirizing the institutions of *opera seria*; judging from the preserved libretti, the two most popular such works were Pietro Metastasio's only contribution to the repertory, *L'impresario delle Canarie* (Dorina and Nibbio), premiered between the acts of his first musical drama, *Didone abbandonata* at Naples in 1724, and Girolamo Gigli's intermezzi of Dirindina, Don Carissimo and Liscione, probably written for production at Rome in 1715.[49]

Metastasio's intermezzo concerns the efforts of Nibbio, impresario of an opera house in the Canary Islands, to engage the singer Dorina as prima donna in his company. The lady is understandably reluctant to journey so far, but enticed by a high salary and numerous fringe benefits, finally agrees to accompany him. Within this slight framework, the young Metastasio directed numerous barbs against what he evidently considered abuses of early eighteenth-century libretti—abuses from which his own later dramas are by no means completely free. Nibbio, the impresario, is also a poet capable of producing "forty dramas in less than a month,"[50] and offers Dorina an outrageous sample of Marinistic verse:

Lilla tiranna amata
   Salamandra infocata,
   All'Etna de'tuoi lumi
   Arder vorrei.
. . . .
Fingi meco rigore
   Sol per prenderti spasso
   So che ai tenero il Core,
   Bell'ostrica d'amore,
   E sembri un sasso.

(Lilla, thou cruel toast!
Salamander of desire!
Thy Aetna-eyes thy lover roast,
And set his heart on fire.
. . . .
Feign'd is your rigour! all but art!
And us'd for mirth alone;
I know you have a tender heart,
[Fair oyster of love,]
Tho' you pretend 'tis stone.)[51]

The intermezzo's most delicious satire, however, is that of a "comparison aria," the text of which Nibbio proposes as the sequel to an *accompagnato scena* Dorina sings for him in the character of Cleopatra. It would be a shame, he suggests, not to follow such a tragic episode with an aria about a "little butterfly" or "small boat"[52] such as:

La Farfalla che all'oscuro
   Và rondando intorno al muro
   Sai che dice a chi l'intende?
   Chi una fiaccola m'accende,
   Chi mi scotta per pietà.
Il Vascello, e la Tartana,
   Fra Siroccho, e Tramontana,
   Con le tavole schiodate
   Va sbalzando, va tirando
   Bù, bù, bù, bù, bù —
   Cannonate in quantità.

(The little moth that darkling hums
Around the walls of lonesome rooms,
Cries who, in pity, as he sings,
Will lend a light to singe my wings?

The vessel thus on seas distrest,
Toss'd from the north, to south, or west,
Her crazy sides near shoal, or cliff,
With bouncing guns, demands relief.)[53]

The satire of Gigli's intermezzo, on the other hand, is directed mainly at the prima donnas and castrati of *opera seria*. Don Carissimo, a singing teacher jealous of his pupil Dirindina's attachment to the castrato Liscione, is chagrined when the latter interrupts their lesson to offer the neophyte singer an operatic contract. Later Don Carissimo returns just in time to overhear Dirindina rehearsing her prospective role of Dido with Liscione. Mistaking for reality the words of the drama's final scene, and believing that Dirindina is actually with child by Liscione and on the point of immolating herself with a stage sword, the singing teacher proposes an unholy matrimony between the pair that leaves them racked with suppressed laughter for the old man's credulity.

This racy little story offers ample opportunity for satirical allusions to the failings of opera singers, including bad intonation, poor acting, memory lapses, and limited range. Gigli also advances some compelling reasons for the castrato's lack of social respectability; Liscione is accused of solecisms ranging from halitosis to appearing before ladies in hot weather clad only in his underwear. The sharpest barbs, however, are directed at the legendary avarice of prima donnas. Liscione assures Dirindina that "protectors" will provide her with a liberal supply of jewelry and gowns when she mounts the operatic stage; she is ready with a plan for increasing the "take":

Farò talor ad arte
Cascar qualche lucerna dalla scena
Sul sottanino, e il mostrerò macchiato,
Perchè un nuovo broccato
Mi si mandi il dì appresso,
Come ben bramerei,
Da alcun de' miei piu fidi Cicisbei.[54]

(Now and then I will contrive to have a footlight fall on my petticoat and show that it is spotted, so that, as I would fondly desire, one of my most faithful protectors will send me a new brocade the next day.)

Disguises, rife in both the *commedia dell'arte* and the comic scenes of *seicento* opera, not only afforded an opportunity in intermezzi for the display of showy costumes, but were useful for creating variety in a drama usually limited to only two singing roles. Thus Bacocco is able to appear as judge at his own trial in *Il marito giocatore*, Erighetta can suggest matrimony to herself as a cure for Don Chilone's ills while impersonating a doctor in *L'ammalato immaginario*, and during the third part of *Cola mal maritato* Drusilla can terrify her henpecked husband while disguised in Turkish costume as her own brother, newly arrived from the East.

Disguises can also create considerable humor through their sheer extravagance and the misunderstanding they create. Possibly the *ne plus ultra* of this type of clowning occurs during the third part of the intermezzi of Brunetta and Burlotto, in which the protagonists encounter one another disguised for their elopement. Brunetta has chosen a man's outfit, complete with mustache; Burlotto, for his part, appears wearing a French cap, German knickers, a Spanish gorget [? *goriglia*] and sword, Turkish turban and whiskers, and a fencing master's chest protector. Neither, of course, recognizes the other, and the following multilingual dialogue ensues:

Bru.	Sen Munsulmansin?
Bur.	Non Sennor.
Bru.	Non Sennor? Sarà Spagnuolo.
	Digame Cavallero
	Es Espagnol V. M.?
Bur.	Nain, Nain
Bru.	Tedesco esso sarà
	Vasfor ein Landasman bist du.
	Bist ein Taicer?
Bur.	Non Monsieur.
Bru.	Ah, Ah, questo è Francese,
	La lingua ancora so di quel Paese.
	Feites moy le Plaisir, Monsieur,
	De me dire, si vous etes Francois?
Bur.	No Sar.
Bru.	O Inglese è questo:
	Tu tell mi ifu aran Inghlis menn?
Bur.	Minime, Nequaquam.
Bru.	Tal linguaggio
	Ora non intend'io.[55]

Dancing by the parti buffe reflects their function of introducing the entr'acte ballets in the seventeenth-century opera. We have seen that shortly after 1700 the comic characters themselves sometimes danced during their scenes together; this custom persists in a number of later intermezzi. Here the flimsiest pretext—or even none at all—is enough to set their feet in motion. Melinda practices a "nuova contradanza" before her master in preparation for carnival;[56] the cook of the Marchese del

Bosco performs a minuet for Madama Dulcinea to demonstrate "il Re
de' balli";[57] and Dorimena forces the unwilling Tuberone to dance by her
occult powers.[58]

Frequently a ballet serves as an intermezzo's finale; at the end of
Il matrimonio per forza Rosmene convinces the reluctant Gerondo to
dance with her to celebrate the joy of their forthcoming nuptials:

Ros.	Orsu via,
	Festegiiam sì lieto giorno,
	E balliam....
Ger.	Balliam un corno.
Ros.	No tant'è, ballar conviene,
	Quando anco cascasse il Mondo.
Ger.	Balliam pur. *balla*
Ros.	O bravo, o bene.
Ros.	Viva Amor, viva Gerondo.
Ger.	*a2.* Viva Amor, viva Rosmene.[59]

(*Ros.*		Come on! Let's celebrate so happy a day and dance—
Ger.		Dance—nonsense!
Ros.		Not at all; it's good to dance even at the end of the world.
Ger.		Let's dance, then. (he dances)
Ros.		Bravo! Good!
Ros.	(together)	Long live love, long live Gerondo.
Ger.		Long live love, long live Rosmene.)

The Pasticcio

The stereotyped situations and recurrent themes just observed
permitted, perhaps to an even greater extent than was the case in
contemporary *opere serie*, the substitution and interchange of verses in
intermezzi to a point where it becomes meaningless to speak of the
"authorship" of a given text. A penchant common in serious operas
published during the first half of the eighteenth century for including
favorite arias from old works in "new" libretti may also help to explain
the practice of pasticcio in intermezzi. Even personal preference of the
parti buffe must be taken into account. A note in the edition of
Vincenzo Grimani's *Agrippina* printed at Naples in 1713 with added
comic scenes for the characters Zaffira and Lesbo states that "the words
of Zaffira's first aria in the final scene of act two, *i.e.*, the one that begins
'Ogni donna è pazza, e stolta,' are those of a most worthy author, and
have been included to please the one who sings them."[60]

Any or all of these factors may account for the fact that one
seldom finds the text of an intermezzo reprinted in original form after its
first edition. The fortunes of *Lidia, e Ircano*, discussed above as an

example of a "disconnected" intermezzo, offer an extreme example of the pasticcio practice. Not a single one of the eleven editions of this piece seen by the present writer was identical to any other; some pairs are so unlike as to be virtually different texts. Table 8 summarizes in graphic form the additions and substitutions of aria and duet texts in various editions of this intermezzo between 1709, when it was first published at Vienna as *scene buffe* in Stampiglia's *L'Abdolomino*, and what seems to have been its final appearance as an independent intermezzo at Bologna in 1747.[61] It will be observed that this last version includes only two verses from the original comic scenes, one of them in considerably altered form.[62]

Most of the texts added to and substituted for those of Stampiglia's *scene buffe* seem to have been newly written for the various later editions of this particular work; more usually, adaptors simply borrowed their substitute numbers from earlier intermezzi. Thus the aria "Con tanto stranutare," which seems to have first appeared in the second of the comic scenes for Flora and Bleso added to Stampiglia's *Mario fuggitivo* for its performance at Naples in 1710 and seven years later was sung by a character named Gildo in the *scene buffe* of an anonymous *La Circe in Italia* (Rome, 1717), turned up as a substitute text in later editions of at least three popular intermezzi published between 1724 and 1748.[63]

Even the first editions of some libretti contained verses from earlier intermezzi or comic scenes. We have seen that at least one of the "new" dramatically independent intermezzi published at Venice during the first decade of the eighteenth century was, in fact, a pasticcio of individual texts and whole parts of *scene buffe* from various *seicento* operas. And the first edition of the popular *Il marito giogatore, e la moglie bacchettona* (Serpilla and Bacocco), published at Venice in 1719, contains at least one borrowed text, that of the duet "Io già sento che il core," drawn from a comic scene in an opera printed at Rome the preceding year.[64]

Libretti of contemporary *opere buffe* were another source of texts for arrangers of intermezzi. The final duet from Gennaro Antonio Federico's full-length comic opera *Flaminio*, first performed at Naples in 1735 with music of Pergolesi, appears in more editions of Federico's *La serva padrona* (Serpina and Uberto) as a substitute text than the intermezzo's original ending, "Contento tu sarai."[65]

Not even the libretti of *opere serie* seem to have been safe from the predatory arrangers of intermezzo texts; the similarity between the first verse of a substitute aria included in the version of *Il tutore* (Lucilla and Pandolfo) performed at Rome's Teatro Argentina during the carnival

TABLE 8

SUBSTITUTE TEXTS IN VARIOUS EDITIONS OF INTERMEZZI OF LIDIA AND IRCANO

		Vienna, 1709	Naples, 1711	Rome, 1715	Ferrara, 1715	Bologna, 1716	Modena 1719	Venice, 1722	Raccolta, 1723	Venice, n.d.	Venice, 1729	Bologna, 1747
Lid.	Madamusella	X										
Irc.	Giallo, e squallido	X	X									
duet	Illustrissimo signor	X	X									
duet	Son pur stanca	X	X									
Lid.	Già parmi	X	X	X								
Irc.	E può la tua bocca	X	X	X								
Lid.	Son giardiniera	X	X	X	O	O	O		O		O	
Irc.	Villanella/Bella	X	X		O	O	O		O		O	
duet	Non v'è rimedio	X	X		O	O	O	O	O	O	O	
duet	Core ingrato	X	X		X	X	X	X	X	X	O	
duet	Perchè dirmi villanella	X	X	X		O	O	O	O			O
duet	La pecorella	X	X		X	X	X	X	X	O		X
Lid.	Che bel piacere		X		O	O	O	O	O	O		
duet	Per acqua			X								
Lid.	Col bel marito			X								
duet	Cara bimba				X	X	X	X	O	O	O	
duet	Arresta, o fanciulla				X	X	X			O		
duet	Bevi, e cresci				X	X	X	X	X	X		O
duet	Villanella/Villanaccio								X			
Lid.	Veder penare											X
Lid.	Se non intendi											X
Lid.	Aspettare? Cospettone!											X
Irc.	Ch'io mai vi possa											X

of 1739 and a verse from Sebastiano Morelli's *rifacimento* of Zeno's *Alessandro Severo* set by Pergolesi under the title *La Salustia* (Naples, 1731) is too close to be coincidental:[66]

La Salustia III.vi	*Il tutore* i
Per queste amare lagrime	Per queste amare lacrime
Figlie del mio dolore,	Figlie del mio dolore,
Si doni al genitore	Si doni o mio Signore
La vita per pietade,	A la tua Dorilletta
O a mè la morte.	Un sguardo per pietà.

One can only marvel at the manner in which intermezzi borrowed dramatic ideas, clothed them in second-hand verse, and then substituted odd bits of apparel at each new appearance. Yet the same stereotyped themes that permitted such substitutions also constituted a type of dramatic framework that no changes of costume could basically alter. The fortunes of an intermezzo libretto provide yet another demonstration of the maxim that "plus ça change, plus c'est la même chose."

THE MUSIC

Volumes could—and doubtless will—be written on the subject of "X als Intermezzokomponist." A preliminary investigation suggests that differences in style noted among the various composers whose scores served as a basis for the present chapter might also be taken as the point of departure for a study comparing distinctive traits of individuals active in the genre. Our present meager knowledge of comic style in dramatic music during the first half of the eighteenth century in general and that of the intermezzo in particular, however, dictates a broader approach. In the following pages, therefore, treatment of individual composers and works will be largely subordinated to a general discussion focused on those elements that distinguish the music of intermezzi from that of contemporary *opere serie.*[1]

It has already been remarked that an intermezzo's overall organization is identical to that of a late seventeenth-century operatic comic scene, *i.e.*, a succession of arias, separated by recitatives, and terminating in a duet. A similar chain of *secco* recitatives and arias characterizes the individual acts of a typical eighteenth-century *opera seria*. Furthermore, we shall see that with few exceptions forms of set pieces are virtually identical in both serious and comic genres.

The distinguishing feature of the intermezzo, then, is not to be found in its organization and forms, but rather in its style—one might even say "spirit." Although the latter is difficult to define with any precision, some observations may serve to suggest what intermezzo composers considered to be effective musical means for the setting of comic texts.

Comic Style

Contemporary accounts of intermezzo performances frequently stress a feature that earlier in the present study has been called "comic realism." In a description of intermezzo singers he heard at Venice around 1720, the English traveler Edward Wright reported that "they laugh, scold, imitate other Sounds, as the cracking of a Whip, the rumbling of Chariot Wheels, and all to Music."[2] The President de Brosses was also impressed by the realistic execution of intermezzi he witnessed in Italy during the years 1739 and 1740. "These comedians," he wrote, "weep, howl, rush madly about, and perform in pantomime of every sort, without ever deviating from the rhythm by a quarter of a second."[3] The German theorist Wilhelm Friedrich Marpurg even found the musical style of intermezzi a bit *too* realistic. "One can already hear conquerors fighting, ducks quacking, and frogs croaking in them," he complained, "and soon it will be possible to hear fleas sneezing and grass growing."[4]

Doubtless much of the realism that eighteenth-century commentators found so delightful (or objectionable) resulted from the singers' performance practices. Directions in libretti occasionally specify that lines of recitative were to be delivered *ridendo* ("laughing"), *con ira* ("angrily"), *sospirando* ("sighing"), *piangendo* ("weeping"), *smaniando* ("raving"), and the like.[5] Other "realistic" modes of vocal delivery specified in libretti and scores include humming[6] and falsetto, the latter an obvious expedient for situations in which the male character appears disguised in woman's dress, as in the third of Francesco Mancini's added *scene buffe* (Zaffira and Lesbo) for the performance of Handel's *Agrippina* at Naples in 1713.[7]

Even a casual inspection of intermezzo scores, however, reveals that a good deal of "realistic" humor is actually written into the music. In a recitative from the second intermezzo of Colombina and Pernicone for his *Trajano* (Naples, 1723), for example, Francesco Mancini is not content merely to direct that Pernicone improvise evidence of his mirth; he provides notes for a "realistic" portrayal of the character's laughter (Example 15). Similarly, the unknown composer of a setting of intermezzi of Pollastrella and Parpagnacco provides a veritable paroxysm of vocal and orchestral sneezes to illustrate Parpagnacco's respiratory distress at the beginning of his aria "Con tanto stranutare" (Example 16).

Example 15
Mancini, Intermezzi of Colombina and Pernicone, part 2

Example 16
Intermezzi of Pollastrella and Parpagnacco, part 1

Con tan - - - - to stra - - - nu-ta-re   mi sen - - - to già   cre-pa-re

Occasionally an entire number is devoted to a "realistic" musical description of its text; graphic portrayal of the palpitations of a love-sick heart is a common subject. Typical of such pieces is the aria "Mi rimbomba dentro il core," (Example 17) sung by the male protagonist in the first of the two intermezzi *La furba, e lo sciocco* (Sofia and Barlacco) for Domenico Sarri's *Artemisia* (Naples, 1731?). Here anapestic rhythms depicting the irregular pulse of the stricken one are followed by a written-out accelerando and rallentando to portray the feverish racing and gradual slowing of his heartbeat.

Example 17
Sarri, *La furba, e lo sciocco*, part 1

Mi rim-bom - - - - - - - - - - - - - - - - - ba dentro il co-re un ru-

- mo-re giusto giusto co-me jl pol-so all'am-ma-la-to quan-do bat-te bat-te bat-te in fretta in fretta in

fret-ta   tic tic tic tic tic tic tic tic tic tic   tic tic tic tic tic tic tic   tic tic tic tic tic tic tic tic tic tic tic tic

tic   poi s'al-len-ta   e   fà   co-si   tic   toc   tic toc   tic

toc tic toc tic toc poi si   fer - ma   toc ttù toc ttù toc ttù   toc ttù

As a final example of "comic realism" let us take an aria from the first intermezzo of *Nana francese, e Armena* (Mirena and Floro) by Francesco Gasparini, performed with Antonio Lotti's *Gl'odj delusi dal sangue* at Dresden in 1718 (Example 18). After a lovers' quarrel, Floro begs his partner's forgiveness: "If you behold me with tender glances, standing beside you, I'll cease my weeping and laugh; if you ignore me, full of sighings I will die." The musical depictions of laughter (mm. 5-6, 15-20), weeping (mm. 7-8), and sighing (mm. 28-30) written into the score are explicit enough, but one imagines they served only as a point of departure for the singer, who may have exaggerated them into a style midway between song and "realistic" noises. In any case, the ironic mood established in the first measure by its unusual accentuation and upward leap was no doubt intensified by a portamento in performance, and singers probably supplied similar effects when composers were less specific.

A second characteristic feature of the *buffo* style in intermezzi is constant repetition. The device, of course, is not unique to music as a means for evincing laughter; as Kathleen Lea observed in regard to the construction of *commedia dell'arte* farces, "when something happens three times in succession we laugh whether it is a joke or not. Why? The professional comedians did not linger over the problem but made use of the fact."[8] Neither did composers of intermezzi trouble themselves over a theoretical justification for the repetition of musical units both large and small, nor did they stop at repeating them a mere three times in succession. Thus Tacollo's five-fold plea for alms in the disguise of a Polish beggar woman near the beginning of Pergolesi's *La contadina astuta* (Livietta and Tracollo) grows more irresistibly risible after each of the intervening recitatives despite its nominally "pathetic" character.

Even in recitatives, composers occasionally intensified the naturalness and humor of the text by repeating words or short phrases for emphasis and comic effect. In his intermezzi of Scintilla and Don Tabarano, for instance, Johann Adolph Hasse reflects the male protagonist's gaucheness at meeting his lady love for the first time with effusions of *mia* and *buon di* (Example 19).

In their arias, intermezzo composers sometimes carried musical repetitions to absurd lengths for special effects. Orcone, the male character in Alessandro Scarlatti's comic scenes for *Il Tigrane* (Naples, 1715), is directed to repeat the same four-note motive during an aria "as many times as he wants, until he shows himself to be out of breath."[9] Even more extreme is the repetition in an aria from Leonardo Vinci's third intermezzo of Servilia and Flacco for his setting of *La caduta de'*

Example 18
F. Gasparini, *Nana francese, e Armena*, part 1

Example 19
Hasse, Intermezzi of Scintilla and Don Tabarano, part 1

Decemviri (Naples, 1727); the whole number consists exclusively of a single rhythmic pattern whose reiterations are broken only at cadential points (Example 20).

More typically, *buffo* pieces in intermezzi are composed of a succession of several such short, frequently related motives, each of which is repeated a number of times to form a mosaic-like type of musical development. As an illustration, let us take a passage from the familiar aria "Sempre in contrasti," sung by Uberto in the first part of Pergolesi's *La serva padrona*. Here an elderly bachelor is depicted pacing the floor, expressing his impatience in short outbursts of rage (a subtler form of "comic realism" than imitations of laughter or weeping). The aria's entire first section (the initial half of which is reproduced in Example 21) is constructed of short, balanced units, each repeated at least once. All share an upbeat beginning and strong cadential effect; further unity results from a repetition of the opening formula to furnish the dominant cadence with which the excerpt ends.

Historians have pointed to the brief, repetitive phrases characteristic of the *buffo* style in opera during the early decades of the eighteenth century as important harbingers of the turn from Baroque to Classical style,[10] but as Edward Downes has observed,

> comic opera and comic opera scenes had been cultivated since the early seventeenth century without exercising such a decisive influence as they appeared to in the eighteenth century. And since this break-up into small units took place simultaneously in a different type of music, namely in the concerto, we cannot necessarily take *opera buffa* to have been its origin. We must assume, rather, that some common esthetic impulse was at the root of both phenomena.[11]

Example 20
Vinci, Intermezzi of Servilia and Flacco, part 3

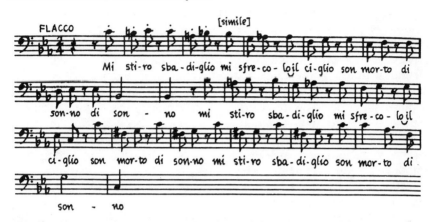

Example 21
Pergolesi, *La serva padrona*, part 1

Whatever the prime impulse behind creation of Classical phrase structure, the reasons for constant repetition of short units in the music of intermezzi are clear: these short, repeated units are a perfect setting for the brief, disjunct verbal phrases found in libretti, where their repetition is often either explicitly called for, or strongly suggested by the nature of the text.[12] And unlike the arias of *opere serie*, which tend to be static in terms of dramatic development, action tends to continue during the course of comic arias; the former invite long melodic lines and melodic development of all types, while the latter require shorter melodic figures and call for motivic development alone.

A third means of creating musical humor prominent in the intermezzo is parody; needless to say, the principal target was contemporary *opera seria*, whose stereotyped conventions and formulas offered composers of intermezzi plentiful targets for musical satire. Doubtless much unintentional parody is present in intermezzo scores; we have seen, after all, that the same composers responsible for the most popular intermezzi were usually also among the most successful exponents of the *seria* tradition, and it would be surprising indeed if these men did not quite innocently incorporate in their comic works certain empty mannerisms of their serious dramatic style completely without parodistic intent.   We must therefore not consider every "meaningless" coloratura and "undramatic" da capo repetition in the music of an intermezzo to be a conscious jibe at the *opera seria*.

Fortunately, the libretto frequently serves as a guide to the composer's intention in this regard.   Thus contemporary audiences must have smiled—or perhaps groaned—knowingly at the end of the rather lengthy duet which terminates part two of the intermezzi of Brunetta and Burlotto to hear the following exchange:

Bur.	Or burli ancor?
Bru.	Sì sì, ch'io burlo.
a 2	Torniamo da capo cara a provar.[13]
	caro

(*Bur.*	Shall we continue our jesting?
Bru.	Oh yes, I'd like to.
Both	Let's go back to the beginning, dear, for practice.)

Similarly, the extravagant similes of the burlesque comparison aria contained in Metastasio's *L'impresario delle Canarie* (Dorina and Nibbio)[14] furnish a clue (if one is needed) that the coloratura in Domenico Sarri's setting of the text is not to be taken too seriously (Example 22).

Example 22
Sarri, Intermezzi of Dorina and Nibbio, part 2

One of the most remarkable and instructive examples of musical satire in the whole intermezzo literature is an aria from Sarri's *scene buffe* for his opera *Arsace* (Naples, 1718). This single number caricatures no fewer than four of the stereotyped affects found in individual arias of contemporary *opera seria*; it not only constitutes a delicious parody of late Baroque aria types, but also furnishes a veritable catalogue of the musical devices (somewhat exaggerated, to be sure) employed in each of these types.

The aria is introduced in a context that leaves no doubt as to its parodistic intent. At the end of the opera's first act, Merilla and Morante, the two *parti buffe* who had performed earlier in the allegorical prologue, enter still dressed in their costumes of Vulcan and Venus. They discuss their previous performance at some length; Morante finally informs Merilla that his talent, fine voice, grace, and good looks are unequaled among his colleagues, and launches into an aria to prove his versatility. The piece begins with a lively section in D major providing Morante an opportunity to demonstrate his mastery of the *buffo* style, at the end of which he declares himself equally adept at portraying the stricken lover. There follows a parody of the "pathetic" style (Example 23), a languorous *siciliano* in the minor mode in which a constant sawing back and forth between the natural and flatted ("Neapolitan") scale degree terminates in a ludicrous melodic sigh on the word *crivellato* ("riddled").

Example 23
Sarri, *Arsace*, comic scene No. 1

But Morante has still other talents; he is also able to play kingly roles, and invites Merilla to admire his *maestà* to the accompaniment of pompous dotted rhythms and string tremolos demonstrating the "trembling" of his vassals. And this is not all. He is equally skilled at hero's parts, as appears from the melodic broad jumps and coloratura that characterize the aria's final section (Example 24). The fact that Morante then proceeds to repeat the whole of the aria's first part (containing the *buffo*, pathetic, and regal styles) in regular da capo fashion is no doubt a bit of unconscious parody the humor of which may have been lost on eighteenth-century audiences.

The extreme changes of tempo and style seen in this example illustrate yet another common feature of comic style in intermezzi. We have already noted that such changes characterize some arias and duets in operatic comic scenes around 1700; they become increasingly more frequent in the scores of *scene buffe* and intermezzi after this date, and by 1720 it is an unusual piece that does not include at least one number containing several changes of musical pace. Unlike the aria we have just observed, however, these changes of tempo and style are generally not occasioned merely by parodistic intent; rather they seem to result from the composer's genuine effort to reflect changing moods of the text. In contrast to set pieces in contemporary *opere serie* where the ideal, at least, was to establish and maintain a single affect throughout an aria, composers of intermezzi seem to have felt no compunction whatsoever about introducing drastic changes of style and tempo within a given number when such changes were suggested by its text.

The aria "Questo a me?" from the second part of Giuseppe Sellitti's *La franchezza delle donne* (Lesbina and Sempronio), first performed at Naples in 1734, furnishes an extreme example of a composer's fidelity to nuances of the libretto. Sempronio, in an effort to avoid punishment for attempting to force his attentions upon Lesbina, has disguised himself as Panstufato, judge at her hearing, with the object of frustrating her suit. The situation is suddenly reversed, however, when Lesbina recognizes the disguised Sempronio, produces a document from Panstufato authorizing her to act in his stead, and (assisted by a burly lawyer) proceeds to place Sempronio under arrest.

His incredulity at this unexpected turn of events ("Questo a me! Questo smacco a un uom d'onore?") is punctuated by an oath ("poter di Bacco!"). He becomes excited and threatens violence "Vuo sbranarti, lacerarti, / Vuo cacciarti...."), but as the lawyer rises to call his bluff, Sempronio backs down and explains his threat was only a figure of speech ("Non Signore / Quest'è un modo di parlar."). In an aside, he threatens fisticuffs ("Vè che bestia di Notario! / Solo seco esser vorrei, / Tuffe tuf..."), but seeing that the lawyer has overheard retreats again ("Non dico a lei / Oh! si lasci maneggiar."). Sellitti's setting designates a

Example 24
Sarri, *Arsace*, comic scene No. 1

different tempo for nearly every line of this mercurial text, producing no
fewer than 18 changes of pace during the course of the aria (counting the
four-fold repetition of its first quintrain dictated by da capo form):

Largo	Questo a me! poter di Bacco!
	Questo smacco a un uom d'onore?
Presto	Vuo sbranarti, lacerarti,
	Vuo cacciarti....
Largo	Non Signore
Andante	Quest'è un modo di parlar.

Largo	Questo a me!
Presto	poter di Bacco!
	Questo smacco a un uom di'onore?
	Vuo sbranarti, lacerarti,
	Vuo cacciarti.... Non Signore
Andante	Quest'è un modo di parlar.
Allegro	(Vè che bestia de Notaro!
	Solo seco esser vorrei,
	Tuffe tuf....
Largo	Non dico a lei
	Oh! si lasci maneggiar.
Presto	Tuffe tuf....
Andante	Non dico a lei
	Oh! si lasci maneggiar.

Extreme changes of musical style accompany each of these tempo alterations; three such changes occur within the aria's first seven measures alone (Example 25). Sempronio expresses his disbelief in a slow, declamatory section reminiscent of an accompanied recitative (mm. 1-2); breathless, rushing scales portray his anger (mm. 3-4), and he makes excuses to the lawyer in a mincing *andante* (mm. 5-7). Similar changes of style characterize the aria's second part, in which 12/8 *allegro* sections alternate with common-time declamatory passages marked *largo*.

The increasing frequency with which one finds numbers of this type in intermezzo scores after 1700 may reflect a growing sensitivity on the part of composers to the possibilities inherent in the texts their librettists provided. The *parti buffe* may also have influenced composers to furnish such pieces for them. Around 1720 Benedetto Marcello admonished intermezzo singers that "they should speed up or slow down the tempo, particularly in duets, due to their preoccupation with the clowning."[15] It is possible, then, that composers were simply following the lead of the performers by liberally sprinkling their set pieces with tempo indications. In any case, the resulting fidelity of music to text is perhaps the most notable feature of comic style in the intemezzo.

Recitative and *Accompagnato*

As in other types of eighteenth-century dramatic music, recitative in the comic intermezzo furnishes an indispensable vehicle for advancing the action in a musical context without sacrificing intelligibility of the text. The special requirements of comedy make the *secco* ("unaccompanied") style particularly indispensable in the intermezzo; fast-paced repartee, witty asides, and lively dialogue depend for their effect upon fleet declamation with a minimum of musical support.

Example 25
Sellitti, *La franchezza delle donne*, part 2

Symptomatic of the importance of *secco* recitative in musical comedy is the fact that this style continued to play a part in *opera buffa* for a considerable time after Italian composers abandoned it in their serious dramatic music. Beginning with *Elisabetta, regina d'Inghilterra* of 1815, for example, Rossini eliminated *secco* recitative altogether in his serious operas, but continued to employ it in later comic works. And Donizetti was still using *secco* in an *opera buffa* (his *Il campanello di notte*) as late as 1835.

We have noted earlier in the present study that *secco* recitative had developed by 1700 into a style nearly ideal for the requirements of comic dialogue—perhaps under the influence of those same requirements. Described briefly, this style is characterized by a syllabically set vocal line with frequent repeated tones moving predominately in eighth notes either stepwise or by simple intervals over a slow-changing bass realized by a harpsichord and doubled by one or more sustaining instruments. Supporting harmonies generally progress among triads closely related by their position in the circle of fifths.

The bulk of *recitativo secco* in comic intermezzi, like that of contemporary *opere serie*, is musically neutral, *i.e.*, except for conventional cadential formulas to mark punctuation,[16] the music generally serves to support the text rather than illustrate it. This is not to say that particularly expressive moments do not receive special musical treatment. Giuseppe Orlandini's setting of *Il marito giocatore* (Serpilla and Bacocco) furnishes an example of such a moment. Serpilla, having been cast out of the house by her gambling husband Bacocco for compromising herself before a magistrate (Bacocco in disguise), pleads forgiveness, reminding her spouse of their courtship "in words that would have liquefied bronze," according to one contemporary account (see above, p. 53). The music (Example 26) reflects this touching text by a descending chromatic scale in the bass and "melting" harmonies that move through the circle of fifths from C$\sharp$ to F, together with drooping appoggiaturas in the vocal line ("do*lo*ri") to which others (e.g., on *fin*) were doubtless added in performance.

Such tender episodes, quite naturally, are comparatively rare in the *secco* recitative texts of most intermezzi. Much more common are occasions that call for quite a different—but no less appropriate—musical treatment. In Johann Adolph Hasse's setting of the intermezzi of Larinda and Vanesio, for example, the male protagonist's mounting exasperation over being deprived at one stroke of bride and dowry is reflected in abrupt, disconnected phrases and a rising vocal line that culminates in an outburst of repeated cries of *dove?* ("where?") (Example 27).

Example 26
Orlandini, *Il marito giocatore*, part 3

Example 27
Hasse, Intermezzi of Larinda and Vanesio, part 3

   Similar outbursts are comparatively rare in the highly stylized recitatives of contemporary *opera seria*; indeed it would appear that at least one composer exercised considerably more force of expression in setting recitative texts for his intermezzi than was the case in his own serious dramatic works. In a perceptive study of Antonio Caldara's *opere serie*, Robert Freeman has found a general "inattention to the finer concerns of recitative composition" reflected in the composer's bland, directionless harmonies and total avoidance of expressive melismas to emphasize crucial words.[17] Yet the same Caldara, in his intermezzi of Pipa and Barlafuso for Antonio Lotti's *Costantino* (Vienna, 1716), was able to write recitative passages such as the one quoted below (Example 28) in which a rising melodic sequence over chromatic harmonies culminating in a melisma on the word "languish" portrays Barlafuso's eagerness to offer his affection to the old hag Pipa in exchange for her hidden treasure. The sentiment, of course, is false; yet its expression is stronger than the composer seems to have allowed more genuine protestations of love by the heroes of his *opere serie*.

Example 28
Caldara, Intermezzi of Pipa and Barlafuso, part 1

   From a comparison of several dozen intermezzo scores with those of the serious operas with which they were first performed, it would appear that such word painting in the vocal lines of recitatives is, in fact, generally more frequent in the *buffo* pieces. In contrast to the gentle emotions and static action that characterize libretti of contemporary *opere serie*, the livelier, more robust language of intermezzi fairly demands such treatment; instances of "action painting" such as the two quoted below (Example 29) from Domenico Sarri's intermezzi of Moschetta and Grullo could be multiplied almost indefinitely.

Example 29
Sarri, Intermezzi of Moschetta and Grullo,
(a) part 1
(b) part 2

Even more peculiar to the intermezzo is use of the continuo instruments for word painting. Doubtless the *cembalo* players of the *opera seria* sometimes added flourishes in their realizations to emphasize key words in the texts of recitatives despite the fact the eighteenth-century theorists were virtually unanimous in banning such word painting along with polyphonic elaboration and other distracting elements from *secco* accompaniments.[18]   In his popular tutor Francesco Gasparini expressly warns the harpsichordists not to "annoy" the singer "with ascending and descending scale passages, as some do," suggesting that pit accompanists did not always observe these prohibitions.[19]

Composers of serious opera active after about 1700, however, seem never to have actually encouraged the practice by writing into the bass lines of their *secco* recitatives musical figures to reflect the meaning of the text. In the recitatives of intermezzi, on the other hand, such word painting is fairly common. It is especially frequent in Hasse's Neapolitan intermezzi, but occurs often enough in the works of his contemporaries active outside of Naples to suggest the practice was fairly widespread and not merely characteristic of this particular composer or local usage. An excerpt from the first part of Hasse's popular intermezzi of Scintilla and Don Tabarano (Example 30) will serve to illustrate a typical use of the device. In an exaggerated protestation of love for Scintilla, Tabarano compares his heart to a ship at sea, while the continuo instruments provide "waves" in the bass.

Example 30
Hasse, Intermezzi of Scintilla and Don Tabarano, part 1

    Another manifestation of the comparative freedom composers exercised in the *secco* recitatives of intermezzi is the occasional appearance there of melodious moments or arioso style. Such passages, although frequent in the recitatives of late seventeenth-century Italian opera, are virtually nonexistent in those of *opere serie* composed after about 1700. It is therefore somewhat surprising to find moments such as that quoted in Example 31 from the intermezzi of Colombina and Pernicone for Francesco Manini's *Trajano* (Naples, 1723) with some frequency in intermezzo scores of such a relatively late date. This and other expressive exaggerations we have just observed may constitute a retrospective feature of the genre, or—more likely—they represent intentional caricature of an outmoded convention at a time when fashion had temporarily banished violent emotional outbursts from the language of other types of dramatic music.

    Passages of accompanied recitative occur in fewer than one third of the scores consulted during preparation of the present study. On the basis of this sample, it would seem that Johann Adolph Hasse, famous during his time for the number and complexity of *accompagnati* in his *opere serie*, tended to employ the device in his intermezzi more frequently than other composers active in the genre. Three of the six surviving scores for his Neapolitan intermezzi contain at least one example of *accompagnato*; *La serva scaltra overo La moglie a forza* (Dorilla and Balanzone) employs the style no fewer than three times.

    Accompanied recitatives in intermezzi serve a variety of miscellaneous dramatic functions; Flacco, the male protagonist of Leonardo Vinci's intermezzi for his opera *La caduta de' Decemviri* (Naples, 1727) recites a poem to his lady love in *accompagnato* style, and

Example 31
Mancini, Intermezzi of Colombina and Pernicone, part 2

the tempestuous Captain Don Galoppo of Hasse's *La fantesca* introduces himself in an accompanied recitative marked *furioso*. In general, however, composers of intermezzi seem to have reserved this style for the same situations as those in which it normally occurs in contemporary *opere serie*, namely with reference to the supernatural and in conditions of extreme moral torment.

One of the most amusing examples of the former usage is the *accompagnato* "Dai cupi vortici" from the first comic scene of Dorilla and Orcone in Alessandro Scarlatti's *Tigrane* (Naples, 1715). Orcone, having played the wizard in a faked evocation of the supposedly dead Meroe during a previous scene, is pursuaded by Dorilla to perform an evocation for her. Fearful that his "magical" powers might actually work this time, Orcone stutters his way through a delicious parody of the traditional *opera seria* incantation scene (Example 32).

A strong parodistic tendency is also evident in *accompagnati* employed to set anguished monologues in intermezzi. Uberto's indecision over whether or not to marry his servant Serpina in the second part of *La serva padrona* is portrayed by vocal histrionics and rushing scale figures in the strings that eighteenth-century audiences probably associated with far more serious operatic crises than the domestic difficulties of Pergolesi's hero.

Like their counterparts in *opere serie*, accompanied recitatives in intermezzi vary in length from a few bars to several dozen measures, and range in style from simple, sustained chords, in which the orchestra merely imitates the function of the harpsichord, to rather elaborate orchestral figurations, including motives which reflect changing moods of the text. In both serious operas and intermezzi produced during the first

Example 32
A. Scarlatti, *Tigrane*, comic scene No. 1

half of the eighteenth century, the shorter, simpler type predominates. As a final example, however, let us take a piece from the second part of Hasse's intermezzi of Larinda and Vanesio which represents the *accompagnato* at its most elaborate. The recitative's text and music depict Vanesio's violent reation to the news that his intended bride is no dowried noble lady, but a commoner like himself (Example 33). Rushing scales and reiterated chords paint his despair over this distressing situation (mm. 1-5); he calls upon malign spirits to gird themselves for battle on his behalf to the accompaniment of a martial motive (mm. 6-11). A mock mad scene ensues. Vanesio imagines himself adrift in a sea of woes whose waves are heard in the orchestra (mm. 13-17). He feels himself drowning (descending scales in the violins, mm. 20-21). Repeated cries for help (mm. 22-26) are answered by arrival of the spirits (*presto*) in a two-octave rising scale. The final measures of the *accompagnato* are devoted to Vanesio's rejoicing over safe delivery from his imaginary aquatic peril.

Example 33
Hasse, Intermezzi of Larinda and Vanesio, part 3

Example 33 (continued)

Example 33 (continued)

The Aria

Arias in intermezzi serve much the same purpose as those of contemporary *opere serie*: they provide an opportunity for sustained commentary or reflection on a dramatic situation within the framework of a closed musical form. Composers seem to have considered the major formal plan of arias in *opera seria* to be equally appropriate for use in intermezzi; in arias from both serious and comic genres, da capo form predominates to the near exclusion of all other types during the entire first half of the eighteenth century. Non da capo forms account for fewer than 15 per cent of arias in intermezzi sampled from this time, a percentage scarcely larger than the one Edward Downes found in a comparable sample of *opera serie* produced during the same period.[20]

During their period of coexistence, moreover, da capo arias in both intermezzi and contemporary *opera serie* followed the same general line of development. Before 1720 they tend to be relatively short pieces whose second part often exceeds that of the first in length and musical elaboration. A cadence in the dominant (or relative major, in the case of arias in the minor mode) generally divides the first part into binary form, but medial ritornelli are either short or lacking altogether. Around 1720, the da capo aria in both intermezzo and *opera seria* assumed the rigidly standardized form that it was to retain for the following 40 or so years of its popularity. A fairly extended ritornello in the dominant divides the first part, now greatly increased in length and relative importance, into two sections. The text of the first section is repeated during the second, during which there is a modulation back to the tonic key. A relatively short second part, often in the relative of the aria's tonic key is followed by the da capo repetition of the whole first part.

Only minor structural details distinguish the da capo arias of intermezzi from their counterparts in *opere serie*. Perhaps the most obvious of these details is the absence of introductory ritornelli in many comic arias. Such introductions are practically never lacking in the arias of serious operas; the first act of the version of Pergolesi's *Adriano in Siria* printed in Caffarelli's edition of the composer's *Opera omnia,* for example, contains not a single aria lacking an initial ritornello. In the first part of the same composer's intermezzo *La contadina astuta* (Livietta and Tracollo), premiered between the acts of *Adriano* at Naples in 1734, introductory ritornelli are absent in two of the four arias and the concluding duet.

The lack of long introductions to arias is, of course, consistent with the "realism" we have so far observed in the music of intermezzi; prolix ritornelli would, after all, interrupt the verbal clowning of the *parti buffe.* And in those numbers that were provided with initial ritornelli, one imagines they devised some humorous "business" rather than strolling downstage, taking snuff, or begging friends' pardon for being out of voice and having a cold, as were customs of singers in the *opera seria* while awaiting the end of orchestral introductions to their arias, if we are to believe Benedetto Marcello.[21]

Like their counterparts in *opera seria*, most arias in intermezzi fall into one or another of several fairly well defined types. Eighteenth-century theorists and commentators were virtually unanimous in declaring the existence of such categories for the arias of serious operas, although they disagree considerably as to their distinctive traits, and there is substantial evidence that in actual practice composers were far from consistent in their application of predetermined musical formulae to set texts of the various emotional qualities distinguished by literati.[22] In view of the intermezzo's neglect by theorists in other respects, it goes almost without saying that its aria types figure in none of their classifications. No matter. The three most common types are so easily distinguished that one hardly needs a guide to recognize them.

Preeminent, of course, are those in *buffo* style, whose general characteristics have already been discussed. We need only add here that within the lively, prevailingly major framework of *buffo* arias the vocabulary of musical effects is nearly endless. Singers may breathlessly recite on a single pitch or leap disjointedly about extremes of the tonal spectrum. The same rhythmic pattern may be repeated with maddening regularity throughout an aria, or a succession of irregularly placed accents may nearly destroy the regular pulse altogether. Settings of text range from the strictly syllabic to extravagant coloratura employed for parody, emphasis of crucial words, or pure exaggeration.

Despite the variety of effects found in *buffo*-style arias, an unbroken succession of lively pieces tends to pall rather quickly, creating a situation analogous to lack of comic relief in a tragedy. It is probably for this reason that librettists seem to have made a point of supplying composers with an occasional opportunity to vary the pace with texts of a mock-serious nature. Such texts generally take the form of laments, protestations of love, pleas for mercy, philosophical reflections and the like.

Late Baroque practice, as we have seen, was for composers to provide for such texts a *siciliano*-like setting in 12/8 meter, generally in the minor mode, with imitation of the vocal line by accompanying instruments, suspensions, and touches of expressive chromaticism. In arias composed after about 1720 the same affect is generally rendered by a musical setting in triple meter and moderate tempo with homophonic accompaniment. Composers of intermezzi active following this date seemed to be in general agreement that such was the most appropriate setting for "pathetic" texts; the aria "Vedovella afflitta e sola," in which the female protagonist expresses her woe at the beginning of the intermezzi of Erighetta and Don Chilone, for example, is remarkably similar stylistically in two thematically unrelated settings by Francesco Conti (Vienna, 1725) and Leonardo Vinci (Naples, 1726) (Example 34).

Arias in this style provide more opportunity than *buffo* pieces for extemporary elaboration of the vocal line; it was probably in the da capo repeats of "pathetic" arias that the singers displayed the improvisational ability attributed to them by Marcello, who suggests that "the *parti buffe* should claim the same salary as the opera's principals, especially if in their singing they introduce swells, coloratura passages, trills, cadenzas, etc. in the style of performers in the *opera seria*."[23]

Less common in intermezzi than *buffo* and pathetic style arias are those modeled on dance rhythms. From their texts and occasional stage directions it appears that the latter were often actually danced by the *parti buffe*, whose favorite step seems to have been the minuet. The aria in which the foolish male character in Hasse's popular intermezzi of Scintilla and Tabarano introduces himself, for example, is marked *tempo di minuetta*, and the text leaves no doubt as to the number's balletic character:

> Alla vita, al portamento
> Sembro giusto un ballerino.
> La la la la. Questo vezzo, questo inchino,
> E' un incanto, un portento, un intento.
> Ah! che passo di minuè.

> (From my figure and bearing,
> I really seem a ballerino;
> La-la-la-la. This gesture, this bow,
> Is a delight, a wonder, a portent.
> Ah! How well I dance the minuet!)

One can only imagine the travesty Tabarano's dancing must have made of Hasse's stately music (Example 35).

Duets

With virtually no exceptions, each part of an intermezzo contains at least one duet; almost invariably it is the final number. Much less frequently another duet between the two singing characters serves to introduce their clowning or appears as a medial number; such duets are generally less extended than the final one. The main function of a duet

Example 34
(a) Conti, Intermezzi of Erighetta and Don Chilone, part 1
(b) Vinci, Intermezzi of Erighetta and Don Chilone, part 1

Example 35
Hasse, Intermezzi of Scintilla and Tabarano, part 1

is thus that of the intermezzo's "ensemble finale"—the largest one possible in the majority of pieces with which we are dealing, since they employ but two singing roles. The analogy between the intermezzo's terminal duet and the ensemble finale of post-1750 *opera buffa* must not be pressed too far, however. In the first place, the latter has for its chief characteristic furtherance of the drama—or at least portrayal of action—within some type of appropriate musical framework. Duets in the intermezzo serve to advance the action no more than do arias, and for the same reason: almost all are cast in da capo form.[24] Nor are the texts of most intermezzo duets notable for representing or suggesting dramatic activity; the vast majority simply expand upon the state of affairs reached at the end of the preceding recitative.

When viewed in the larger context of eighteenth-century dramatic music, moreover, the persistence of duets in intermezzi written after about 1720 is an anachronism. As Edward Downes has pointed out, relative profusion of duets and other vocal ensembles was a hallmark of late seventeenth- and early eighteenth-century serious dramatic music, but after about 1720 such ensembles declined in number to an average of one per opera.[25] Since no such decline occurred in intermezzi after this date (nor did duets *increase* in frequency or importance), one must consider their continued use to be yet another retrospective feature of the genre.

As was the case in their counterparts from contemporary *opera seria*, da capo duets in intermezzi differ only slightly from arias. The most obvious distinguishing feature from a formal standpoint is the general absence of medial ritornelli from the first part of intermezzo duets; such ritornelli are also customarily lacking in duets from contemporary serious opera. Typically, introductory ritornelli, which we have seen are often omitted in the arias of intermezzi, are also frequently lacking in their duets.

The vast majority of duet texts in intermezzi fall into one of two categories: one portrays an argument or conflict of interest between the characters; the other expresses harmonious agreement or mutual affection. Generally a situation of the first type obtains at the end of an intermezzo's initial part; the second is present at the end of its final section. As examples, let us take the first and last duets from Antonio Salvi's *Il marito giocatore* (Serpilla and Bacocco). The intermezzo's first part terminates with a duet in which Serpilla vows to divorce her gambling husband despite his promises of reform:

Bac.	Serpilla diletta
	A dadi, a bassetta
	Mai più giocherò.
Ser.	Son'anni, ch'io sento
	Un tal giuramento
	Più creder non vò.
Bac.	Se più questi torti
	Ricevi da mè—
Ser	Non vò che mi porti
	Il Diavol con tè.
Bac.	Consorzio, consorzio
	Sì cara mercè.
Ser.	Divorzio, divorzio
	Ciascuno da se.
Bac.	Ti giuro, e prometto
	Giocar non vò più.
Ser.	Dividasi il letto
	Bugiardo sei tù.
Bac.	Te'l giuro ⎫
	⎬ alla fè.
Ser.	No'l credo ⎭

(*Bac.*	Serpilla, my dearest
	Not a die, not a card
	Will I ever touch more!
Ser.	Too often I've heard,
	How the same you have swore,
	But troth! I shall trust you no more!
Bac.	If ever again
	I deceive you in either!
Ser.	When I trust you again
	The devil shall take us together.
Bac.	Come, come let's agree!
Ser.	A divorce, Sir, for me!
Bac.	Your pardon, my goddess! forgive it.
Ser.	In a wholesome divorce you shall have it.
Bac.	I vow and I swear, from this day—
Ser.	Our beds are asunder!
Bac.	I never, no never, will play.
Ser.	You lye loud as thunder.
Bac.	I swear on this dearest, dear breast.
Ser.	No, no, Sir, your oaths are a jest.)[26]

During the intermezzo's second part Bacocco turns the tables on his wife by disguising himself as judge at his own divorce trial and forcing the unwitting Serpilla into the embarrassing position of agreeing to be his (the judge's) mistress in return for a verdict favorable to her. Bacocco then tears off his disguise, upbraids her for "faithlessness," and sends her away. But in the intermezzo's final part, Serpilla's pleadings soften her husband's heart; all is forgiven, and the two join in a duo of reconciliation:

Ser.	Io sento
	Che il mio core
	Per amore del tuo amore
	Tappe tappe il cor mi fa.
Bac.	Io già sento
	Gioja mia,
	Che il mio cor per l'allegrìa
	Tuppe tuppe il cor mi fà.
Ser.	Non temer ò mio diletto.
Bac.	No temer idolo caro.
Ser.	Ti prometto,
Bac.	Mi dichiaro,
a 2.	Che fedele il cor sarà.
Ser.	Or di nuovo gioja mia
Bac.	Tutto piena d'allegria
A 2.	Tappe, tuppe il cor mi fà.

(*Ser.*   From the fear in my breast,
            I vow and protest,
            My heart, to pant, pit-a-pat,
                Does incline.

Bac.   From the same fear with thee,
            My past jealousy
            Gives a thump-a-thump, thump
            Too in mine.

Both { Away with our doubts then } my dearest
       For I swear   my fairest
       And declare
       From this time, I'll only be thine.

       And, now, my dear, dear!
       I with pleasure can swear,
       My heart is all light as a toy.
Both {   That it's thump, a thump, thump,
          And it's soft pit-a-pat,
          Is the product of joy.)[27]

How to dispose the vocal lines so as to differentiate musically between the diametrically opposite emotions expressed in these two types of texts seems not to have struck composers of intermezzi as a problem worth solving. We have seen in Chapter I of the present study that duets in comic scenes composed around 1700 display at least some attempt to reflect the character of texts by the relationships of their vocal parts; in later intermezzi, duets, regardless of the nature of their texts, are generally treated alike in this respect according to a formula described by Charles Burney as the "modern plan," which he defines as "reserving the junction of voices till near the close."[28] According to Burney, Handel adopted this type of duet beginning with the number "Vivo senz'alma" from his *Muzio Scevola* (1721);[29] it commences to appear in the scores of intermezzi somewhat earlier, and may be described as follows: the first voice sings an extended solo phrase which is immediately repeated by the second; the two then alternate in short phrases, and combine briefly only at the end of the da capo form's first part. In the second part there is more consistent combination of the voices, generally in parallel thirds and sixths.

Quite clearly, this rigid framework is a more appropriate setting for the cooing of smitten lovers in the *opera seria*, where it was developed, then the battles—or even lively amorous exchanges—of characters in the intermezzo. Composers availed themselves of all the devices of *buffo* style to animate duets in their comic works; the combination of voices near the end of the *prima parte* in Orlandini's first duet for *Il marito giocatore* (Example 36) depicts a family argument realistically enough, but one searches in vain through scores of intermezzi

Example 36
Orlandini, *Il marito giocatore*, part 1

for methods of handling two voices that would permit real musical differentiation of character. Even the conservative Burney seems to have tired of the "modern plan," apparently still used in *opere serie* over thirty years after the demise of the operatic intermezzo: "modern dramatic duets are all cast in the same mould; which though a good one, yet others should be sought and tried."[30]

Accompaniment and Instrumental Music

There is no evidence that an exodus from the orchestra pit occurred when the intermezzo singers replaced those of the serious opera on stage between the acts of the latter; contemporary full scores of both intermezzi and *opere serie* produced in Italy during the first half of the eighteenth century customarily call for an ensemble whose core consists of four-part strings (first and second violins, violas, and cellos and basses doubled at the octave) plus harpsichord, and in which flutes, oboes, bassoons, trumpets, and horns occasionally figure in solo parts, or (more frequently) reinforce the string instruments.[31]

It would appear, however, that composers utilized this ensemble considerably less frequently and completely in intermezzi than in serious operas. We have seen in Chapter I of the present study that continuo arias and duets account for a majority of set pieces of operatic *scene buffe* composed around the turn of the century; in the years following 1700 such pieces gradually declined numerically in intermezzi until about 1730, when they disappeared entirely, but this decline seems to have been less rapid in set pieces from intermezzi than in those of contemporary *opere serie*. Continuo numbers averaged about one per intermezzo during the decade of the twenties at Naples, although they were virtually extinct by then in the operas of composers active in that city; two of the five numbers from Antonio Caldara's intermezzi of Alisca and Bleso (Graz, 1728) are accompanied by continuo only, at a time when such pieces account for less than three per cent of the arias in that composer's *opere serie*;[32] and even Hasse, who according to Rudolph Gerber employed not a single continuo number in his more than one hundred operas,[33] composed at least one such piece for an intermezzo.[34]

Three reasons may be advanced for the persistence of numbers accompanied by continuo only in scores of intermezzi. In the first place, such pieces are customarily reserved in late seventeenth- and eighteenth-century operas for the less important roles; composers may have automatically considered characters of the intermezzo to be second-class citizens of the opera because of their descent from the latter's comic

servants.   Secondly, it goes almost without saying that textual intelligibility, a prime requirement in any type of musical comedy, may have
constrained composers to score their numbers as lightly as possible to
avoid obscuring the words.   Finally, the extreme flexibility of tempo that
apparently characterized the performance of set pieces in intermezzi may
have militated against elaborate instrumental accompaniments.   It is
probably significant in this connection that duets, which according to
Marcello were especially susceptible to tempo variations in performance,[35]
are more frequently accompanied only by the continuo instruments than
are arias, despite the fact that the latter far outnumber duets in most
scores.   In their duets, composers of intermezzi occasionally even omitted
the accompaniment altogether for several measures, allowing the *parti
buffe* to chatter away ad libitum, as in the passage from Scarlatti's comic
scenes of Pericca and Varrone for his opera *Scipione nelle Spagne* quoted
below (Example 37).

An ensemble of string instruments is the medium most generally
specified in set pieces employing more than continuo accompaniment.
This ensemble may consist only of unison violins employed concertato-
fashion in ritornelli and between vocal phrases in arias and duets (usual
in intermezzi composed during the first two decades of the eighteenth
century); after 1720 it may comprise the full string section (first and
second violins, violas, cellos and basses doubled at the octave) of the late
Baroque orchestra, so disposed as to provide continuous harmonic
support for the singers.   In the latter case, however, the texture very
seldom reaches four independent parts; if the violas are provided with a
separate line, the first and second violins will usually be doubled, and if
the two violin parts are independent, the violas generally double the bass
instruments at the octave.

Even in those numbers employing accompaniments of only string
instruments, intermezzo composers frequently enlivened their scores with
deft touches that reflect the genre's characteristic realism.   During the
first part of Giuseppe Sellitti's *La franchezza della donne*, Sempronio,
dressed as a Venetian gondolier, serenades his lady love to the accompaniment of pizzicato strings, and violin tremolos graphically portray
Tracollo's quaking in the face of punishment for his misdeeds in the
second part of Pergolesi's *La contadina astuta*.

Perhaps the most interesting of these special effects found by the
present writer in the string parts of intermezzi occurs in an accompanied
recitative from Johann Adolph Hasse's *La serva scaltra overo La moglie a
forza* (Dorilla and Balanzone), first performed at Naples in 1729.   Here
glissandos covering the range of a third portray a jilted lover's distraction
(Example 38).   From the composer's explicit directions for executing the

Example 37
A. Scarlatti, *Scipione nelle Spagne*, comic scene No. 5

Example 38
Hasse, *La serva scaltra overo La moglie a forza*, part 3

passage ("slide with only one finger" [between the two notes]), it would appear that the device was relatively new, since traditionally the novelty of a given orchestral effect is directly proportional to the explicitness with which it is described.[36]

The wind instruments most often mentioned in musical scores of intermezzi are oboes. Often the reference is a negative one, i.e., "senza oubi" in the violin line, leading one to suppose that these instruments may have regularly doubled the upper string parts. On the other hand, directions specifying such doubling also appear with some frequency in scores; these directions would, presumably, be unnecessary if doubling throughout were a matter of course. Probably the matter depended upon local custom—or even more likely—the decision of the orchestra's director. In a very few instances the oboes are given a line of the score to themselves, but in such cases their part is not particularly idiomatic, but merely imitates the unison violin line or doubles it at the third or sixth.[37]

Analogous to the role of the oboe is that of the bassoon. Although seldom given a solo role, and practically never a separate line in scores, the direction "senza fagotti" or "stromenti d'arco [soli]" appears with enough frequency in the bass lines of intermezzo accompaniments to suggest that the bassoons regularly doubled this part. Here again the matter was probably one of local custom or individual preference, since doubling by bassoons is also specifically called for in some scores.

In a few cases the bassoon is treated so as to deserve its later sobriquet as "clown of the orchestra"; a pair of examples will serve to illustrate the typically none-too-subtle use of this instrument for humorous effect. In the first (Example 39) it mocks the extravagant coloratura sung by the male character in Antonio Caldara's intermezzi of Alisca and Bleso (Graz, 1728); in the second (Example 40), from Hasse's Le fantesca (Merlina and Don Galoppo) two bassoons portray Galoppo's contempt of the Spanish captain who threatens to "disembowel" him.

Other wind instruments are called for so seldom by composers of intermezzi that their use alone must have constituted a coloristic special effect. A particularly lovely example of such wind writing occurs in the second part of Francesco Gasparini's intermezzi of Lisetta and Astrobolo. The former, awaiting her lover in a parco reale, sings an aria ("Canaries, nightingales, goldfinches, dwellers in so lovely a place, . . . pray, if pity reigns among birds, tell me if my beloved is here") to an accompaniment of due piccoli flautini (Example 41) that anticipates the descriptive writing found in the solo obbligato parts of Rameau's familiar "Rossignols amoureux."

Example 39
Caldara, Intermezzi of Alisca and Bleso, part 1

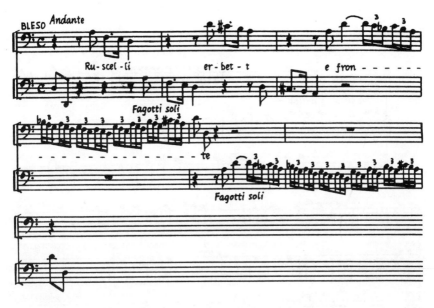

Example 40
Hasse, *La fantesca*, part 2

Independent orchestral music is a rarity in scores of intermezzi. A few manuscripts contain introductory *sinfonie*, but these all seem to be later additions by composers other than those of the intermezzo in question. Thus a *Sinfonia a 6* by Galuppi prefaces the version of Pietro Chiarini's *Il geloso schernito* (Dorina and Masocco) published by Caffarelli in the *Opera omnia* of Pergolesi.[38] In such a case, the score invariably turns out to be one employed for the performance of an intermezzo in a non-operatic context;[39] the present writer has not found a single score of an intermezzo containing an overture that can be proved to have been played between the acts of an *opera seria*.

Example 41
F. Gasparini, Intermezzi of Lisetta and Astrobolo, part 2

The only type of independent instrumental music found with any frequency in these scores is that which served to accompany dancing of the *parti buffe*; these ballets generally fall at the end of the intermezzo's final section, although a few appear in the midst of a part. Dance music was found in fewer than 20 percent of a representative sample of preserved scores, but this figure is scarcely reliable as an indication of the frequency of dances in actual practice, since ballet music included in one manuscript of a given piece may be lacking in another.[40] Whether its absence indicates that dancing was not a feature of the particular performance for which the score served, or simply that the dance music for that performance was separately bound and subsequently lost is, of course, impossible to state with any certainty. Nor is it possible to determine in those rare cases where only the bass line of a dance piece appears in a score[41] whether the upper parts were improvised, performed on stage, or even played by one or both of the intermezzo singers themselves to accompany their own dancing.

The most extensive ballet music in any score seen by the present writer is contained in a version of Johann Adolph Hasse's intermezzi of

Scintilla and Don Tabarano preserved in Rome's Biblioteca
Casanatense.[42]   This ballet consists of four entrées: a minuet with
obbligato horns, a rustic *ballo dì villano* (*allegro alla breve*), a *ballo dà
Turcho* (marked *grave*), and a da capo repeat of the initial minuet. The
personalities and costumes of the intermezzo's dramatis personae
probably explain the seemingly disparate nature of these pieces. Don
Tabarano is presented as a vain, boorish nobleman (he introduces himself
singing and dancing a minuet); Scintilla is a humble (but crafty) peasant
girl; and during the intermezzo's second part Tabarano disguises himself
as a Turkish pirate in order to abduct her.

No such connections bind ballet music and drama in the
majority of intermezzi that contain dance pieces. The minuet, to judge
from its frequency of appearance in preserved scores, was the favorite
step of the *parti buffe*, although the protagonists of Giuseppe Sellitti's *La
franchezza delle donne* (Lesbina and Sempronio) terminate their antics by
dancing a *furlana*, and a few scores contain unidentified *balli* in duple
meter. Usually the intermezzo's ballet consists of one or two short pieces
in binary form; instrumentation and tempo are frequently unspecified.
Example 42 reproduces in its entirety a typical dance movement, the
minuet from the fifth of Alessandro Scarlatti's *scene buffe* for his *Scipione
nelle Spagne* (Naples, 1714).

Example 42
A. Scarlatti, *Scipione nelle Spagne,* comic scene No. 5

From the foregoing survey it is apparent that composers of intermezzi lavished some of their most novel and effective music on the genre. These composers' adherence to formal stereotypes more appropriate to the spirit of Metastasian libretti than that of most comic texts makes the novelty and effectiveness of this music all the more remarkable. Whether these stereotypes might have given way after 1750 to more innovative and flexible approaches to the setting of comic texts as was the case in *opera buffa* after this date is a moot point; by the midpoint of the eighteenth century the intermezzo as an entr'acte entertainment in *opere serie* had fallen into almost total decline. It now remains to examine the circumstances which led to that decline and to consider what influences—if any—the genre exerted on the "new" Italian comic opera.

CONCLUSION

DECLINE AND INFLUENCE

The grotesque alternation of tragedy and comedy created by performance of intermezzi between the acts of *opere serie* seems in retrospect one of the most bizarre features of an art form replete with eccentricities, yet one must search diligently to find contemporary condemnations of this practice. As usual in such matters, the earliest and most vehement criticism came from non-Italian sources. The English traveler Edward Wright obviously enjoyed the intermezzi he heard in Italy during the early years of the 1720's, but observed in his published diary that "such Entertainments, between the Acts of an Opera, somewhat like it in the Manner, but different in the Subject, seem to interrupt the Unity of the Opera itself; and if they will have such laughing Work, it shou'd seem better at the end of the Entertainment; as the *Petite piece* in *France*, at the End of their Comedy, and the Farces with us sometimes are."[1]

The French themselves had harsher words for the combination of *opere serie* and intermezzi. Josse de Villeneuve, while praising the latter's "musique brillante & singuliérement caractérisée," and admitting they mitigated the "ennui" and "langueur" of the serious operas with which were presented, declared that the resulting "monstrous jumble of serious [drama] and outrageous comedy . . . is revolting to reason." "Just imagine," he shuddered, "seeing a representation of the death of Caesar and [the antics of] Pourceaugnac, in which an act of each is performed in alternation."[2] Even an observer so partial to Italian music as Jean-Jacques Rousseau believed intermezzi were "so out of place in the midst of a tragic work that the two pieces were mutually prejudicial, and one of the two could never help being more interesting at the expense of the other."[3]

Such objections are practically nonexistent in the writings of Italian critics. Even Benedetto Marcello's satirical *Il teatro alla moda* [Venice, ca. 1720] directs no barbs at the practice of filling the intervals between acts of a musical tragedy with comic pieces. For the first significant criticism of this practice in the Italian language one must turn to the second edition of Stefano Arteaga's *Le rivoluzioni del treatro musicale italiano*, published some time after musical intermezzi had ceased to figure in performances of *opere serie*. In hindsight, the Spanish Jesuit saw the "indiscriminate" use of intermezzi as a cause of "disordine negli spettacoli." He quotes with evident tolerance several seventeenth-century examples of intermezzi that corresponded in subject or dramatic genre to the operas with which they were performed (e.g., *Dafne conversa in Lauro* with the tragicommedia [pastorale] *L'amorosa clemenza* [Bologna, 1623], but laments that "soon corruption set in, the adjuncts became the principal attraction, intermezzi multiplied without rhyme or reason, and the spectacle became a monstrosity."[4]

This state of affairs seems to have troubled Italian audiences not at all. Indeed, we have seen that Venetian impresarios around 1740 were content to repeat operas from previous seasons, knowing that intermezzi alone would attract audiences to their theaters.[5] Only for Naples is there any evidence that lack of interest or change of taste caused a decline in intermezzi. Performances of the latter ceased there abruptly in 1735, due to displeasure of the new king, Carlo di Borbone,[6] who apparently preferred for his entr'acte diversion the presentation of dances—"sumptuous ballets [of a kind] never seen before in this capital," according to one contemporary report.[7]

Although evidence of royal or popular disfavor is lacking for other cities of Italy, they too soon followed Naples' lead in dispensing with intermezzi during performances of *opere serie*. Table 9 lists statistics relative to those Italian cities for which the present writer found enough evidence to establish with some certainty the date of the last intermezzo presented in conjunction with a serious opera. Doubtless, the evidence of libretti and theatrical chronologies is imperfectly preserved and incomplete, yet any later performances that may have escaped notice could not have been very numerous or frequent.

Existing theatrical records, at least, leave no doubt that the custom of performing comic intermezzi with *opere serie* died a lingering death in Italy during the decade of the forties. To judge from the same records, there is also no question as to how the intermezzo met its fate: it was slowly drowned under the tide of comic operas that swept over the theaters of Italy during the same decade. Repertories of some principal opera houses supply the evidence. The last intermezzo performed at Bologna's Teatro Formagliari was heard during carnival of 1747; for the rest of that year and all of the following, the theater was given over for the first time to *drammi giocosi* by such popular exponents of that style as Pietro Auletta and Gioacchino Cocchi.[8] Similarly, the first season devoted principally to *drammi giocosi* immediately followed that in which the last recorded intermezzo was performed at Genoa's Teatro del Falcone.[9] And it seems hardly coincidental that the presentation of intermezzi with *opere serie* at Venice ceased just one year after the first season in which *opere buffe* outnumbered serious operas at that city's theaters.[10]

TABLE 9

LAST PERFORMANCES OF INTERMEZZI WITH *OPERE SERIE*

Year	City	Theater
1738	Milan	Regio Ducal
1740	Rome	della Pace
1740	Lucca	Pubblico
1741	Rimini	Pubblico
1743	Ferrara	S. Stefano
1743	Genoa	Falcone
1746	Pisa	Pubblico
1746	Pesaro	del Sole
1746	Florence	Cocomero
1747	Bologna	Formagliari
1747	Pistoia	Risvegliati
1749	Brescia	Nuovo
1750	Venice	S. Cassiano and S. Samuele
1753	Messina	della Munizione

If an increase in the number of full-length *opere buffe*, which satisfied the popular appetite for comic musical entertainment more thoroughly than intermezzi, was indeed responsible for the latter's decline, one might ask whether the intermezzo may have stimulated production of—or at least left its mark on—the genre that eventually replaced it as the most important type of Italian musical comedy. We must first dispose of the common misconception that comic intermezzi were somehow "children" to the "adult" *opera buffa*. This erroneous concept seems to have originated with no less an authority than Carlo Goldoni, who described intermezzi in his *Mémoires* as "the forerunners of Italian comic operas."[11] By the end of the nineteenth century this idea had become an article of faith for writers such as Nicola D'Arienzo, who states flatly that "undoubtedly, the *opera buffa* is nothing more than an expanded intermezzo,"[12] and Francesco Florimo, who misquotes Michele Scherillo to the effect that "our *opera buffa* was only a development, an expansion of the *intermezzo per musica*."[13] More recently, Manfred Bukofzer has asserted that

> the formal establishment of the *opera buffa* cannot be dissociated from that of the *opera seria*. Although comic scenes were a traditional feature of Italian opera in the seventeenth century, the *opera buffa* did not become a form in its own right before the early eighteenth century. Only with the relegation of the comic elements from the *opera seria* to the burlesque intermezzo, played between its three acts, was the contrast between the two types recognized in principle.[14]

As early as 1923, Andrea della Corte decisively refuted these notions by pointing out that independent, full-length comic operas were produced in abundance during the seventeenth century, long before comic intermezzi reached their maturity and that in the period of its mature form the intermezzo in no way presents a preliminary, inferior, or gestational aspect.[15]   Nonetheless, recent popular texts continue to assert in one chapter that the *opera buffa* developed from intermezzi of the early eighteenth century, while recording elsewhere Mazzocchi and Marazzoli's *Chi soffre, speri* of 1637 as the first comic opera, noting its distinctive *buffo* style, and listing some of its seventeenth-century successors—all, apparently, without noticing the inconsistency.[16]

More rational would be the conjecture that appearance of the first independent intermezzi may somehow have stimulated an increased production of full-length *opere buffe*.   Circumstantial evidence would indicate that this, in fact, was the case.   We have noted earlier that independent intermezzi first began appearing at Venice with some frequency around 1706.   That same year witnessed at Naples the premiere of *La Cilla*, the first dialect *comedia in musica*, a genre that by 1714 had become popular enough to force all serious operas from the boards of that city's Teatro dei Fiorentini.[17]

Unfortunately, these two developments occurred at opposite ends of the Italian peninsula, and seem to have had no mutual influence even in their own respective locales.   In spite of the large number of independent intermezzi produced after 1706 at Venice, only a handful of full-length *opere buffe* were performed there before 1743, when the first examples of comic operas by such Neapolitan composers as Gaetano Latilla and Rinaldo da Capua began to reach Venetian stages.[18]   And despite the model of independent *buffo* pieces *La Cilla* and its numerous successors provided, we have seen that poets and composers at Naples continued to consider comic scenes an integral part of the *opere serie* performed at the Teatro San Bartolomeo and Royal Palace until the mid 1720's.

Although no causal relationship seems to exist between intermezzo and *opera buffa*, it would be only reasonable in view of the strong penchant for pasticcio during the first half of the eighteenth century to assume that the two genres may have borrowed text and music from one another with some frequency during their period of coexistence.   We have already noted that the duet "Per te ho io nel core" from Pergolesi's *Flaminio*, a full-length *comedia per musica*, was frequently substituted for the original final number of the same composer's intermezzo *La serva padrona*.   Due to the scarcity of scores for *opere buffe* from the first half of the eighteenth century, however, it seems unlikely that we shall ever come to any definite conclusion as to whether this was an exceptional case, or representative of common practice during the period. In 1910 Edward Dent published a list of all the then-known eighteenth-century *opera buffa* scores up to 1760 preserved in European libraries; only 13 of them date from before 1750.[19] Recent searches have turned up several more, but hardly enough to furnish material for a comprehensive study of mutual borrowing by composers of intermezzi and *opere buffe.*

In regard to such borrowing of texts, a researcher is faced by the opposite problem, an embarrassment of riches. Libretti of intermezzi and *opere buffe* published during the first half of the eighteenth century exist in such profusion that only creation of an automated index of text incipits will permit a thorough investigation of this subject. In advance of that happy event, the present writer can offer only one sample of the interrelationships between intermezzo and *opera buffa,* a series of related texts discovered quite fortuitously during an examination of several thousand libretti printed before 1750.

The chain of related texts begins with Metastasio's *L'impresario delle Canarie*, already discussed in Chapter III of the present study. One year after its first publication at Naples in 1724, the libretto was reprinted in Bologna for reasons that are not entirely clear, since, contrary to eighteenth-century practice, no cast, theater, or other information regarding a performance is mentioned in the booklet.[20] In any case, it may have been this edition of Metastasio's intermezzo that served as a textual source for Giuseppe Maria Buini, librettist and composer of *Il savio delirante,* a *comico divertimento per musica* mainly in Bolognese dialect performed at Bologna's Teatro Formagliari during the carnival of 1726.[21]

Now *Il savio delirante* is nothing less than an expansion of Metastasio's *L'impresario delle Canarie* into the text of a full-length comic opera. Needless to say Buini effected numerous changes and additions to amplify the little farce with its two singing roles and two short parts into a three-act *opera buffa* with a cast of five. Dorina, Metastasio's haughty prima donna, becomes a novice soprano named Lisetta, daughter of an impecunious widow, Crespa, and in love with her singing teacher, Lindoro. The latter's rivals for her affection are a Ferrarese Doctor (the "delirious sage" of the opera's title, a Doctor Gratiano type straight from the *commedia dell'arte*) and Lindoro's dilettantish friend Flema, who corresponds roughly to Nibbio, the impresario of Metastasio's intermezzo.

The intrigue generated within this amorous quadrilateral is, of course, all lacking in the intermezzo, but most of it results from Flema's efforts to lure away Lisetta as the leading lady in a Tyrolean opera company, just as Metastasio's Nibbio attempts to engage Dorina as prima donna for his theater in the Canary Islands. This central episode of the Buini version closely paraphrases Metastasio's language and verse (with Dorina's part translated into Bolognese dialect). Thus the scene in which the impresario reassures his prospective prima donna that language will be no barrier to her appearance on a foreign stage is virtually identical in the two settings, but gains additional humor in the adaptation from Lisetta's inability to express herself in Tuscan:

L'impresario delle Canarie i	*Il savio delirante* II.i
Nib. Eh! non si prenda affanno. Il libretto non deve esser capito; Il gusto è repulito, E non si bada a questo: Si canti bene, e non importi il resto.	*Fle.* Questo già niente importa, Perchè oggidi la moda de' Teatri Non vuol più, che s'intendan le parole; Basta solo chi canta, Faccia passi di crome, e di biscrome, Con sdrocciolante gusto.
Dor. Nell'arie io son con lei, Ma ne' recitativi è un'altra cosa.	*Lis.* Int' el i arj al cunced, Mò in ti recitativ l' è un'altra cosa.
Nib. Anzi in questi potrà Cantar con quella lingua che le pare, Che allor, com'Ella sa, Per solito l'udienza ha da ciarlare.	*Fle.* Già per lo più questi non sono intesi, Perchè ogn'uno in quel tempo vuol chiarlare.

A contemporary English translation of the Metastasian version[22] will serve to convey the sense of both:

> *Nib.* Ah! madam, that, with us, is no objection!
> An opera book should not be understood.
> We have refin'd our taste to that degree,
> That sense is the least part of our concern:
> Sing you but well, the rest will ne'er be minded.
>
> *Dor.* In airs, I grant you, sir, this may be true:
> But recitative is quite another thing.
>
> *Nib.* Not of half the consequence! that may be sung
> In what language you please; for then, you know,
> The audience love, too, to talk in their turn.

Even Metastasio's burlesque comparison aria appears so slightly altered in the *opera buffa* that one is led to wonder whether Buini might also have borrowed some music from a previous setting of the intermezzo libretto along with the text:[23]

L'impresario delle Canarie ii	*Il savio delirante* III.i
Nib. La farfalla, che allo scuro Va ronzando intorno al muro, Sai che dice a chi l'intende? "Chi una fiaccola m'accende. Chi mi scotta per pietà?"	*Fle.* La Farfalla senza il lume Non si stacca mai dal muro, Che per esser allo scuro, Più volar' ella non sà.
Il vascello e la tartana, Fra scirocco e tramontana, Con le tavole schiodate Va sbalzando, va sparando Cannonate in quantità.	Così ancor la Navicella, Che abbattuta da procella, Perch' e lungi dalla sponda, O' s'affonda, O' smarrita se ne và.

The close relationship between intermezzo and *opera buffa* illustrated by these two libretti is striking enough, but there is yet another link in the chain of related texts. During May and June of 1726, the same year that *Il savio delirante* received its premiere at Bologna, the *opera buffa* was performed virtually unchanged under the title *Le frenesie d'amore* at Venice.[24] Just five years later, there appeared at that same city's Teatro San Angelo in conjunction with a revival of Vivaldi's *La costanza trionfante degl'amore, e degl'odii*[25] an intermezzo entitled *Melinda*, the text of which turns out to be a *reduction* of Buini's *Il savio delirante* to three short parts with only two singing roles.[26] The latter are our old friends, the dilettantish impresario and his prospective prima donna, named, respectively, Melinda and Flema in this latest reincarnation.[27] In addition to eliminating all the other roles and amorous intrigue of Buini's *opera buffa,* the arranger of *Melinda* translated the Bolognese dialect of his model into literary Italian, and added a third part, lacking in both previous versions of the libretto, in which the singer drives her would-be employer to near distraction with extravagant demands.

The text of the intermezzo's first two parts is a skillful pastiche of scenes from *Il savio delirante* rearranged so as to make a self-contained drama reminiscent of *L'impresario delle Canarie*, but more closely related in language and verse to Buini's paraphrase of Metastasio's intermezzo than to the original model itself.[28] The redactor's tour de force is the obligatory duet that terminates the intermezzo's second part. Since such a text is lacking in the scenes from *Il savio delirante* that serve as the basis for this part of *Melinda*, the arranger constructed one from the text of a Buini aria (in which the impresario assures the vacillating prima donna of his continued favor regardless of her decision) by "farcing" the text with her pointed observations on the "favors" she will continue to expect from him:[29]

Il savio delirante II.vii   *Melinda* ii

Fle. Pensi, e risolva,	*Fle.* Pensa, e risolva
Mi fa gran favore	Mi fà gran favore
In tutti li modi,	In tutti li modi
che risponderà,	Che risolverà.
	Mel. Attonita penso
	Ai grandi favori,
	Che in tutti li modi
	Sempre ella mi fà.
Se accetta, ò rifiuta,	*Fle.* Se accetta; o rifiuta.
Io sono lo stesso	Io sono lo stesso,
Che quì mi professo	Che quì mi proffesso
Suo buon servitore,	Suo buon Servitore
Se pur mi vorra.	Se pur mi vorrà.
	Mel. Se accetto, o rinuncio
	Io sono la stessa
	Sua serva indefessa
	Di tutto buon cuore
	Con ingenuità.
	Fle. Io sono lo stesso
	Che qui mi professo
	Suo buon servitore
	Se pur mi vorrà.
Intanto per segno	Intanto per segno
Del mio grand'ossequio,	Del mio grand'ossequio
M'umilio, m'inchino,	Mi umilio, e m'inchino.
	Mel. Le son serva vera.
Le fo riverenze	*Fle.* Le fò riverenze
In gran quantità.	in gran quantità.

From this particular chain of related libretti stretching from 1724 at Naples to 1731 in Venice, it appears that texts (and quite possibly music) of intermezzi and *opere serie* were considered interchangeable during their period of coexistence. Still unanswered is the question of whether any distinctive features of the intermezzo may have left their mark on the *opera buffa*. To discover any such influence we must first consider the *opera seria* and intermezzo with which it was performed as a single unit, and then concentrate on developments leading to the creation of a new type of *opera buffa* generally considered a product of the association between Carlo Goldoni and Baldassare Galuppi that began around 1750.

Goldoni's contribution has been summarized by Donald Grout in the following manner:

> His influence on the libretto marked a turning point in the history of the opera buffa, which from this time on became more dignified,

more orderly in structure, and more refined in action and language. New kinds of comic opera librettos began to appear—works which must be called dramas rather than farces, and which were often sentimental or even pathetic in character. These newer tendencies did not, of course, replace the old comic element altogether but rather existed side by side or intermingled with them, so that the comic opera libretto in the second half of the eighteenth century was distinctly varied and, on the whole, much more interesting than that of the opera seria.[30]

Symptomatic of the "more orderly structure" of post-1750 *opere buffe* libretti is the customary division of roles in their lists of dramatis personae into *parti serie* and *parti buffe*. At Venice, this practice seems to have begun in 1747 and become quite regular by 1754 in the comic works of Goldoni and his contemporaries.[31]

For his part, Galuppi is credited with musically organizing the rather extended finales that customarily fall at the ends of acts one and two of these libretti in a' series of short sections varying in meter and tempo to reflect the changing moods of the text.[32] Although this so-called "chain finale" may involve as many as five participants, the latter are always drawn from among the opera's *parti buffe*.[33]

It is striking that these developments occurred almost simultaneously with the abandonment of intermezzi in conjunction with the performance of *opere serie*. Did this conjunction provide the model for dramatic construction of the new type of *opera buffa*? And did the intermezzo's traditional closing duet furnish a pattern for the *opera buffa's* ensemble finale? Conclusive affirmation of these questions would require a study at least the length of the present one and the availability of more scores from the early decades of the eighteenth century than seem to have survived.

Yet some time ago Edward Dent called attention to at least one bit of convincing evidence that the *opera seria*-intermezzo tradition and the dramaturgy and ensemble finales of mid-eighteenth-century *opera buffa* are related. In an article published in 1909 Dent properly observed that *opera buffa* and the intermezzo *per se* pursued quite different lines of development during the century's early decades, but he remarked of Alessandro Scarlatti's *Il trionfo d'onore* (1718), the earliest full-length Neapolitan comic opera for which the music has been preserved, that

it is curious to see that . . . there are scenes which deserve to be called "intermezzi" as much as any in his serious works. The two servants Rodimarte and Rosina differ from the comic characters in "Tigrane" or any other [serious] opera only in being more realistically treated, and in having more to do.

But since comedy is the general style of the opera, it was necessary to exaggerate the "parti buffe" into farce, if they were to be kept proportionate to the other characters. We find therefore that the two comic duets are very extended in form, and that their humour is more than usually grotesque. The specimen which I have already quoted [in *Alessandro Scarlatti: His Life and Works* (London, 1906), p. 129]—"Ferma, ferma, o cospettaccio"—comes in its natural place at the end of Act I. After the principal characters have unfolded the exposition of the play, Rodimarte, who is a sort of Leporello to a Don Giovanni called Riccardo, looks about for a suitable partner, and encounters Rosina, the servant of the old lady Cornelia. He sings a parody of the "Siciliano" type; she responds with a lively air in which she calls to him—"tè tè tè"—as if calling a dog to heel. Finally they join in a duet. The style of this duet is sufficiently indicated in the bars quoted. It should be observed that it is not in Da Capo form, and that it works up to a more or less exciting climax at the end.[34]

It should be immediately apparent to readers of the present study that Dent's description of this scene, with its quasi-improvisatory horseplay, parodistic elements, and terminal duet—all falling at the end of an act—would apply to any comic intermezzo produced during the first half of the eighteenth century. It is equally obvious that the isolation of the serious from the comic characters, and the little duet of the latter, with its greater extension, musico-dramatic stretto, and avoidance of da capo form, looks forward to the plot construction and ensemble finales of Goldoni and Galuppi, not to mention those of Mozart and his librettists. *Il trionfo d'onore* is still miles from the dramaturgy and finales of Goldoni-Galuppi, much less those of da Ponte-Mozart, and most of the intervening territory still remains unmapped; yet it seems possible that the model furnished by performances of *opere serie* with intermezzi may have initiated the long journey.

APPENDIX A

SOME FREQUENTLY REVIVED INTERMEZZI

The following pages list those intermezzi for which the present writer was able to find libretti or notices of at least five revivals in as many different cities. They are arranged alphabetically by dramatis personae (female role first), since the intermezzo not only shared with serious operas of the period a proclivity for changes of title at every new production, but often lacked one altogether. Such "titles" as "Intermezzi cantati dai signori___" (with the singers' names frequently misspelled) or "Intermezzi nel teatro___" that sometimes appear on the covers of libretti have been disregarded. Data for what appears to be the first edition of each text preceeds the city, date, title, and composer mentioned in the libretti or notices for revivals.

This list is not to be considered a catalogue of all the most popular comic intermezzi produced during the eighteenth century, nor is it claimed to register every revival of each piece included; rather it was compiled as a representative sample to serve as the basis for a discussion of the repertory and its diffusion (see Chapter II). For this reason, information other than that contained in libretti seen by the present writer is enclosed in brackets and its source identified, to distinguish the evidence of primary sources from the frequently questionable data to be found in the secondary literature. Titles given in the latter are so often patently corrupt that they have in most cases been omitted. Finally, it should be noted that the degree of similarity between two versions of the same libretto tends to diminish as their separation in time and place of publication increases, so that texts for some later revivals of intermezzi recorded here bear only a tenuous resemblance to those of their respective premieres.

BRUNETTA AND BURLOTTO

Venice; Carnival, 1708; Teatro San Cassiano, as *La capricciosa e il credulo*,[1] with [Francesco Gasparini's][2] *Engelberta*. [Music by Francesco Gasparini?][3]

Naples	1720		[Domenico Sarri][4]
Rome	1724		
Venice	1725	La capricciosa e il credulo[1]	
Hamburg	1725	La capriciosa e il credulo	Georg Philipp Telemann
Urbino	1741	La fuga di Burlotto con Brunetta	

CARLOTTA AND PANTALEONE

Naples; Spring, 1728; Teatro San Bartolomeo, with Johann Adolph Hasse's *Attalo re di Bitinia*. Music by Johann Adolph Hasse.

Florence	1729	La finta tedesca	
Naples	1734		
[St. Petersburg	1734][5]		
Hamburg	1746	La finta tedesca	J. A. Hasse *et al.*
Pescia	1748	La finta tedesca	
Potsdam	1749	La finta tedesca	
[Copenhagen	1756-57][6]		

DORINA AND NIBBIO, libretto by Pietro Metastasio[7]

Naples; Carnival, 1724; Teatro San Bartolomeo, with Domenico Sarri's *Didone abandonata*. Music by Domenico Sarri.

Venice	1725	L'impresario delle Canarie	
Bologna	1725	L'impresario delle Canarie	
[Genoa	1726][8]		
Venice	1731	L'impresario delle Canarie	
[Venice	1732][9]		
[St. Petersburg	1733][10]		
[Lucca	1735][11]		
London	1737	L'impresario	Domenico Sarri
Madrid	1738	L'impressario delle Canarie	
Pardo	1739	L'impressario delle Canarie	
Venice	1741	L'impresario dell'Isole Canarie	Leonardo Leo
Bologna	1744	L'impresario delle Canarie	
Vienna	1747	L'impresario dell'Isole Canarie	
Potsdam	1748	L'impresario dell'Isole Canarie	
[Madrid	1749][12]		
Venice	1749	L'impressario dell'Isole Canarie	
Parma	1750	L'impresario dell'Isole Canarie	
Ravenna	1752	L'impresario dell'Isole Canarie	

[Hamburg   1752][13]
Copenhagen   ?[14]   L'impresario, dell'Isole Canarie   Giuseppe Maria
                                                               Orlandini
[Schwetzingen   ?][15]

DRUSILLA AND STRAMBONE, libretto by Tomaso Mariani[16]

[Naples; 1735; Teatro San Bartolomeo, with Domenico Sarri and Leonardo Leo's *Demofoonte*. Music Giuseppe Sellitti.][17]

Malta	1741	La vedova ingegnosa
S. Giovanni	1741	La vedova ingegnosa
Bergamo	1743	La vedova ingegnosa
Hamburg	1743	La vedova ingegnosa
Venice	1746	La vedova ingegnosa
Dresden	1747	La vedova ingegnosa
[Prague	1747][18]	
[Leipzig	1748][19]	
[Potsdam	1748][20]	
Rome	1749	La vedova ingegnosa
[Copenhagen	1755-58][21]	
[Schwetzingen	?][22]	
[Brunswick	?][23]	

ERIGHETTA AND DON CHILONE

Venice; Autumn, 1707; Teatro San Cassiano, with Francesco Gasparini's *Anfitrione*. [Music by Francesco Gasparini?][24]

[Florence	1718][25]		
Ferrara	1724	L'ammalato immaginario o sia l'ipocondriaco[26]	
[Pistoia	1725][27]		
Vienna	1725	Don Chilone	
Naples	1726		Leonardo Vinci
[Mannheim	1726][28]		
Perugia	1727	L'ammalato immaginario	
[Genoa	1727][29]		
Brussels	1728	Il malato immaginario	
Florence	1732	L'ammalato immaginario	
[St. Petersburg	1734][30]		
Venice	1748	L'ammalato immaginario	
Brescia	1749[31]		

FIAMMETTA AND PANCRAZIO, [libretto by Antonio Salvi][32]

[Florence; 1720; as *L'avaro*.][32]

Venice	1720	L'avaro	[Francesco Gasparini][33]
[Pesaro	1723][34]		
[Lucca	1724][35]		
Cento	1725	Il vecchio avaro	
Naples	1726		
S. Giovanni	1729	L'avaro	
[St. Petersburg	1733][36]		

GRILLETTA AND PORSUGNACCO

Milan; Carnival, 1727; Teatro Regio Ducal, as *Monsieur di Porsugnacchi*, with Giuseppe Vignati's *Girita*.

Venice	1727[37]	Monsieur di Porsugnacco	
Florence	1727[38]	Monsieur di Porsugnacco	
Naples	1727[39]		Johann Adolph Hasse
Perugia	1728	Monsieur di Porsugnacco	
Faenza	1728	Monsieur di Porsugnacco	
Rome	1729		
[Pistoia	1730][40]		
[St. Petersburg	173?][41]		
[Lucca	1735][42]		
London	1737	Porceaugnac and Grilletta	Giuseppe Maria Orlandini
S. Giovanni	1740	Monsieur de Porsugnacco ingannato da Grilletta	
Venice	1741	Monsieur de Porsugnac	
[Venice	1742][43]		
Hamburg	1745	Monsieur de Porsugnacco ingannato da Grilletta	
[Hamburg	1746][44]		
[Dresden	1747][45]		
[Potsdam	1750][46]		
[Copenhagen	1752][47]		
[Schwetzingen	1752][48]		
[Hamburg	1753][49]		
[Copenhagen	1754-58][50]		
[Brunswick	?][51]		

LARINDA AND VANESIO, [libretto by Antonio Salvi][52]

[Florence; 1722; as *L'artigiano gentiluomo.*][52]

Naples	1726		[Johann Adolph Hasse][53]
Florence	1732	Le bourgeois gentilhomme	
Rome	1732		
[Palermo	1732][54]		

Dresden	1734	Der Handwercks-Mann ein Edel-Mann	
[St. Petersburg	1734][55]		
London	1737	Le bourgois gentilhomme; or, Vanesio and Larinda	Giuseppe Maria Orlandini
Cortona	1738	La baronessa	
Venice	1739	Il bottegaro gentiluomo	Johann Adolph Hasse

LIDIA AND IRCANO, libretto by Silvio Stampiglia [and Belisario Valeriani][56]

Vienna; Carnival, 1709; Hoftheater, and Naples; Autumn, 1711; Teatro San Bartolomeo, as comic scenes in Giovanni Bononcini's *L'Abdolomino*. Music by Giovanni Bononcini.

Rome	1715	
Ferrara	1715	Ircano innamorato
Bologna	1716	Ircano innamorato
Modena	1719	Lidia, e Ircano
Venice	1722	Ircano innamorato
[Venice	1726][57]	
Venice	1729	Ircano inamorato
[Bologna	1730][58]	
[Venice	1730][59]	
[Venice	1731][60]	
[Moscow	1731][61]	
Bologna	1747	Li amori d'Ircano, e Lidia

LISETTA AND ASTROBOLO

Venice; 1707; Teatro San Cassiano, with Francesco Gasparini's *Taican rè della Cina*. [Music by Francesco Gasparini.][62]

Naples	1709	
Rome	1711	Astrobolo, e Lisetta
Parma	1714	Lisetta, & Astrobolo
Modena	1714	
Bologna	1716	
Vienna	1717	Lisetta, ed Astrobolo
Bologna	1719	
Venice	1725	Lisetta, e Astrobolo
Barcelona	?[63]	Lisetta, ed Astrobolo

LIVIETTA AND TRACOLLO

Naples; October, 1734; Teatro San Bartolomeo, as *La contadina astuta*, with Giovanni Battista Pergolesi's *Adriano in Siria*. Music by Giovanni Battista Pergolesi.

[Rome	1737][64]		
[Milan	1739][65]		
Venice	1741	Il finto pazzo	[G.B. Pergolesi][66]
Verona	1742][67]		
Genoa	1742	Amor fa l'uomo cieco	
Hamburg	1743	Amor fà l'uomo cieco	
Venice	1744	La contadina astuta	G.B. Pergolesi
[Hamburg	1744][68]		
Prague	1744	Amor fa l'uomo cieco	
Leipzig	1744	Amor fa l'uomo cieco	
Bologna	1746	Il Tracollo	
[Dresden	1747][69]		
[Prague	1748][70]		
[Madrid	1748][71]		
[Vienna	1748][72]		
[Rome	1748][73]		
[Leipzig	1748][74]		
[Postdam	1748][75]		
Brunswick	[1749][76]	Il finto pazzo	G. B. Pergolesi
Copenhagen	1749	Il Tracollo	
Venice	1750	Il ladro convertito per amore	
[Peterhof	1750][77]		
Paris	1753	Tracollo medico ignorante	G. B. Pergolesi
[Barcelona	1754][78]		
[Schwetzingen	1754][79]		
[Copenhagen	1757][80]		

LUCILLA AND PANDOLFO

Naples; 1730; Teatro San Bartolomeo, as *Il tutore*, with Johann Adolph Hasse's *Ezio*. [Music by Johann Adolph Hasse.][81]

Dresden	1738	Il tutore	
Venice	1739	Pandolfo	J. A. Hasse
Rome	1739	Il tutore[82]	
Pardo	1740	Il tutore, o sia la pupilla	
Hamburg	1744	Il tutore e la pupilla	
Bologna	1746	Il tutore	J. A. Hasse
Vienna	1747	Il tutore, e la pupilla	J. A. Hasse

MADAMA DULCINEA AND IL CUOCO DEL MARCHESE DEL BOSCO, libretto by Marchese Trotti[83]

Rome; Carnival, 1712; Teatro Capranica, with *La fede tradita e vendicata.*

Naples	1715	La preziosa ridicola	Giuseppe Maria Orlandini

Reggio	1715	La preziosa ridicola	
Modena	1717	La preziosa ridicola	
Bologna	1718	La preziosa ridicola	
Venice	1719	La preziosa ridicola	
Ricanati	1720	La preziosa ridicola, ed il Cuoco del Marchese del Bosco	
Vienna	1724	Cuoco, e Madama	
Florence	1728	La preziosa ridicola	
[Moscow	1731][84]		
[Pesaro	1733][85]		
Milan	1735		
Hamburg	1746	La preziosa ridicola	Giuseppe Maria Orlandini
Venice	1747	Il Marchese del Bosco	
Venice	1750	La preziosa ridicola[86]	
[Peterhof	1750][87]		
[Moscow	1753][88]		
[Copenhagen	1756-57][89]		
[Aranjuez	?][90]		

MELISSA AND SERPILLO[91]

Venice; Autumn, 1707; Teatro San Cassiano, as *Melissa schernita,* with Francesco Gasparini's *L'amor generoso.* [Music by Francesco Gasparini.][92]

Bologna	1708	Melissa	
Naples	1709	Melissa schernita	
Verona	1710	Melissa	
Genoa	1712		
Modena	1716		
[Prague	1724][93]		
[Hamburg	1731	Herr Fändrich Nothdurfft aus dem Lager bey Mühlberg	Georg Philipp Telemann][94]
Graz	1738	Melissa	
[Munich	1739	Melissa tradita	Joseph Anton (?) Camerloher][95]

MOSCHETTA AND GRULLO

Naples; Carnival, 1727; Teatro San Bartolomeo, with Domenico Sarri's *Siroe rè di Persia.* Music by Domenico Sarri?[96]

Brussels	1729	La trufaldina	
Venice	1732	Grullo, e Moschetta	[Giuseppe Maria Orlandini][97]
Genoa	1734		
London	1737	Grullo and Moschetta	Giuseppe Maria Orlandini

[Lucca	1740][98]		
Florence	1744	(?)[99]	
Hamburg	[1746][100]	Le gelosie frà Grullo, e Moschetta	Domenico Paradies[101]
[Hamburg	1748][102]		
Copenhagen	1748	La gelosie fra Grullo e Moschetta	Domenico Paradies[101]
[Luebeck	1746][103]		
[Copenhagen	1756-58][104]		

PALANDRANA AND ZAMBERLUCCO

Venice; Autumn, 1709; Treatro San Cassiano, as *Zamberlucco*, with [Francesco Gasparini's][105] *La principessa fedele.* [Music by Francesco Gasparini?][106]

Genoa	1712	Zamberlucco
Modena	1713	
Reggio	1715	Palandrana, e Zamberlucco
Naples	1716	
Bologna	1717	Intermezzi di Zamberlucco, e di Palandrana
[Massa	1717][107]	
Florence	1719	
Ferrara	1721	Intermezzi di Zamberlucco, e Palandrana
Bologna	1724	Intermezzi di Zamberlucco, e Palandrana
Parma	1726	Intermezzi di Zamberlucco, e Palandrana

POLLASTRELLA AND PARPAGNACCO

Venice; Carnival, 1708; Teatro San Cassiano, as *Parpagnacco*, with [Francesco Gasparini's][108] *L'Engelberta.* [Music by Francesco Gasparini?][109]

Florence	1713		
Verona	1713	Parpagnaco e Polastrella	
[Brunswick	1717][110]		
[Ferrara	1722][111]		
Cento	1724		
[Bologna	1724][112]		
Venice	1731	L'astrologo	
[Moscow	1731][113]		
Parma	1733		
Stuttgart	1737		
Bologna	1743	L'astrologo ritroso in amore	Angiolo Maria Mazzanti

Vicenza	1753
Udine	1754
[Dresden	1762][114]

ROSMENE AND GERONDO[115]

Venice	1729	Il matrimonio per forza	
[Venice	1731][116]		
[S. Giovanni	1731][117]		
Reggio	1732	Il matrimonio per forza	Giuseppe Maria Buini
Ravenna	1732	Il matrimonio per forza	
[Lucca	1735][118]		
Graz	1739	Il matrimonio per forza	
Potsdam	1748	Il matrimonio per forza	

SCINTILLA AND DON TABARANO, libretto by Bernardo Saddumene[119]

Naples; Autumn, 1728; Teatro San Bartolomeo, as *La contadina*, with Pietro Scarlatti's *Clitarco, o sia il più fedel tra gli amici.* [Music by Johann Adolph Hasse.][120]

Venice	1731	La contadina	[Johann Adolph Hasse][121]
[Rome	1731][122]		
Trieste	1731	La contadina	Johann Adolph Hasse
Treviso	1731	La contadina	
Naples	1733	La contadina	
Genoa	1733		
Parma	1734	La contadina	
[St. Petersburg	1734][123]		
Bologna	1734		
[Dresden	1737][124]		
[Madrid	1738][125]		
Bologna	1738	La contadina	Johann Adolph Hasse
Lucca	1740	La contadina	
Sinigaglia	1741	D. Tabarano	
Bologna	1744	Il Tabarano	Johann Adolph Hasse
[Hamburg	1744][126]		
Hamburg	1745	Il Tabarano	
[Dresden	1745][127]		
[Dresden	1746][128]		
[Venice	1746][129]		
Dresden	1747	Don Tabarrano	
[Potsdam	1748][130]		
Copenhagen	1748	Il Tabarano	Johann Adolph Hasse
Brunswick	1749	Il Tabarano	
[Charlottenburg	1750][131]		
[Prague	1750][132]		

Treviso	1755	Don Tabarano
[Copenhagen	1756][133]	
[Dresden	1762][134]	
[Dresden	1763][135]	
[Aranjuez	?][136]	

SERPILLA AND BACOCCO, libretto by Antonio Salvi[137]

Venice; Carnival, 1719; Teatro San Angelo, as *Il marito giogatore, e la moglie bacchettona*, with Fortunato Chelleri's *Amalasunta*.

[Florence	1720][138]		
Rome	1721		
[Venice	1721][139]		
[Ferrera	1722][140]		
Munich	1722	Serpilla, e Bacocco	
Genoa	1723	Serpilla è Bacocco	
[Lucca	1724][141]		
Bologna	1725	Il giocatore	
[Pistoia	1725][142]		
Naples	1725		
[Palermo	1726][143]		
Venice	1727	Il marito giocatore, e la moglie bacchettona	
[Breslau	1727][144]		
Brussels	1728	Serpilla e Baiocco, o vero il marito giocatore e la moglie bacchettona	
Paris	1729	Bajocco e Serpilla	
[Venice	1729][145]		
Trieste	1730	Serpilla, e Bacocco	
Venice	1730	Serpilla, e Bacocco	
[Moscow	1731][146]		
[Venice	1732][147]		
Reggio	1733	Il gioccatore	
[Vienna	1733][148]		
[St. Petersburg	1733][149]		
[Lisbon	1736][150]		
[Hamburg	1736][151]		
London	1737	Il giocatore	Giuseppe Maria Orlandini
Venice	1739	Il marito giocatore, e la moglie bacchettona	
[Lucca	1740][152]		
[Venice	1741		Giuseppe Maria Orlandini][153]
Hamburg	1741	Das einander werthe Ehe-Paar, oder Bacocco und Serpilla	

[Venice	1742		Giuseppe Maria Orlandini][154]
Prague	1744	Il marito ciocatore, e la moglie bacchettona	
[Hamburg	1746][155]		
[Dresden	1746][156]		
[Augsburg	1746][157]		
Bologna	1748	Il Bacocco o sia Il giuocatore	
Potsdam	1748	Il glocatore	
[Potsdam	1751][158]		
Paris	1752	Il giocatore	
Rome	1753	Il marito giocatore	
[Hamburg	1753][159]		
[Copenhagen	1755][160]		
[St. Petersburg	1757][161]		
[Copenhagen	1757][162]		
[Hamburg	1767][163]		

SERPINA AND UBERTO, libretto by Gennaro Antonio Federico[164]

Naples; Autumn, 1733; Teatro San Bartolomeo, as *La serva padrona*, with Giovanni Battista Pergolesi's *Il prigionier superbo*. Music by Giovanni Battista Pergolesi.

Rome	1735	La serva padrona	G. B. Pergolesi
[Rome	1738][165]		
[Parma	1738][166]		
S. Giovanni	1739	La serva padrona	
[Bologna	1739][167]		
Graz	1739	La serva padrona	G. B. Pergolesi
[Lucca	1740][168]		
Venice	1740	La serva padrona	[Pergolesi and Vinci][169]
Dresden	1740	Das Magd als Frau im Hause	
Modena	1741	La serva padrona	
Venice	1741	La serva padrona	[G. B. Pergolesi][170]
Gorizia	1742	La serva padrona	G. B. Pergolesi
Florence	1742	La serva padrona	
Ferrara	1743	La serva padrona	
Hamburg	1743	La serva padrona	
Hamburg	1744	La serva padrona	
Prague	1744	La serva padrona	
[Venice	1745][171]		
Hamburg	1745][172]		
[Hamburg	1746][173]		
Paris	1746	La serva padrona	
Vienna	1746	La serva padrona	
[Augsburg	1746][174]		
Padua	1747	La serva padrona	
Reggio	1748	La serva padrona	
Venice	1748	La serva padrona	

Potsdam	1748	La serva padrona
[Hamburg	1748][175]
[Leipzig	1748][176]
[Piacenza	1749][177]
Brunswick	1749	La serva padrona
[London	1750][178]
[Barcelona	1750][179]
[Nuremberg	1751][180]
[Berlin	1752][181]
[Hamburg	1752][182]
[Schwetzingen	1752][183]
Paris	1752	La serva padrona

VESPETTA AND PIMPINONE, libretto by Pietro Pariati[184]

Venice; Autumn, 1708; Teatro San Cassiano, as *Pimpinone*, with Tomaso Albinoni's *Astarto*. [Music by Tomaso Albinoni?][185]

Naples	1709		
Rome	1711		
Ferrara	1711	Pimpinone, e Vespetta	
Padua	1712		
Parma	1714		
[Modena	1714][186]		
Turin	1716		
Vienna	1717[187]		Francesco Conti
Bologna	1717	La serva astuta	
Florence	1718		
[Brunswick	1720][187, 188]		
Munich	1722	Vespetta, e Pimpinone	
[Pesaro	1723][189]		
[Lucca	1724][190]		
S. Giovanni	1725	La serva astuta	
Venice	1725	Pimpinone	
Hamburg	1725	Die ungleiche Heyrath zwischen Vespetta und Pimpinone	[Georg Philipp Telemann][191]
Bologna	1728	La serva astuta	
[Breslau	1728][192]		
Brussels	1728		
[Hamburg	1730][193]		
[Brunswick	1731][194, 187]		
[Moscow	1731][195]		
Lanbach	1740		
Brescia	?	Pimpinone	

APPENDIX B

SOME COMIC SCENES AND INTERMEZZI PRINTED IN LIBRETTI OF *OPERE SERIE*, 1700-1753

The following pages list alphabetically by dramatis personae (female role first) a corpus of dramatic poetry generally not classified in libretto catalogues. The list makes no pretense to completeness, nor does it attempt to group together all variants of similar texts with different roles—or for that matter, differentiate among those with the same dramatis personae and substantially dissimilar texts (for an indication of the difficulties such an attempt would entail, see above, p. 38-39).

Nonetheless, this list may serve to identify the sources of at least some separately printed intermezzo libretti. Pietro Toldo (*L'OEuvre de Molière et sa fortune en Italie* [Turin, 1910], p. 425), for example, suspected that the Marchese Trotti's popular *La preziosa ridicola* (Madama Dulcinea and il cuoco del Marchese del Bosco) must have received its premiere in a city more important than Reggio, where the text was apparently separately published for the first time in 1715. As may be seen from the present list, this intermezzo was, in fact, printed three years earlier at Rome, but in an untitled version as part of an anonymous *La fede tradita, e vendicata*, a circumstance that has kept it from inclusion in standard bibliographies.

Titles (in parentheses) and attributions of text and music following some entries are those contained in libretti.

ACRISIA AND ERIDIONE
Teodosio il giovane (Rome, [1711]), pp. 28-30, 51-55, 74-75.

ALCEA AND ELPINO
Apostolo Zeno, *Aminta* (Florence, [1703]), pp. 36-38, 62-65, 71-73.

ALCEA AND LISO
[Nicola Pagano], *La Rosmene overo L'infedeltà fedele* (Naples, 1709), pp. 11-12, 20-21, 25-26, 32-34.

ALCEA AND MILO
[Francesco Silvani], *La fede tradita, e vendicata* (Livorno, 1706), pp. 18-20, 35-37, 56-59.

ALCEA AND RULLO
Francesco Silvani *et al.*, *La fortezza al cimento* (Florence, 1702), pp. 17-19, 40-41, 54-59.

ALFEA AND NESSO
[Giacomo Maggi], *Mitridate in Sebastia* (Genoa, 1701), pp. 19-21, 42-44, 58-61.

ALFEA AND NESSO
Giacomo Maggi, *Mitridate in Sabastia* (Turin, [1702]), pp. 27-31, 53-55, 66-69.

ALISCA AND BLESO Music by Antonio Caldara.
Giovanni Claudio Pasquini, *La forza dell'amicizia, ovvero Pilade, ed Oreste* (Vienna, [1728]), [pp. 25-32, 55-60].

ARDEA AND BAGOLO
Bartolomeo Pedoni, *La Rosilda* (Venice, 1707), pp. 18-21, 33-36.

ARETE AND TRASONE
[Franceso Silvani], *La Zoe, ovvero Il comando non inteso, ed ubidito* (Rome, 1721), pp. 30-34, 50-52, 57-59, 76-78.

ARGILLA AND NESSO Music by Giuseppe Vignola.
Il Mitridate (Naples, 1706), pp. 17-19, 38-39, 53-55.

ARGILLETTA AND BUBBALO
Circe delusa (Naples, 1731), pp. 14-16, 21-23, 31-35, 41-44.

ARGILLETTA AND GILDO
La Circe in Italia (Rome, 1717), pp. 22-26, 33-35, 40-43, 49-50, 54-56.

ARGILLETTA AND GILDO Music by Carlo Manza *et al.*
La Circe in Italia (Ancona, [1722]), pp. 13-14, 20-24, 30-33, 37-38, 43-44, 48-50.

APPENDIX B

ARMILLA AND BLESO
[Francesco Silvani], *Carlo rè d'Alemagna* (Naples, 1716), pp. 24-29, 33-35, 45-51, 64-68.

ARMILLA AND PLANCO
[Nicolò Guivo], *L'Agrippina* (Naples, 1708), pp. 16-18, 25-29, 33-34, 50-53.

ARMILLA AND RAFO Text by Angiolo Birini.
Domenico Lalli and Angiolo Birini, *Il Gran Mogol* (Naples, 1713), pp. 16-19, 28-30, 37-40, 46-50.

ARMILLA AND SANCIO
Il D. Chischiotte (Bologna, 1729), pp. 16-18, 22-23, 39-40, 50-52.

ARRIGHETTA AND SEMPRONIO *(Il vedovo)* Music by Francesco Feo.
Il Tamese (Naples, 1729), pp. 56-72.

ATTILIA AND MEMMIO
[Apostolo Zeno], *La Griselda* (Pavia, [1710]), pp. 17-20, 39-43, 54-57.

AURETTA AND GILDO Text by Giovanni Domenico Pioli.
[Apostolo Zeno and] Pietro Pariati, *La forza dell'innocenza* (Florence, 1710), pp. 29-32, 52-56, 64-68.

AURETTA AND GILDO
[Apostolo Zeno and Pietro Pariati], *L'Engelberta o sia La forza dell'innocenza* (Rome, 1711), pp. 21-23, 30-31, 38-41, 51-53, 65-68, 73-75.

AURILLA AND COLA
Francesco Antonio Novi, *Il pescatore fortunato principe d'Ischia* (Bologna, [1716]), pp. 22-24, 34-36.

AURILLA AND FILENO Text by Giuseppe Papis *et al.*
Giovanni Domenico Pioli, *L'amor volubile, e tiranno* (Naples, 1709), pp. 19-22, 46-50, 55-56, 64-66.

AURILLA AND FILENO
Giovanni Domenico Pioli, *La Dorisbe, overo L'amor volubile, e tiranno* (Rome, 1711), pp. 28-31, 56-60, 74-76.

BAGATELLA, MAMALUCCA AND PATTATOCCO Music by Francesco Conti.
Pietro Pariati, *Ciro* (Vienna, [1715]), pp. 57-64.

BELINDA AND RULLO
L'Eraclio (Naples, 1711), pp. 8-9, 14-17, 25-28, 33-36, 40-44.

BELISA AND DORILLO
Giulio Convò, *L'Ottavia ristitvita al trono* (Naples, 1703), pp. 23-25, 34-35.

BELLINA AND ARMINO
Francesco Antonio Novi, *Il Cesare e Tolomeo in Egitto* (Bologna, [1716]), pp. 23-25, 36-37, 48-50.

BELLINA AND CREPERIO Text by Giulio Convò and Silvio Stampiglia.
[Francesco Silvani] and Giulio Convò, *Il più fedel tra vassalli* (Naples, 1705), pp. 13-15, 31-33, 44-47.

BELLINA AND GOLO
Ariovisto (Naples, 1702), pp. 25-27, 40-41, 47-48, 58-61.

BELLINA AND LENNO Text by Giuseppe Papis.
Nicolò Minato and Giuseppe Papis, *Il Maurizio* (Naples, 1708), pp. 16-18, 27-30, 38-39, 49-52, 63-66.

BETTINA AND MARCONE (*Li sposi contenziosi*)
Tito Manlio (Messina, 1753), pp. 54-66.

BINDA AND DELBO
Silvio Stampiglia, *L'Etearco* (Rome, 1719), pp. 21-23, 37-39, 45-47, 54-56.

BLENA AND DESBO
[Aurelio Aureli], *Gerone tiranno di Siracvsa* (Genoa, [1700]), pp. 27-30, 47-49, 71-73.

BLENA AND GILBO
[Carlo Sigismondo Capece], *Il figlio delle selve* (Modena, [1701]), pp. 16-17, 27-30.

BLENA AND NISO
L'Analinda ovvero Le nozze col nemico (Florence, 1702), pp. 19-22, 46-49, 75-77.

BLESA AND FLORO
Silvio Stampiglia, *Mario Fuggitivo* (Vienna, [1708]), pp. 17-20, 72-74.

BLESA AND FLORO
Almahide (London, 1710), pp. 22-24.

BRUNETTA AND BURLOTTO
[Antonio Salvi], *Ginevra principessa di Scozia* (Naples, 1720), pp. 25-30, 45-50, 62-67.

BRUNETTA AND BURLOTTO (*La fuga di Burlotto con Brunetta*)
Pier-Jacopo Martello *et al.*, *Gli amici* (Urbino, 1741), pp. 35-53.

CALANDRA AND NILO
[Apostolo Zeno and Pietro Pariati], *Alessandro in Sidone* (Vienna, [1721]), pp. 35-37, 70-72.

CALISTA AND NISO
   La Teodora Augusta (Naples, 1709), pp. 14-16, 24-26, 35-38.

CARILDA AND BRENO
   [Andrea Rossini], *Silla* (Naples, 1703), pp. 16-17, 25-27, 42-44, 48-50, 56-69.

CARINA AND MILONE
   Matteo Norris *et al.*, *L'odio, e l'amore* (Naples, 1704), pp. 12-14, 29-31, 41-45, 53-55.

CARLOTTA AND PANTALEONE Music by Johann Adolph Hasse.
   [Francesco Silvani], *Attalo re di Bitinia* (Naples, 1728), pp. 41-58.

CARLOTTA AND PANTALEONE
   Pietro Pariati, *Cajo Marzio Coriolano* (Naples, 1734), pp. 55-70.

CIRILLA AND ARPASSO
   Domenico Lalli *et al.*, *Pisistrato* (Naples, 1714), pp. 14-16, 25-27, 32-35, 43-45, 49-52.

CLEANTA, SOFIA AND MERCURIO
   Pietro Pariati, *Anfitrione* (Venice, [1707]), pp. 23-25, 33-36, 43-47, 57-60.

COCCHETTA AND DON PASQUALE (*Intermezzi di Cocchetta, e di Don Pasquale*)
   [Giovanni Palazzi], *L'Armida al campo* (Ravenna, [1726]), pp. [49]-71.

COLOMBINA AND MARMOTTO
   Sidonio (Naples, 1714), pp. 10-12, 20-21, 27-29, 33-35.

COLOMBINA AND PERNICONE
   Trajano (Naples, 1723), pp. 23-27, 43-49, 61-56 (*sic* 65).

CORIMBA AND MILONE
   Le gare generose trà Pompeo, e Cesare (Naples, 1706), pp. 14-16, 32-35, 45-47.

CORINNA AND FAVONIO
   Alesandro il Grande in Sidone (Naples, 1706), pp. 21-22, 38-40, 57-59.

CORISCA AND SATIRO
   [Domenico Lalli], *Elisa* (Rome, [1738]), pp. 25-27, 44-46.

DALINA AND BALBO
   Apostolo Zeno *et al.*, *Teuzone* (Naples, 1720), pp. 16-20, 37-41, 50-55.

DALINDA AND ALFASIO
   Giovanni Domenico Pioli, *Selim rè d'Ormuz* (Naples, 1712), pp. 18-21, 38-40, 45-48, 52-55.

DALISA AND BRENO
[Antonio Salvi], *Arminio* (Naples, 1714), pp. 17-19, 24-27, 43-46, 54-58.

DALISA AND TULLIO
L'Arminio (Genoa, [1705]), pp. 27-29, 63-66.

DAMARI AND DORILLO
Amore tutto puole (Bologna, [1738]), pp. 17-20, 30-33, 44-47.

DAMARI AND MIRIDE
[Angelo Carasale], *Il Sesostrate* (Naples, [1726]), pp. 18-22, 41-45.

DELBA AND ORALBO
[Vincenzo Grimani], *Il Teodosio* (Livorno, 1705), pp. 15-17, 33-35, 48-50.

DELFINA AND BESSO Music by Giuseppe Vignola.
[Francesco Silvani], *La forza del sangue* (Naples, 1712), pp. 6-8, 22-24, 32-34, 45-47, 59-60.

DESPINA AND CORIANDOLO
Girolamo Gigli, *Amore frà gli impossibili* (Padua, [1707]), pp. 30, 43-45.

DESPINA AND FORBANTE, Music by Leonardo Leo.
[Pietro Pariati], *Arianna e Teseo* (Naples, 1722), pp. 13-15, 21-25, 41-47, 54-59.

DESPINA AND GILDONE
Ataulfo re de' Goti, ovvero La forza della virtù (Rome, 1712), pp. 16-18, 26-29, 41-44, 53-55, 67-69.

DESPINA AND NISO
L'amor generoso (Naples, 1714), pp. 15-18, 28-31, 41-42, 51-54, 63-66.

DINA AND BRENO
Tito Manlio (Rome, 1720), pp. 20-23, 35-36, 50-51, 62-64.

DORI AND NUTO Text by Nicola Barbapiccola, music by Domenico Scarlatti.
[Girolamo Frigimelica-Roberti] and Nicola Barbapiccola, *L'Irene* (Naples, 1704), pp. 13-14, 21-22, 41-43.

DORILLA AND BALANZONE (*La serva scaltra ovvero La moglie a forza*) Music by Johann Adolph Hasse.
[Francesco Silvani], *Il Tigrane* (Naples, [1729]), pp. 56-72.

DORILLA AND BIRENO
Silvio Stampiglia, *Tito Sempronio Gracco* (Naples, 1702), pp. 3-5, 19-20, 26-28, 40-41, 44-45, 51-52.

DORILLA AND BRENNO
[Agostino Piovene], *Publio Cornelio Scipione* (Rome, 1713), pp. 21-23, 44-46, 66-67, 81-82.

DORILLA AND DELBO
Il Teodosio (Naples, 1709), pp. 17-19, 33-36, 51-54.

DORILLA AND NESSO
[Giovanni Battista Neri?], *Basilio rè d'Oriente* (Naples, 1713), pp. 18-19, 28-31, 36-38, 47-50, 60-63.

DORILLA AND NESSO (*Dorilla, e Nesso*)
[Apostolo Zeno], *Eumene* (Rome, 1721), pp. 71-81.

DORILLA AND ORCONE
Domenico Lalli, *Tigrane, overo: L'egual impegno d'amore, e di fede* (Naples, 1715), pp. 30-33, 49-53, 64-68.

DORILLA AND TERSITE
Pietro Pariati, *Penelope* (Vienna, [1724]), pp. 17-20, 34-36.

DORILLA AND ZERBINO Music by Giuseppe Vignola.
Apostolo Zeno *et al.*, *L'inganno vinto dalla ragione* (Naples, 1708), p. 23-25, 35-36, 41-43.

DORIMENA AND TUBERONE Music by Francesco Conti.
Apostolo Zeno, *L'Atenaide* (Vienna, [1714]), pp. 35-39, 63-68.

DORINA AND DELBO
Nicolò Giuvo, *La Cassandra indovina* (Piedimonte, 1711), pp. 16-18, 26-27, 39-43, 51-53, 59-60.

DORINA AND DELBO
Nicolò Giuvo, *La Cassandra indovina* (Naples, 1713), pp. 7-9, 19-21, 27-29, 41-44, 51-54, 58-60.

DORINA AND GRULLO
[Girolamo Gigli], *L'Anagilda* (Rome, [1711]), pp. 17-22, 27-32, 46-51, 57-59, 67-69, 77-80.

DORINA AND GRULLO
[Girolamo Gigli], *L'Anagilda* (Foligno, [1722]), pp. 15-19, 35-38, 48-50, 56-58.

DORINA AND LICO
[Tommaso Ristori], *Pallade trionfante in Arcadia* (Padua, 1713), pp. 20-21, 33-34.

DORINA AND NIBBIO
[Pietro Metastasio], *Didone abandonata* (Naples, 1724), pp. 28-34, 52-57.

DORINDA AND MILO
[Adriano Morselli] and Carlo de Pretis, *Il Tullo Ostilio* (Naples, 1707), pp. 28-30, 55-57.

DORISBE AND CREPERIO Text by Carlo de Pretis, music by Giuseppe Vignola.
[Apostolo Zeno, Pietro Pariati], and Carlo de Pretis, *Le regine di Macedonia* (Naples, [1708]), pp 17-18, 30-32, 57-59.

DORISBE AND LESBO
Stratonica (Florence, 1707), pp. 27-29, 40-42, 57-60.

DROSILLA AND GIACCO
Il Silandro (Milan, [1707]), pp. 38-40, 53-55.

DROSILLA AND IRCANO Text by Silvio Stampiglia and Giulio Convò.
Gli amanti generosi (Naples, 1705), pp. 8-10, 17-18, 30-31, 38-41.

DROSILLA AND IRCANO
Gli amanti generosi (Genoa, 1711), pp. 9-11, 18-20, 33-35, 42-46.

DROSILLA AND NESSO
Carlo de Palma, *L'Orismene overo Dalli sdegni l'amore* (Naples, 1726), pp. 15-18, 26-30, 49-52, 58-61.

DRUSILLA AND STRABONE (*La vedova ingegnosa*) Text by Tomaso Mariani.
Emira (Naples, 1735), pp. 46-60.

DRUSILLA AND STRAMBONE (*La vedova ingegnosa*)
Francesco Passarini, *Diomeda* (Bologna, [1741]), pp. 46-60.

DRUSILLA AND VALASCO
Giulio Cesare Corradi *et al.*, *La pastorella al soglio* (Naples, 1710), pp. 8-11, 16-18, 26-28, 36-40, 53-56.

DRUSILLA AND D. VELASCO Text by Pietro Mozzi.
[Francesco Silvani], *La innocenza giustificata* (Palermo, 1714), pp. 17-19, 28-30, 49-51, 64-67.

DRUSILLA AND VELASCO
Il Fernando (Modena 1717), pp. 25-27, 42-47, 65-68.

DRUSILLA AND VELASCO
[Giulio Cesare Corradi], *La pastorella al soglio* (Rome, 1718), pp. 17-20, 26-29, 37-40, 49-52, 64-67.

ELISA AND GORO
[Apostolo Zeno *et al.*], *I rivali generosi* (Naples, 1700), pp. 25-27, 30-32, 38-40, 46-47, 50-52, 56-58.

ELISA AND TULLO
Apostolo Zeno, *Zenobia in Palmira* (Naples, 1725), pp. 22-27, 40-46, 54-56.

ELPINA AND FALCONE
La fede riconosciuta (Naples, 1710), pp. 14-17, 22-23, 32-35, 40-42.

ERIGHETTA AND D. CHILONE (*L'ammalato immaginario o sia L'ipocondriaco*)
Domenico Lalli, *L'amor tirannico ò sia Il Farasmane* (Ferrara, [1724]), pp. 20-24, 34-38, 48-50, 60-63.

ERIGHETTA AND D. CHILONE Music by Leonardo Vinci.
[Francesco Silvani] and Carlo de Palma, *L'Ernelinda* (Naples, [1726]), pp. 24-27, 43-47, 52-53.

ERINDA AND BRILLO
Orfeo a torto geloso (Genoa, [1706]), pp. 29-31, 36-37, 62-64.

ERMOSILLA AND BACOCCO Text by Bernardo Saddumene.
Publio Cornelio Scipione (Naples, 1722), pp. 15-19, 37-41, 50-56.

EURILLA AND BELTRAMME
Silvio Stampiglia, *Partenope* (Naples, 1722), pp. 27-31, 43-49, 59-[62].

EURILLA AND LEONZIO
[Matteo Noris], *M. Attilio Regolo* (Rome, 1719), pp. 18-21, 31-34, 58-61, 70-72, 83-84.

EURILLA AND NESSO
Francesco Maria Paglia, *La Semiramide* (Naples, 1702), pp. 42-44, 53-55, 63-66.

EURINDA AND CURIO
[Apostolo Zeno], *Alessandro Severo* (Naples, 1719), pp. 23-26, 40-44, 55-58.

FARFALLETTA AND DRAGASSO Music by Francesco Mancini.
[Francesco Silvani], *Artaserse rè di Persia* (Naples, 1713), pp. 19-22, 33-35, 41-43, 51-53.

FARFALLETTA, LIRONE AND TERREMOTO Music by Francesco Conti.
[Apostolo Zeno], *Astarto* (Vienna, [1718]), pp. 77-91.

FERINDA AND AMARANTO
Armida abbandonata (Naples, 1719), pp. 18-23, 38-43, 49-53.

FIAMMETTA AND CURULLO
Apostolo Zeno, *Lucio-Vero* (Naples, 1707), pp. 23-25, 32-34, 54-57.

FIAMMETTA AND PANCRAZIO
Apostolo Zeno, *La Lucinda fedele* (Naples, [1726]), pp. 19-23, 38-42, 49-52.

FIORDILINA AND BESSO
Amare per regnare (Naples, 1723), pp. 25-29, 44-48.

FIORLISA AND GRIPPO
Francesco Silvani *et al.*, *La fortezza al cimento* (Naples, 1721), pp. 23-28, 37-38, 43-48, 54-59.

FLORA AND BLESO
Silvio Stampiglia, *Mario fuggitivo* (Naples, 1710), pp. 7-8, 18-21, 38-40, 49-51.

FLORA AND BLESO
Il Massimo Puppieno (Rome, 1718), pp. 24-26, 37-40, 46-49, 56-58, 62-65.

FLORA AND BLESO
[Apostolo Zeno], *Lucio Vero* (Macerata, 1728), pp. 20-22, 40-42.

FLORA AND D. GIROLDO
[Antonio] Salvi, *Il carceriero di se stresso* (Turin, 1720), pp. 25-29, 55-58.

GALANTINA AND PAMPALUGO Music by Francesco Conti.
Pietro Pariati, *Teseo in Creta* (Vienna, [1715]), pp. 70-78.

GARBINA, AMET AND FLORIO
[Francesco Silvani *et al.*], *Sofonisba* (Naples, 1718), pp. 18-20, 29-32, 36-38, 47-53, 64-69.

GELIDIA AND BRILLO
Il Giustino (Naples, 1703), pp. 44-45.

GELLIA AND ZELTO
[Matteo Noris], *L'Agrippina* (Milan, 1703), pp 5-7, 50-52, 67-68.

GERILDA AND GILDO
[Apostolo Zeno *et al.*], *Vincislao* (Naples, 1714), pp. 20-23, 27-30, 39-42, 50-53, 62-65.

GERILDA AND GILDO Music by Francesco Mancini and Francesco Gasparini.
[Apostolo Zeno], *Il Vincislao* (Rome, 1716), pp. 22-24, 28-31, 42-44, 55-57, 69-72.

GERINA AND MUSTAFA'
[Agostino Piovene], *La principessa fedele* (Naples, 1710), pp. 26-29, 43-45, 56-58, 83-87.

GRESPILLA AND FANFARONE
Il Germanico Marte (Salzburg, n.d.), pp. 38-43, 69-72.

GRILLETTA AND LINCO Music by Giuseppe Vignola.
[Apostolo Zeno and Pietro Pariati], *Ambleto* (Naples, 1711), pp. 13-15, 21-24, 36-37, 43-45, 59-62.

GRILLETTA AND PORSUGNACCO (*Monsieur di Porsugnacco*)
La caccia in Etolia (Florence, 1727), pp. [43]-64.

GRILLETTA AND PORSUGNACCO Music by Johann Adolph Hasse.
[Aurelio Aureli *et al.*], *Gerone tiranno di Siracusa* (Naples, 1727), pp. 22-26, 41-45, 54-58.

GRILLETTA AND PORSUGNACCO (*Monsieur de Porsugnacco ingannato da Grilletta*)
La costanza vincitrice (Bologna, [1740]), pp. [39]-51.

GRIMORA AND ERBOSCO
[Pietro Pariati], *Sidonio* (Venice, 1706), pp. 25-26, 35-36, 44-46, 56-58.

IRENE AND MILLO
[Adriano Morselli], *Il Tullo Ostilio* (Siena, 1702), pp. 23-27, 37-40, 60-64.

LARINDA AND VANESIO
[Apostolo Zeno and Pietro Pariati], *L'Astarto* (Naples, [1726]), pp. 22-26, 40-43, 53-56.

LARINDA AND VANESIO (*Der Handwercks-Mann ein Edel-Mann*)
Cajus Fabritius (Dresden 1734), pp. 81-88.

LAURETTA AND CORRADO Music by Francesco Feo *et al.*
[Francesco Silvani], *Il duello d'amore, e di vendetta* (Naples, 1715), pp. 28-31, 45-49, 52-56, 62-65.

LESBINA AND ADOLFO
A[postolo] Z[eno], *Odoardo* (Naples, 1700), p. 18-20, 27-31, 35-36, 45, 59-60.

LESBINA AND ADOLFO
Il Gordiano (Palermo, 1700), pp. 5-7, 16-19, 28-30, 35-36, 49-51.

LESBINA AND BRENO Music by Ignazio Prota.
[Matteo Noris], *Tito Manlio* (Naples, 1720), pp. 18-22, 38-42, 53-56.

LESBINA AND CHIUCHIOLO
Il trionfo d'amore (Mantua, [1704]), pp. 23-25, 45-47.

LESBINA AND CREPERIO
Le regine di Macedonia (Messina, 1710), pp. 18-19, 37-38, 61-64.

LESBINA AND D. CREPERIO
Il premio dell'innocenza overo Le perdite dell'inganno (Naples, 1725), pp. 21-25, 42-47, 55-56.

LESBINA AND MILO
Tiberio imperatore d'Oriente (Naples, 1702), pp. 3-5, 10-11, 22-23, 31-33, 38-40, 54-56.

LESBINA AND MILO
[Francesco Silvani], *La fede tradita e vendicata* (Florence, 1704), pp. 16-18, 42-45, 58-60, 67-70.

LESBINA AND MILO
[Francesco Silvani], *La fede tradita, e vendicata* (Lucca, 1706), pp. 18-20, 41-44, 57-58, 64-67.

LESBINA AND MILO
[Francesco Silvani] and Carlo de Pretis, *La fede tradita e vendicata* (Naples, 1707), pp. 21-23, 44-47, 64-65.

LESBINA AND MILO
[Silvio Stampiglia], *Alba Cornelia* (Vienna, [1714]), pp. 28-31, 55-57, 68-71.

LESBINA AND MILO
Pietro Pariati, *Alba Cornelia* ([Breslau, 1726]), [pp. 39-46, 81-84, 99-104].

LESBINA AND NESSO Music by Leonardo Leo.
[Giacomo Rossi and Nicola Serino], *Rinaldo* (Naples, 1718), pp. 21-25, 36-40, 47-51, 53-54.

LESBINA AND SEMPRONIO (*La franchezza delle donne*) Text by Tomaso Mariani, music by Giuseppe Sellitti.
[Pietro Metastasio], *Siface* (Naples, 1734), pp. 58-72.

LESBINA AND ZELTO
Giulio Cesare Corradi and Carlo de Pretis, *Il Vespesiano* (Naples, 1707), pp. 22-23, 31-33, 44-47, 60-62.

LESBINA AND ZELTO
[Apostolo Zeno], *I rivali generosi* (Messina, 1712), pp. 19-23, 31-34, 52-56, 66-70.

LIDIA AND CALISTONE
L'Eusonia overo La dama stravagante (Palermo, 1702), pp. 14-16, 19-22, 42-44, 50-53, 70-73.

LIDIA AND CIMONE (*La maga per vendetta, e per amore*) Text by Tomaso Mariani.
La nemica amante (Naples, 1735), pp. 51-60.

LIDIA AND IRCANO
Silvio Stampiglia, *L'Abdolomino* (Vienna, [1709]), pp. 17-21, 28-30, 41-45, 63-66, 71-72.

LIDIA AND IRCANO
Silvio Stampiglia, *L'Abdolomino* (Naples, 1711), pp. 8-11, 16-18, 26-29, 44-45, 48-49.

LIDIA AND IRCANO
[Apostolo Zeno and Pietro Pariati], *Astarto* (Rome, 1715), pp. 31-35, 57-60.

LIDIA AND IRCANO (*Li amori d'Ircano, e Lidia*)
Aleria (Bologna, 1746), pp. 18-21, 32-35.

LIDIA AND NESSO
[Apostolo Zeno], *Merope* (Rome, 1721), pp. 27-30, 51 54, 68 70.

LIDIA AND SERGIO
Domenico Lalli, *Cambise* (Naples, 1719), pp. 25-28, 47-51, 65-70.

LINDORA AND BALZO
L'Eraclea (Genoa [1705]), pp. 26-28, 36-39.

LISETTA AND ASTROBOLO
[Apostolo Zeno and Pietro Pariati], *Astarto* (Naples, 1709), pp. 29-32, 40-44, 56-59, 77-80.

LISETTA AND ASTROBOLO
[Antonio Marchi], *Il Radamisto* (Modena, 1714), pp. 61-75.

LISETTA AND ASTROBOLO (*Intermezzi di Lisetta, ed Astrobolo*)
[Francesco Silvani], *La verità nell'inganno* (Vienna, [1717]), pp. 84-95.

LISETTA AND BATTO
Francesco Ballerini, *Il trionfo dell'amicizia, e dell'amore* (Vienna, [1711]), pp. 35-37, 78-80.

LISETTA AND BATTO
I gemelli rivali (Naples, 1713), pp. 19-21, 28-31, 52-54.

LISETTA AND BLESO
La Floridea regina di Cipro (Ancona, [1722]), pp. [18]-20, 23-26, 30-31, 37-40, 45-47.

LISETTA AND DELFO
[Domenico Lalli], *L'amor tirannico* (Rome, 1713), pp. 31-34, 58-61, 73-77.

LISETTA AND DELFO
Dagl'inganni alle nozze (Perugia, 1725), pp. 47-56.

LISETTA AND DORI
Cefalo (Brescia, [1715]), pp. 23-26, 41-43.

LISETTA AND MILO
Alba soggiogata da' Romani (Genoa, [1703]), pp. 13-17, 62-64, 81-85.

LISETTA AND NISO
Carlo de Palma, *Il trionfo d'amore ò vero Le nozze trà nemici* (Naples, 1725), pp. 14-15, 24-28, 46-50, 57-60.

LISETTA AND RICCARDO (*La Zingaretta*)
Argene (Naples, 1731), pp. 57-71.

LIVIETTA AND CARDONE (*L'amor fa l'uomo cieco*)
[Pietro Metastasio], *L'Artaserse* (Genoa, [1742]), pp. 23-29, 53-61.

LIVIETTA AND TRACOLLO (*La contadina astuta*)
[Pietro Metastasio], *Adriano in Siria* (Naples, 1734), pp. 56-72.

LIVIO AND ALFEO
Silvio Stampiglia, *L'Eraclea* (Naples, 1700), pp. 24-26, 36-37, 47-48, 59-60, 71-73.

LIVIO AND ALFEO
Silvio Stampiglia, *L'Eraclea* (Parma, 1700), pp. 27-28, 37-40, 45-47, 69-73, 80-82, 95-97.

LIZA AND BLESO
Flavio Cuniberto (Genoa, [1702]), pp. 21-22.

LUCILLA AND ELPINO
Apostolo Zeno *et al.*, *La Griselda* (Perugia, 1707), pp. 31-33, 47-49, 74-75.

LUCILLA AND NIBBIO
[Francesco] Silvani *et al.*, *Rosiclea in Dania* (Naples, 1721), pp. 18-23, 41-45, 58-61.

LUCILLA AND PANDOLFO (*Il tutore*)
Pietro Metastasio, *Ezio* (Naples, 1730), pp. 79-93.

LUCINDA AND BRAGONE
L'Ateone (Naples, 1708), pp. 11-14, 18-20, 23-24, 27-28, 43-46.

MADAMA DULCINEA AND IL CUOCO DEL MARCHESE DEL BOSCO
[Francesco Silvani], *La fede tradita, e vendicata* (Rome, 1712), pp. 27-31, 50-55, 69-74.

MADAMA DULCINEA AND IL CUOCO DEL MARCHESE DEL BOSCO (*La preziosa ridicola*) Music by Giuseppe Orlandini.
[Domenico Lalli], *I veri amici* (Naples, 1715), pp. 25-28, 45-48, 53-57.

MADAMA DULCINEA AND IL CUOCO DEL MARCHESE DEL BOSCO (*La preziosa ridicola*)
[Antonio Marchi], *Il Radamisto* (Florence, 1728), pp. 71-88.

LA MARCHESINA DI NANCHIN AND IL CONTE DI PELUSIO
Domenico Lalli, *Camaide imperatore della China, o vero Li figliuoli rivali del padre* (Salzburg, [1722]), pp. 23-29, 59-65.

MARITORNE AND SANCIO
[Apostolo Zeno and Pietro Pariati], *Don Chisciotte in Sierra Morena* (Vienna, [1719]), pp. 33-36, 73-74.

MEDULLINA AND CARASSO
[Nicolò Giuvo], *Il Radamisto* (Florence, 1709), pp. 14-18, 55-58, 75-80.

MEDULLINA AND CARASSO
[Grazio Braccioli], *La costanza in cimento o sia Il Radamisto* (Bologna, 1714), pp. 13-16, 48-50, 63-66.

MEDULLINA AND CARASSO Music by Cintio Vinchioni *et al.*
[Grazio Braccioli], *La costanza in cimento, o sia Il Radamisto* (Rome, 1721), pp. 14-18, 30-34, 53-56, 70-75.

MELISSA AND SERPILLO (*Melissa schernita*)
[Apostolo Zeno and Pietro Pariati], *L'Engelberta, o sia La forza dell'innocenza* (Naples, 1709), pp. 61-72.

MELISSA AND SERPILLO
Il Faramondo (Genoa [1712]), pp. 24-27, 52-56, 75-79.

MELISSA AND SERPILLO
La caccia in Etolia (Modena, 1715), pp. 47-58.

MERILLA AND GILBO
[Apostolo Zeno], *Faramondo* (Naples, 1719), pp. 26-29, 49-53, 62-68.

MERILLA AND MORANTE
Antonio Salvi *et al.*, *Arsace* (Naples, 1718), pp. 25-28, 45-49, 56-60.

MERLINA AND CURIO
[Francesco Silvani], *Armida al campo* (Naples, 1718), pp. 20-22, 26-31, 39-42, 48-51, 58-62.

MERLINA AND GALOPPO (*La fantesca*)
L'Ulderica (Naples, 1729), pp. 55-72.

MIRENA AND SINOPIO
Pietro Pariati, *Archelao, re di Cappadocia* (Vienna, [1722]), pp. 26-28, 60-62.

MODESTINA AND POMPONIO (*Il corteggiano affettato*)
[Apostolo Zeno and Pietro Pariati], *Flavio Anicio Olibrio* (Naples, 1728), pp. 55-69.

MOSCHETTA AND GRULLO
[Pietro Metastasio], *Siroe rè di Persia* (Naples, 1727), pp. 57-64.

NAPOLINA, VENERE AND SPACCAVIENTO
Francesco Antonio Novi, *Il Diomede* (Bologna, [1716]), pp. 24-26, 37-40.

NERINA AND D. CHISCHIOTTO Music by Francesco Feo.
Tomaso Mariani, *Il castello d'Atlante* (Naples, 1734), pp. 48-59.

NERINA AND GILDO
[Francesco Silvani], *L'innocenza difesa* (Rome, 1720), pp. 15-16, 20-22, 42-44, 61-63.

NERINA AND GILDO
[Francesco Silvani], *L'innocenza difesa* (Turin, [1722]), pp. 15-16, 27-29, 36-37, 50-51, 63-64.

NERINA AND LISO
Paride sull'Ida, overo Gl'amori di Paride con Enone (Mantua, [1704]), pp. 17-19, 25-29, 48-52, 71-73.

NERINA AND LISO
[Francesco Mazzari], *Paride in Ida* (Venice, 1706), pp. 15-16, 20-21, 37, 51-52.

NERINA AND NIBBIO
[Apostolo Zeno and Sebastiano Morelli], *La Salustia* (Naples, 1731), [pp. 63-72].

NERIZIA AND DRESO
Dal finto nasce il vero (Bologna, 1715), pp. 13-16, 25-28, 42-44.

NESA AND LESBO
Il trionfo della fedeltà (Turin, [1723]), pp. 10-12, 20-22, 44-45, 57-60.

NICE AND COLA
La fede ne' tradimenti (Bologna, [1720]), pp. 11-14, 30-32, 52-53.

NICE AND COLA
La fede ne' tradimenti (Modena, 1723), pp. 12-15, 32-34, 57-58.

NISA AND DELBO
Silvio Stampiglia, *Etearco* (Naples, 1708), pp. 20-21, 34-36, 43-45, 50-52.

NISA AND GLOCO
[Pietro d'Averara], *Angelica nel Cataj* (Milan, [1702]), pp. 21-23, 63-64.

PALANCHA AND ATOMO (*Intermezzi di Atomo huomo vecchio, e Palancha giovine*)
Antonio Maria Luchini, *L'inganno tradito dall'amore* (Salzburg, [172?]), pp. 26-29, 54-57.

PALANDRANA AND ZAMBERLUCCO
[Francesco Silvani], *Carlo rè d'Alemagna* (Naples, 1716), [pp. 73-82].

PASQUELLA AND PASQUINO
Achille in Sciro (Prague, [1727]), [pp. 34-37, 60-63, 74-77].

PERICCA AND VARRONE
[Apostolo Zeno], *Scipione nelle Spagne* (Naples, 1714), pp. 16-18, 26-29, 35-38, 49-52, 58-62.

PERICHITTA AND BERTONE
[Claudio Nicola Stampa], *L'Oronta* (Naples, 1728), pp. 21-26, 38-43, 51-56, 60.

PERINOTTA AND BOMBO
Pietro Metastasio *et al.*, *Il Demetrio* (Naples, 1732), pp. 66-76.

PERLETTA AND LISO
[Apostolo Zeno] *et al.*, *Flavio Anicio Olibrio* (Naples, 1711), pp. 14-16, 26-29, 32-33, 40-41, 48-51, 57-60, 70-71.

PERNELLA AND ELPINO
Apostolo Zeno *et al.*, *Griselda* (Florence, 1703), pp. 31-34, 49-53, 79-82.

PERNELLA AND ELPINO
[Apostolo Zeno], *Griselda* (Livorno, [1704]), pp. 27-30, 41-43, 56-58.

PERNELLA AND ELPINO Text by Carlo de Pretis, music by Domenico Sarri.
Apostolo Zeno and Carlo de Pretis, *La Griselda* (Naples, 1706), pp. 29-32, 41-43, 56-68.

PERNELL AND ELPINO
Apostolo Zeno, *La Griselda* (Piacenza, [1708]), pp. 27-29, 50-51, 64-67.

PIMPINELLA AND MARCANTONIO Music by Johann Adolph Hasse.
[Stefano Benedetto Pallavicini], *Numa* ([Dresden, 1743]), [pp. 55-68].

PIPA AND BARLAFUSO (*Barlafuso, e Pipa*) Text by Francesco Rinaldi Cantù, music by Antonio Caldara.
[Apostolo Zeno], *Costantino* (Vienna, [1716]), pp [79]-96.

PLAUTILLA AND ALBINO
Silla dittatore (Naples, 1732), pp. 22-25, 43-48, 57-62.

POLLASTRELLA AND PARPAGNACCO
[Apostolo Zeno] *et al.*, *Merope* (Florence, 1713), pp. 77-90.

POLLASTRELLA AND PARPAGNACCO
[Pietro Metastasio], *Adriano in Siria* ([Stuttgart, 1737]), pp. 196-237.

QUARTILLA AND TIRONE
Pietro Pariati, *Cajo Marzio Coriolano* (Vienna, [1717]), pp. 33-35, 59-61, 76-78.

REGILLA AND FILOCRATE Text by Silvio Stampiglia *et al.*
Silvio Stampiglia *et al.*, *Cajo Gracco* (Naples, 1720), pp. 16-18, 25-29, 35-37, 51-54, 65-68.

RIVETTA AND RUSTENO
Domenico Renda, *L'Adrasto* (Rome, 1702), pp. 43-44, 59-61.

RODISBE AND ARISTONE
L'Incoronazione di Dario (Naples, 1705), pp. 27-29, 37-39, 57-59.

RODISBE AND ARISTONE
Silvio Stampiglia, *Li trè rivali al soglio* (Bologna, 1710), pp. 24-26, 43-45, 51-52.

ROSETTA AND MALORCO Music by Carmine Giordano.
La vittoria d'amor conjugale (Naples, 1712), pp. 26-29, 34-36, 45-47, 54-56.

ROSICCA AND MORANO
[Pietro Metastasio], *Siface* (Naples, 1723), p. 23-29, 45-49.

ROSICCA AND PADIGLIO
[Girolamo Gigli], *La fede ne' tradimenti* (Naples, 1718), pp. 23-26, 36-39, 52-55.

ROSINA AND FLACCO
[Agostino Piovene], *Porsenna* (Naples, 1713), pp. 25-28, 39-42, 54-58.

ROSINA AND LESBO Music by Leonardo Leo.
[Apostolo Zeno], *Sesostri re di Egitto* (Naples, 1717), pp. 19-21, 30-33, 46-50, 58-62.

ROSINDA AND NESSO Music by Leonardo Leo.
[Apostolo Zeno *et al.*], *L'Eumene* (Naples, 1715), pp. 16-19, 36-40, 49-52.

ROSMENE AND GERONDO (*Il matrimonio per forza*)
[Antoni Salvi *et al.*], *Stratonica* (Bologna [1732]), pp. 47-62.

ROSMENE, ZINGARA, AND GERONDO (*Il matrimonio per forza*) Music by Giuseppe Maria Buini.
[Giuseppe Maria Buini], *Il regno posposto ad amore* (Reggio, [1732]), pp. [45]-60.

RUBINA AND PINCONE
[Domenico Lalli] *et al.*, *Amor tirannico* (Naples, 1713), pp. 27-31, 46-51, 64-68.

SCINTILLA AND TABARANO (*La contadina*)
Clitarco, o sia Il più fedel fra gli amici (Naples, 1728), pp. 55-70.

SCINTILLA AND TABARANO *(La contadina)*
Apostolo Zeno, *Cajo Fabricio* (Naples, 1733), pp. 56-71.

SCINTILLA AND TABARRANO
Pietro Metastasio, *L'Olimpiade* (Genoa, 1733), pp. 66-84.

SCINTILLA AND TABARANO
Pier-Jacopo Martello et al., *Gli amici* (Bologna, [1734]), pp. 17-24, 37-44.

SELVAGGIA AND DAMETA
Dafni (Naples, 1700), pp. 12-13, 19-20, 24-25, 29-30, 36-37.

SEMIDEA AND LIDO
[Apostolo Zeno and Pietro Pariati], *Artaserse* (Livorno, 1706), pp. 17-29, 34-35, 55-58.

SEMIDEA AND LIDO Text by A[ndrea del] P[ò], music by Francesco Mancini.
[Apostolo Zeno and Pietro Pariati], *Artaserse* (Naples, 1708), pp. 13-16, 29-31, 43-46.

SERPILLA AND BACOCCO
Artaserse (Rome, 1721), pp. 29-32, 53-56.

SERPILLA AND BACOCCO
Amore, e fortuna (Naples, 1725), pp. 16-29, 30-34, 40-43.

SERPILLA AND DIDACO Music by Giovanni Battista Stuch.
Rodrigo in Algieri (Naples, 1702), pp. 20-22, 28-30, 37-39, 49-51, 58-59, 64-65.

SERPILLA AND SERPOLLO
Francesco Maria Paglia, *Il pastor di Corinto* (Naples, 1701), pp. 12-13, 17-19, 28-29, 32-33, 39-41, 44-46.

SERPILLA AND SERPOLLO
Francesco Maria Paglia, *Il pastor di Corinto* (Palermo 1702), pp. 11-13, 18-20, 33-35, 37-39, 47-49, 55-57.

SERPILLA AND SERPOLLO
Francesco Maria Paglia, *Il pastor di Corinto* (Naples, 1705), pp. 8-10, 14-16, 25-27, 29-31, 33-34, 38-40, 44-46.

SERPILLA AND VOLPASTRO
Pietro Pariati, *Il finto Policare* (Vienna, [1716]), pp. 32-33, 52-54, 68-69.

SERPINA AND UBERTO (*La serva padrona*) Text by Gennaro Antonio Federico.
Il prigionier superbo (Naples, 1733), pp. 48-[60].

SERPINA AND UBERTO (*La serva padrona*) Music by Giovanni Battista Pergolesi.
Francesco Passarini, *L'odio vinto dall'amore* (Udine, 1741), pp. 45-62.

SERPINA AND UBERTO (*La serva padrona*)
Pietro Metastasio, *La clemenza di Tito* (Bologna, [1743]), pp. 72-88.

SERVILIA AND FLACCO
[Silvio Stampiglia], *La caduta de' Decemviri* (Florence, 1700), pp. 15-17, 38-39.

SERVILLA AND FLACCO
[Silvio Stampiglia], *La caduta de' Decemviri* (Siena, [1704]), pp. 16-18, 29-30, 39-41.

SERVILIA AND FLACCO
[Silvio Stampiglia] *et al.*, *La caduta de' Decemviri* (Naples, 1727), pp. 22-24, 39-44, 56-58.

SIBILLINA AND MENENIO
[Antonio Salvi], *Berenice regina di Egitto, o vero Le gare di amore, e di politica* (Rome, 1718), pp. 17-19, 29-32, 41-43, 50-53, 63-66.

SILVINA AND TERSITE
Carlo Sigismondo Capeci, *Telemaco* (Rome, 1718), pp. 16-18, 36-38, 49-50, 61-63.

SLAPINA AND BARILOTTO
Antonio Salvi, *Lucio Papirio* (Rome, 1714) pp. 65-74.

SPILLETTA AND FRULLO Music by Domenico Sarri.
[Francesco Silvani] *et al.*, *Il comando non inteso, et ubbidito* (Naples, 1713), pp. 17-20, 29-31, 37-39, 44-48, 53-55.

STELLINA AND NESSO
Apostolo Zeno, *L'Eumene* (Palermo, 1706), pp. 11-14, 29-32, 63-66.

TILLA AND CIVETTONE Text by Carlo de Pretis.
L'humanità nelle fere, overo Il Lucullo (Naples, [1708]), pp. 20-22, 39-24 [*sic* 42], 54-58.

TILLA AND DELFO
[Girolamo Gigli], *La fede ne' tradimenti* (Bologna, [1732]), pp. 12-27, 39-43, 55-58.

TISBE AND BRENNO
[Apostolo Zeno], *Gl'inganni felici* (Palermo, 1700), pp. 12-13, 35-38, 55-57.

TISBE AND BRENNO
[Apostolo Zeno], *L'Agarista ovvero Gl'inganni felici* (Florence, 1704), pp. 16-18, 40-42, 52-54.

TISBE AND GILBO
[Apostolo Zeno and Pietro Pariati], *Ambleto* (Florence, 1707), pp. 26-28, 38-40, 67-70.

TULLIA AND LINCO
Silvio Stampiglia, *Li [sic] trionfo di Camilla regina de' Volsci* (Lucca, 1702), pp. 24-26, 40-43, 52-54, 57, 75-77.

TULLIA AND LINCO
[Silvio Stampiglia], *La fede in cimento, ò sia La Camilla regina de' Volsci* (Bologna, [1719]), pp. 30-32, 47-49, 67-69, 80-82.

URANIA AND CLITO
Antonio Salvi, *Astianatte* (Naples, 1725), pp. 20-24, 39-44, 51-56.

VENTURINA AND SCIARAPPA Text by Bernardo Saddumene, music by Leonardo Leo. *Bajazete imperador de' Turchi* (Naples, 1722), pp 15-19, 34-40, 49-51.

VESPETTA AND BELLOCCO
Antonio Zaniboni, *Amor nato trà l'ombre* (Bologna, [1723]), pp. 16-17, 25-26, 34-37, 42.

VESPETTA AND CARINO Music by Giuseppe de Bottis.
Apostolo Zeno *et al, L'amor generoso* (Naples, 1708), pp. 20-22, 34-36, 42-43, 49-51.

VESPETTA AND DELBO
M[atteo] N[orris], *Laodicea, e Berenice* (Naples, 1701), pp. 18-20, 30-32, 53-55.

VESPETTA AND DELBO
Allesandro amante eroe (Genoa, [1706]), pp. 23-25, 50-53, 66-67.

VESPETTA AND FRULLONE
Angelo Donato Rossi, *La costanza in amore* (Rome, [1715]), pp. 15-20, 43-47, 67-71.

VESPETTA AND LESBO
[Francesco di Lemene and Pier-Jacopo Martelli], *Lo scherno degli dei* (Bologna [1708]), pp. 19-22, 33-36, 42-46.

VESPETTA AND NESSO Music by Francesco Feo.
[Antonio Salvi], *Lucio Papirio* (Naples, 1717), pp 26-30, 37-39, 43-49, 60-66.

VESPETTA AND PIMPINONE
[Apostolo Zeno and Pietro Pariati], *L'Engelberta, o sia La forza dell'innocenza* (Naples, 1709), pp. 61-72.

VESPETTA AND PIMPINONE
La costanza in amor vince l'inganno (Rome, [1711]), pp. 21-24, 41-44, 65-68.

VESPETTA AND PIMPINONE Text by Pietro Pariati, music by Francesco Conti.
Pietro Pariati, *Sesostri re di Egitto* (Vienna, [1717]), pp. 69-80.

VESPETTA AND VALASCO
Stratonica (Naples, [1727]), pp. 19-23, 35-39.

VESPILLA AND LICO
Pietro Pariati, *Creso* (Vienna, 1723), pp. 29-31, 57-59.

VESPINA, SERPILLO AND ZELTO
Il Seleuco (Messina, 1711), pp. 75-[80].

VIOLETTA AND PISTOLFO
Caligula delirante (Naples, 1714), pp. 12-14, 22-23, 30-32, 45-46, 52-55.

ZAFFIRA AND LESBO Music by Francesco Mancini.
[Vincenzo Grimani], *Agrippina* (Naples, 1713), pp. 28-31, 49-53, 62-66.

ZAFFIRA AND LESBO
[Francesco Silvani], *La fede tradita, e vendicata* (Turin, [1719]), pp. 24-29, 48-52, 67-72.

ZAIDA AND SIFONE
Publio Cornelio Scipione (Livorno [1704]), pp. 17-19, 40-42, 63-67.

ZAIRA AND CLEONZIO
Artenice (Turin, [1723]), pp. 11-13, 49-51, 70-73.

ZELTA AND BALZO
[Apostolo Zeno], *Amar per virtù, overo I generosi rivali* (Turin, [1702]), pp. 19-21, 53-55, 73-75.

ZELTA AND BRENO
Matteo Noris *et al., Tito-Manlio* (Turin, [1703]), pp. 19-21, 65-67, 83-94.

ZELTA AND DELBO
Silvio Stampiglia, *L'Etearco* (Vienna, [1707]), pp. 24-27, 45-47, 56-58, 66-68.

NOTES

INTRODUCTION

[1]See Alfred Loewenberg, *Annals of Opera: 1597-1940* (2d ed.; Geneva, 1955), I, coll. 173-78.

[2]*A General History of Music from the Earliest Ages to the Present Period* (London, 1776-89), IV, 132. An anonymous intermezzo with the title *La serva padrona* is, in fact, recorded by the *Drammaturgia di Lione Allacci accresciuta e continuata fino all'anno MDCCLV* (Venice, 1755), col. 715, as having been performed at Venice in 1740. According to an eighteenth-century manuscript catalogue of Venetian opera that is authoritative for the period, the music for this performance was "del Pergolese Napolitano, a riserva dell'ultimo dueto il quale fu del Vinci." Antonio Groppo, "Catalogo purgatissimo di tutti li drammi per musica recitatisi ne' teatri di Venezia dall'anno MDCXXXVII sin oggi [1767].... accresciuto di tutti gli scenari, varie edizioni, aggiunte a drammi, e intermedi con la notizia di alcuni drammi nuovamente scoperti, e di altre rare particolarità," Venice, Biblioteca Marciana, MS Cl. VII, No. 2326, p. 254.

[3]".... a studio di maggior brevità, il passarli sotto silenzio,..." *Le glorie della poesia, e della musica contenute nell'esatta notitia de teatri della città di Venezia,...* (Venice, [1730]), p. 150.

[4]"Sono gl'Intermedj un'adjacenza de' Drami accidentale ed incerta. Non sono stampati unitamente alli Drami; ne il loro titolo come quello dei Drami è esposto sopra li pubblici Cartelli. Si mutano a capriccio degl'Attori; ed a misura dell'approvazione che incontrano; quindi per saperne il cambiamento bisognerebbe frequentare ogni sera tutti li Teatri d'Opera. Ecco giustificata la difficoltà di trovarli, dalla difficoltà di saperli." "Cattalogo di tutti li Drami rappresentati in musica in Venezia dall'anno 1637 fino al presente [1790] col nome de' compositori della poesia, e della musica e coll'indicazione de' teatri, ove furono rappresentati illustrato con particolari annotazioni," Venice, Biblioteca Marciana, MS Cl. VII, Nos. 1613-14, II, fol. 25.

[5]*Proceedings of the Musical Association*, XLIII (1916-17), 139-63.

[6]*Ibid.*, p. 153.

[7]For a bibliography of contemporary and later writings see Louisette Reichenburg, *Contribution à l'histoire de la "Querelle des Bouffons"* (Philadelphia, 1937), pp. 100-133.

[8][Venice, *ca.* 1720], p. 40.

[9]"Loderanno infinitamente li *Virtuosi dell'Opera, la Musica, il Libretto, le Comparse, le Scene, l'Orso, i Terremoti, &c.* attribuendo però a se soli la *Fortuna* del *Teatro.*" *Ibid.*, p. 54.

[10]"Les Entrepreneurs ne voulant point courir les risques de la nouveauté, remettent presque tous les ans les Opéra qui ont eu du succès quelques années auparavant, ... on fait encore plus; car on remet quelquefois le même Opéra deux fois de suite; ce qui déplaît aux Spectateurs, & qui ternit beaucoup la gloire des Théatres d'Italie, autrefois si fertiles en nouveautés." *Réflexions historiques et critiques sur les differens théâtres de*

l'Europe (Amsterdam, 1740), pp. 42-43; trans. in *An Historical and Critical Account of the Theaters in Europe* (London, 1741), p. 83.

[11]"Non e meraviglia se in questi ultimi anni si veggono così rari i nuovi Drammi, e così frequenti le reppliche de' vecchi più che ne' passati; poiche al presente il meno a cui si applica sono i Drammi. Lo Spettatore è tutto portato da' balli, e da gli Intermedii, e considera l'Opera che dov[r]ebbe essere il principale, come un'aggiunto, ed un sollievo a ballerini, ed ai Buffoni." "Catalogo purgatissimo," p. 255.

[12]The libretto for a setting of Girolamo Gigli's *Anagilda* by Luca Antonio Predieri (Turin, 1719) states that "per convenienti motivi" the intermezzi were not printed, but this is one of a very few exceptions.

[13]Libretti of eighteenth-century operas were occasionally printed in a city and/or year other than that of the actual performance. In such a case, information concerning the performance usually appears after the title, with the city and date of publication following as usual at the bottom of the title page. A similar distinction will be observed in the present study. Cities and dates enclosed by parentheses in its text refer to those of the performance; in the notes, they pertain to publication data of the printed libretto.

[14]See *La scuola musicale di Napoli e i suoi conservatorii* (Naples, 1880-82), IV, 18.

[15]See, for example, [Pietro Metastasio], *Didone abandonata* (Naples, 1724), pp. [8], 28, 52.

[16]Francesco Silvani, *Armida abbandonata* (Venice, n.d.), p. 8.

[17]See, for example, the intermezzi described in [Adriano Morselli], *La forza della fedeltà* (Fano, 1716), performed at the Teatro della Fortuna during the carnival of 1716 with "musica del Sig. Alessandro Scarlatti con aggiunta d'Arie di diversi Primarij Autori vnite dal Sig. Angelo Massarotti Virtuoso di Violoncello." (It was a pasticcio based upon Scarlatti's *Pirro e Demetrio*, first performed at Naples in 1694.)

[18]See the intermezzi of the anonymous *L'Erasitea* (Parma, 1710), a *favola boschereccia* performed "all'arrivo in Piacenza della serenissima Signora Principessa Carlotta Aglaide di Valois sposa del serenissimo signor Principe ereditario di Modona fatta rappresentare dal serenissimo signor Duca di Parma, &c."

[19]Giuseppe Papis, *Trattenimento musicale in lode della maestà cattolica di Elisabetta regina delle Spagna* (Naples, 1709), p. 12.

[20]But, as in operas of this period, one occasionally finds allegorical intermedi with machines performed between the acts of prose plays. See, for example, the description of intermedi for *Romolo e Remo*, a *tragicomedia* acted at Rome's Teatro Tordinona in 1754, quoted in Alberto Cametti, *Il teatro Tordinona poi di Apollo* (Tivoli, 1938), II, 382.

[21]The two types are separately indexed in his "Catalogo purgatissimo."

[22]See his *Mémoires ... pour servir a l'histoire de sa vie, et a celle de son théâtre* (Paris, 1787), I, 275-76.

[23]"Catalogo purgatissimo," p. 169. The date of this early example, "Gnagnaro e China," Venice, Biblioteca Marciana, Dramm. 900.16, has been altered from 1707 to 1706 by another hand on the title page of the MS. The earlier date would make it contemporary with the first preserved Venetian *intermezzi dramatici.*

[24]Most of them are preserved in the Collezione Rossi of the Biblioteca Marciana.

[25]*Mémoires,* I, 275-76.

[26]"Ne Connoissoient pas une note de musique, ..." *Ibid.,* p. 276.

[27]"Attore assai comico e caratteristico per gl'Intermezzi. Non sapea di musica; ma cantava passabilmente,... apprendeva a orecchio la parte,... e supplia al difetto della scienza e della voce coll'abilità personale, colle caricature degli abiti, e colla cognizion dei caratteri che sapeva ben sostenere." *Delle commedie* (Venice, 1761-78), XIII, 2.

[28]*Libretti d'opera in musica* ("Catalogo dello biblioteca del Liceo Musicale di Bologna," Vol. V [Bologna, 1943]).

[29]See Giulia De Dominicis, "I teatri di Roma nell'età di Pio VI," *Archivio della R. Società Romana di Storia Patria,* XLVI (1923), 136, 209-227.

[30]Of the Roman intermezzi and *farsette in musica* recorded by Sesini (see note 28), most of those performed before 1760 had four or fewer characters; between 1760 and 1780 the number increased to five, and after 1780 casts of up to seven may be found.

[31]See, for example, the notices recorded in Taddeo Wiel, *I teatri musicali veneziani del settecento* (Venice, 1897), p. 230.

[32]This example and several other similar ones are cited by Cametti, II, 387-88, 402, 405.

CHAPTER I

[1]"Quando la Compositione si distribuirà in tre Atti, i quali per esperienza fatta deuono bastare, si puotrebbono aggiungere quattro Intermedij apparenti, compartiti, che il primo sia auanti del Proemio, e gli altri ogn'vno sia al fine del suo Atto, osseruando quest'ordine, che dentro la Scena si faccia vna piena Musica, & armoniosa sinfonia di stromenti, al suono de' quali siano concertati i moti dell'Intermedio, hauendo riguardo, che non habbia bisogno di recitatione, come non haurebbe, per essempio, rappresentandosi li Giganti, quando vollero far guerra à Gioue, ò cosa simile. Et in ciascheduno si potrebbe fare quella mutatione di Scena, che apportasse l'occasione dell'Intermedio: il quale è d'auuertire, che non può esser capace di descendenza di nuuole, non potendosi cosi conformare il moto col tempo della Sinfonia, come acconciamente seguirebbe doue interuenissero passi di Moresca, ò d'altri Balli." Facsimile, ed. Francesco Mantica ("Prime fioriture del melodramma italiano," Vol. I [Rome, 1912], [fol. 2]).

[2]On the history and bibliography of the Renaissance intermedio, see Nino Pirrotta, "Intermedium," *MGG*, VI, coll. 1310-26, and more recently his *Li due Orfei* (Turin, 1969).

[3]They are described in the score (Venice, 1626), pp. 18, 63.

[4]".... ciascun Atto di questa bellissima Fauola fu terminato con merauigliosi Balletti fatti da nobilissimi Caualieri della Corte di Toscana:..." Andrea Salvadori, *La Flora* (Florence, 1628), [fol. 2'].

[5]See Alessandro Ademollo, *I teatri di Roma nel secolo decimosettimo* (Rome, 1888), pp. 20-22.

[6]".... per fine dell'Atto [primo] si cantò prima di dentro vn Madrigale à più voci, concertato con Istrumenti diuersi; e poi tre bellissimi Giouinetti, in habito d'Amore, vscirono à fare, per Intermezzo, vna gratiosissima danza." Benedetto Ferrari, *L'Andromeda* (Venice, 1637), pp. 8-9.

[7]".... dodici Seluaggi vscirono à fare,... vn strauagantissimo, e gustosissimo ballo di moti, e gesti." *Ibid.*, p. 10.

[8]".... mezzi ignudi, e ricoperti solo da vna gran pelle di lupo ceruiero, armati di arco, col cimiero in testa fatto del capo similmente di lupo, e terranno vna torcia accesa.... intrecciandosi con molta vaghezza." Giulio Strozzzi, *La finta savia* (Venice, 1643), p. 140.

[9]Marc' Antonio Tirabosco, *L'Alcate* (Venice, 1642), p. 49.

[10]*Ibid.*

[11](Venice, 1659), p. 44.

[12]".... tratto da la curiosità ad aprire vn libro consegnatoli da vn Mago di corte per portarlo ad Idraspe suo Signore. Non a pena egli l'apre, che si mouono alcune statue della Galleria, ond'egli atterrito sen fugge, & quelle formano il ballo per fine dell'Atto Secondo." *Scenario dell'Erismena di Avrelio Avreli* (n.p., n.d.), p. 17. Not a word about this is mentioned in the opera's libretto; quite possibly such pantomimes figured even more frequently in seventeenth-century operas than their libretti indicate.

[13]*Alessandro Scarlatti: His Life and Works* (London, 1960), p. 50.

[14]"Apre il Libro, e nell'aprirlo il tauolino si cangia in vn Carro tirato da due Draghi Infernali comparendo dalle par[e]ti della Stanza molti Demonj." (Venice, 1697), p. 22.

[15]"Parte soura il Carro per l'Aria, e segue vn Ballo di Spiriti Infernali." *Ibid.*

[16]Niccolò Minato, *La prosperità di Elio Seiano* (Venice, 1667), pp. 31-32.

[17]See, for example, the intermedi of Francesco Maria Paglia, *Comodo Antonio* (Naples, 1696), pp. 16-17, 35-37.

[18]".... con la ostensione di varij mobili ridicoli, che erano dentro vna cassa, tra' quali vn libro per cauare i tesori, & alcuni sottanini. che si trasformano in Damigelle, le quali regalano Bleso di varie cose, e formano il Ballo." (Rome, n.d.), p. 34.

[19]".... li Buffi vengono col libro à cauare il tesoro, e trouano vna statua d'oro. Bleso credendo abbracciar la statua per portarla via, si troua à cauallo di vn'Asino, il quale mette l'ali, e lo porta via per aria &c." *Ibid.*, p. 34.

[20]"Nelle Contrascene delle Parti Bufe, se non incontrerai quella viuezza, che si aspettaua dal tuo spirito, ti sarà facile compatire, considerandole come cose obligate, e quasi sempre dependenti dall'operazione degl'Intermedij." *Ibid.*, pp. 5-6.

[21]Charon's song and the pages' duet are printed in Hugo Goldschmidt, *Studien zur Geschichte der italienischen Oper im 17. Jahrhundert* (Leipzig, 1901-1904), I, 201, 210-11.

[22]See also those discussed in N[icola] D'Arienzo, "Origini dell'opera comica," *Rivista musicale italiana*, II (1895), 613-28; G[ian] G[iuseppe] Bernardi, "Contributo allo studio dell'elemento comico nell'opera seria veneziana del secolo XVII," *Musica d'oggi*, XII (1935), 53-61; and Nino Pirrotta, "Buffo, buffi," *Enciclopedia dello spettacolo*, II, coll. 1300-1301.

[23]For an early example, see the scene between Fidalpa and Bleso in Francesco Sbarra, *Alessandro vincitor di se stesso* (Venice, 1651), pp. 39-41.

[24]*Claudio Monteverdi und das musikalische Drama* (Lippstadt, 1954), p. 147.

[25]*Die venezianische Oper in der zweiten Hälfte des 17. Jahrhunderts* (Berlin, 1937), p. 115.

[26]The entire scene is published, ed. Robert Eitner, *Die Oper von ihren erlten Anfängen bis zur Mitte des 18. Jahrhunderts*, pt. 2 ("Publikation älterer praktischer und theoretischer Musikwerke," Vol. XII [Berlin, 1883], pp. 123-27.

[27]Apolloni, *La Dori* (Venice, 1663), p. 11.

[28]*Ibid.*

[29]Naples, Biblioteca del Conservatorio S. Pietro a Majella, MS 32.3.32, foll. 83-89', 159-64', 198-203. Neither the score nor the libretto (Naples, 1684) names either the author or composer of the added comic scenes.

[30]*Alessandro Scarlatti*, pp. 53-55.

[31]"Il presente Drama.... dalla famosa penna del Sign. Noris,... sempre ricevuto con somma plauso da' più cospicui Teatri d'Italia, non hà potuto à meno, che di patire, qualche accidental mutatione, ogni volta, che è stato rappresentato. Vn abito per presioso ch'egli si sia, e ben tagliato da man perita, forza è che sofra qualche leggìer colpo di forbice, e puntura d'ago, quando hà da vestir più d'un corpo, e ciò, non per diffetto di chi lo fece, mà per la necessità d'accommodarsi à più d'una statura. Si sono hora aggionte le parti di Fausta, e di Alcea, per servire semplicemente al numero delli Attori." *Tito-Manlio* (Turin, 1703), p. 5.

[32]See Francesco Florimo, *La scuola musicale di Napoli e i suoi conservatorii* (Naples, 1880-82), IV, 7-9, and cast lists of the following libretti: Matteo Noris, *Il Flavio Cuniberto* (Rome, [1696]); [Aurelio Aureli], *Gerone tiranno di Siracvsa* (Genoa, [1700]); *Stratonica* (Florence, 1707); and *L'Engelberta* (Milan, 1708). Francesco Maria Paglia, *Il prigioniero fortunato* (Naples, 1698) and other libretti from about this time describe him as "Virtuoso del Serenissimo di Parma." In claiming that he also wrote music, Ademollo, *I teatri di Roma*, p. 193, and Benedetto Croce, *I teatri di Napoli* (3d ed.; Bari, 1926), p. 125, evidently confuse him with the younger Bolognese composer Luca Antonio Predieri.

[33]MSS 1/F/39,1 and 1/F/39,2.

[34]See Otto Jahn, *W. A. Mozart* (2d. ed.; Leipzig, 1867), I, 203.

[35]Nietan, pp. 5-6, 19.

[36]See, for example, Werner Bollert, *Die Buffoopern Baldassare Galuppis: Ein Beitrag zur Geschichte der italienischen komischen Oper im 18. Jahrhundert* (Bottrop, 1935), pp. 16-17.

[37]See, for example, [Silvio Stampiglia], *Camilla, regina de' Volsci* (Venice, 1698); Matteo Noris, *Tito Manlio* (Venice, 1697); [Silvio Stampiglia], *La Partenope* (Venice, [1707]); Domenico David, *La forza della virtù* [= *Creonte tiranno di Tebe*] (Venice, 1693); A[postolo] Z[eno], *Gl'inganni felici* (Venice, 1696); and Apostolo Zeno, *Odoardo* (Venice, 1698).

[38]See, for example, the libretto for a revival of Alessandro Scarlatti's setting of Silvio Stampiglia, *L'Eraclea* (Parma, 1700), pp. 37-40, 69-73, where the word is used to denote only the comic scenes in which magic and scenic spectacle play a part. These two "intermezzi," which end the opera's first and second acts, were additions to the Neapolitan version of *L'Eraclea*; the text of the second is similar to that of the fourth comic scenes of Mirena and Floro contained in Vol. I of the Dresden collection.

[39]"Chi hà dovuto per un grande comandamento ridurlo all'uso di queste Scene hà servata religiosamente l'intention del celeberrimo Auttore, che l'hà composto, non alteratovi punto l'ordine delle Scene, nè con accrescervi del suo, nè con lo scemarvi cos'alcuna di ciò ch'hà ritrovato nell'Esemplare Stampato in Napoli l'anno 1699. che fù il primo, in cui fù rappresentato. Solamente ci hò levato gl'intramezzi, ed alcune ariette à titolo della voluta brevità nel luogo dell quali hà posto due versi di recitativo." (Venice, [1707]), p. 4.

[40]See those of Tullia and Linco, Niceta and Morasso, Zelta and Breno, Lucilla and Delbo, Anfrisa and Beltramme, and Dircea and Pindoro.

[41]See those of Lidia and Gilbo, Servilia and Flacco, Lesbina and Milo, and all the scenes of Vol. I.

[42]See, for example, Francesco Maria Paglia, *Cesare in Alessandria* (Naples, 1699). Soubrette roles in comic scenes of Neapolitan operas appeared as early as 1697, but they were sung by a castrato, Giulio Cavalletti; see Silvio Stampiglia, *La caduta de' Decemviri* (Naples, 1697).

[43]Andrea Perrucci, *Dell'arte rappresentativa premeditata, ed all'improviso* (Naples, 1699), p. 374, in reference to improvised intermedi, states that "il lor tema,... sarà una burla di Servi, e parti Ridicole con la Serva.... con qualche furbaria finta magia, Tesoro di Demonii, e con simili burle,..."

[44]See also Lidia and Gilbo, Nos. 2-4; Dorilla and Bireno, No. 2; and Servilia and Flacco, No. 6.

[45]For statistical evidence of this trend in Venetian opera see Robert Freeman, "Opera without Drama: Currents of Change in Italian Opera, 1675-1725, and the Roles Played Therein by Zeno, Caldara, and Others" (Princeton University Dissertation, 1967), I, 27-29, 113-44. Libretti seen by the present writer tend to support Freeman's thesis for operas performed in Naples during the same period—if one disregards the traditional *scene buffe*.

[46]In particular, recitatives in comic scenes from around 1700 tend to avoid syncopated passages such as that in measure 3 of the *Giustino* example.

[47]See Edward Downes, *"Secco* recitative in Early Classical Opera Seria (1720-80)," *Journal of the American Musicological Society,* XIV (1961), 57-58.

[48]*Alessandro Scarlatti,* p. 51.

[49]See also the "page of breathless 'patter' worthy of Sullivan" in a *buffo* aria from Scarlatti's *Tiberio imperatore d'Oriente* quoted by Dent, *Alessandro Scarlatti,* p. 52.

[50]So called because the division of its text by ritornelli and harmonic scheme into five sections (including repetition of the first two); see Rudolf Gerber, "Aria," *MGG,* I, coll. 619-20.

[51]See Dent, *Alessandro Scarlatti,* pp. 53-55; and "Ensembles and Finales in 18th-Century Italian Opera," *Sammelbände der Internationalen Musikgesellschaft,* XI (1909-1910), 544.

[52]Dent, "Ensembles and Finales," pp. 543-55.

[53]This conclusion could be rather protracted; two duets in the *Emireno* scenes lack a final cadence; directions inform the singers that they may chatter away "in sin che li piacerà" and "sin che vorrà."

[54]Typically, Venetian opera libretti during the last quarter of the seventeenth century included one character—a servant, page, shepherd, equerry, or confidant—whose presence in the drama served a variety of functions, including that of comic relief. But such episodes as were possible with only one comic role are unrelated to the Neapolitan *scene buffe* just described and to the independent intermezzi of the following discussion.

[55]Establishing just which intermezzi were performed with what opera at Venice is a difficult task (see p. 1). The present study relies upon the pairings contained in an autograph repertory of Venetian theaters by Antonio Groppo, "Catalogo purgatissimo di tutti li drammi per musica recitatisi ne' teatri di Venezia dall'anno MDCXXXVII sin

oggi [1767].... accresciuto di tutti gli scenarj, varie edizioni, aggiunte a drammi, e intermedi con la notizia di alcuni drammi nouvamente scoperti, e di altre rare particolarità," Venice, Biblioteca Marciana, MS Cl. VII, No. 2326 (8263). This chronology, much less well known than Groppo's own published *Catalogo di tutti i drammi per musica...* (Venice, [1745?]), which omits notices of intermezzi altogether, contains seemingly more exact—and perhaps more accurate—information regarding them than other contemporary or modern Venetian theatrical repertories.

[56]"Per lasciar tempo à gl'intramezzi ridicoli, & a' balli, si taceranno nella Musica tutti li versi, che vedrai segnati nel margine." [Urbano Rizzi], *Taican rè della Cina* (Venice, 1707), p. 8. Most of the intermezzi performed during this period with three-act operas are in three parts. Opera libretti give no indication as to where the third intermezzo was placed, but later Venetian practice was to perform it before the final scene of the opera's last act (see p. 63).

[57]Included in the former category are *Il nuovo mondo, Le rovine di Troja, Tulipano,* and *Zamberlucco;* for examples of the latter, see *La capricciosa e il credulo, Lisetta, e Astrobolo, Pimpinone,* and intermezzi of Catulla and Lardone.

[58]But they are unlike the comic scenes with these characters added to Niccolò Minato's *Il Muzio Scevola* for performances in Rome (1695) and Naples (1697); nor are they similar to the comic scenes of Lesbina and Milo in *Tiberio imperatore d'Oriente* (Naples, 1702) and *La fede tradita e vendicata* (Naples, 1707).

[59]One aria text of the latter, "Ragazze appassionate," was taken from the second comic scene of Dircea and Pindoro added to [Domenico David], *Creonte tiranno di Tebe* (Naples, 1699). It is likely that other texts in the versions printed for Florence and Lucca have antecedents in various scenes from around the turn of the century.

[60]Printed under the title *L'Agrippina* (Milan, 1703).

[61]The latter is completely unlike any of the three intermezzi with the same characters performed with *Il premio dell'innocenza ovvero Le perdite dell'inganno* (Naples, 1725).

[62]The word is used here and elsewhere in the present study not only in its usual meaning, but also to denote "inter-regional" in reference to the Italian peninsula.

CHAPTER II

[1]See Edward Downes and Helmuth Hucke, "The Neapolitan Tradition in Opera" *International Musicological Society: Report of the Eighth Congress, New York 1961* (Kassel, 1961-62), I, 253-84; II, 132-34.

[2]Brussels, Bibliothèque royal de Belgique, Coll. Fétis, No. 2567.

[3]Rome, Biblioteca Apostolica Vaticana, Codex Barb. lat., 4231, foll. 151-85′.

[4]Antonio Groppo, "Catalogo purgatissimi di tutti li drammi per musica recitatisi ne' teatri di Venezia dall'anno MDCXXXVII sin oggi [1767].... accresciuto di tutti gli scenarj, varie edizioni, aggiunte a drammi, e intermedi con la notizia di alcuni drammi

nuovamente scoperti, e di altre rare particolatità, "Venice, Biblioteca Marciana, MS Cl. VII, No. 2326, p. 155.

[5]According to the card catalogue of the Sächsische Landesbibliothek, Dresden. The scores, MS Mus. 1/F/71, were destroyed in the air raid of 1944.

[6]Groppo, pp. 158-59.

[7]By the same token, the earliest setting of *Pimpinone* (Vespetta and Pimpinone) may be attributed to Tomaso Albinoni, with whose *Astarto* it received its first performance at the Teatro San Cassiano during the autumn of 1708. According to a notice in the libretto for his setting of [Apostolo Zeno and Pietro Pariati], *Statira* (Rome, [1726]), Albinoni was also the composer of an intermezzo with the characters Fiammetta and Malsazio. It is unfortunate that the libretto for this intermezzo has not come to light; it might prove to be a version of *L'avaro* (Fiammetta and Pancrazio), included among the popular works listed in Appendix A.

[8]See Monte Cassino, Biblioteca dell'Abbazia, MS 124-I-4. According to the libretto for a revival of Francesco Mancini's setting of *Il Vincislao* (Rome, 1716), Gasparini also composed parts of the added comic scenes betwen Gerilda and Gildo; and the score of Antonio Lotti's *Gl'odj delusi dal sangue* [=*L'Ascanio*] (Dresden, Sächsische Landesbibliothek, MS Mus. 2159/F/5) names him as composer of the first two intermezzi of Mirena and Floro, performed with that opera at Dresden in 1718.

[9]*Cf.*, for example, *L'Alfier Fanfarone* (Venice, 1716) and (Reggio, 1714); *Lisetta, e Delfo* (Venice, 1718) and the intermezzi of [Domenico Lalli], *L'amor tirannico* (Rome, 1713), pp. 31-34, 56-61, 73-77; *La preziosa ridicola* (Venice, 1719) and the intermezzi of [Francesco Silvani], *La fede tradita, e vendicata* (Rome, 1712), pp. 27-31, 50-55, 69-74; those of Elpina and Silvano (Venice, [1720]) and *Intermedj pastorali...* (Rome, 1715); the intermezzi of Aurilla and Cola (Venice, 1720) and those of Francesco Antonio Novi, *Il pescatore fortunato principe d'Ischia* (Bologna, [1716]), pp. 22-24, 34-36.

[10]Comic scenes in Giuseppe Aldrovandini's *Il Mitridate* (Teatro San Bartolomeo, 1706), [Francesco Gasparini's] *Le regine di Macedonia* (S. Bartolomeo, 1708), Antonio Lotti's *L'inganno vinto dalla ragione* (Teatro Fiorentini, 1708), Francesco Gasparini's *Ambleto* (S. Bartolomeo, 1711), and Antonio Lotti's *La forza del sangue* (S. Bartolomeo, 1712).

[11]Comic scenes in Giuseppe Maria Orlandini's *Artaserse* (Teatro San Bartolomeo, 1708), George Frideric Handel's *Agrippina* (S. Bartolomeo, 1713), and Antonio Lotti's *Artaserse rè di Persia* (Teatro del Real Palazzo, 1713).

[12]Comic scenes in the pasticcio *Il duello d'amore, e di vendeta* (Teatro San Bartolomeo, 1715, and Giuseppe Maria Orlandini's *Lucio Papirio* (S. Bartolomeo, 1717).

[13]Comic scenes in Francesco Gasparini's *L'Eumene* (Teatro del Real Plazzo, 1715) and *Sesostri re di Egitto* (Real Palazzo, 1717), George Frideric Handel's *Rinaldo* (Real Palazzo, 1718), the pasticcio *Arianna e Teseo* (Teatro San Bartolomeo, 1721), and an anonymous *Bajazete imperador de' Turchi* (Real Palazzo, 1722).

[14]Other comic scenes from Neapolitan operas by Scarlatti performed elsewhere as intermezzi in works by other composers include the second and fourth episodes of

Despina and Niso from his *L'amor generoso* (Naples, 1714), heard with Giuseppe Maria Orlandini's *Antigona* (Venice, [1724]), and the scenes of Pericca and Varrone from his *Scipione nelle Spagne* (Naples, 1714), parts of which were given at Bologna in 1730 as intermezzi in an opera of Giovanni Porta under the title *La dama spagnola ed il cavalier romano.*

[15]No composer is named in the Venetian libretto for either, but they were performed by the intermezzo singers from the Teatro San Bartolomeo, Santa Marchesini and Gioacchino Corrado. It seems unlikely that these singers would have been brought to Venice to sing another composer's resetting of a piece that they had performed shortly before in Naples.

[16]See the intermezzi of Carlotta and Pantaleone, Grilletta and Porsugnacco, Larinda and Vanesio, Lucilla and Pandolfo, and Scintilla and Don Tabarano listed in Appendix A. *La fantesca* (Merlina and Capitan D. Galoppo) and *La serva scaltra ovvero La moglie a forza* (Dorilla and Balanzone), first performed, respectively, with Hasse's *L'Ulderica* (Teatro San Bartolomeo; carnival, 1729) and *Il Tigrane* (S. Bartolomeo; November, 1729) were only slightly less popular. A version of the former was heard as late as 1753 in Salvaterra, a Portuguese city near Lisbon (see Joaquim José Marques, *Cronologia da ópera em Portugal* (Lisbon, 1947), p. 95.

[17]According to Frank Walker, "Two Centuries of Pergolesi Forgeries and Misattributions," *Music and Letters,* XXX (1949), 311, "the work published by [Francesco] Caffarelli as Pergolesi's 'La contadina astuta', from a score in Fétis's library, consists of Hasse's 'La contadina', with two arias from Hasse's 'Il tutore' and the duet 'Per te ho io nel core' from Pergolesi's 'Flaminio' substituted for the original arias and duets of the second part. The inclusion of the well-known duet of Pergolesi's probably accounts for the misattribution to this composer of the whole score." See Paolo-Emilio Ferrari, *Spettacoli drammatico-musicali e coreografici in Parma dall'anno 1628 all'anno 1883* (Parma, 1884), p. 32, for an example of a misattribution to Pergolesi of this piece on the basis of no discernable evidence; the libretto on which Ferrari evidently based his entry lacks the name of a composer and bears no resemblance to Mariani's text for *La contadina astuta.*

[18]See the lacunae in Francesco Florimi, *La scuola musicale di Napoli e i suoi conservatorii* (Naples, 1880-82), IV, 24, for the years following 1730. Other Neapolitans named as intermezzo composers in the few surviving libretti from this period include Giuseppe Sellitti (See Tomaso Mariani, *La franchezza delle donne* [Lesbina and Sempronio] in [Pietro Metastasio], *Siface* [Naples, 1734], pp. 58-72), and Francesco Feo (see the untitled intermezzi with the characters Nerina and D. Chischiotto in Tomaso Mariani, *Il castello d'Atlante* [Naples, 1734], pp. 48-59).

[19]See Walker, "Two Centuries," pp. 309-320, and below, p. 203, note 17.

[20]Goldoni and Pergolesi," *Monthly Musical Record,* LXXX (1950), 202.

[21]See Alfred Loewenberg, *Annals of Opera: 1597-1940,* (2nd ed.; Geneva, 1955), I, cols. 181-82, and the list of revivals for intermezzi of Livietta and Tracollo in Appendix A.

[22]"Goldoni and Pergolesi," pp. 204-205.

[23]For the scant biographical information known about Orlandini, see articles by Luigi Ferdinando Tagliavini in *MGG*, X, cols. 389-400; and *Enciclopedia dello spettacolo*, VII, cols. 1401-1402.

[24]".... fu singolare a' suoi tempi nell'adattare la Musica alle Cose Buffe." *Della storia e della regione d'ogni poesia* (Bologna and Milan, 1739-52), Index, p. 249.

[25]*A General History of Music from the Earliest Ages to the Present Period* (London, 1776-89), IV, 535.

[26]"Il excellait dans la composition des intermedes." [Jean Benjamin de Laborde], *Essai sur la musique ancienne et moderne* (Paris, 1780), III, 207.

[27]See the intermezzi of Dorina and Nibbio, Grilletta and Porsugnacco, Larinda and Vanesio, Madama Dulcinea and il cuoco del Marchese del Bosco, Moschetta and Grullo, and Serpilla and Bacocco. In addition, Orlandini is identified as composer of the comic scenes between Zaira and Cleonzio in the libretto for his and Giovanni Giaij's setting of *Artenice* (Turin, [1723]), and those for the intermezzi *La donna nobile* (Melinda and Tiburzio) (Venice, 1730) and *Il marito geloso* (Giletta and Ombrone) (Venice, 1742). According to Ugo Morini, *La R. Accademia degli Immobili ed il suo teatro "La Pergola" (1649-1925)* (Pisa, 1926), p. 41, Orlandini also composed an intermezzo entitled *Un vecchio innamorato*, performed at Florence in 1725. The present writer is unable to say on what basis Tagliavini, "Orlandini," *MGG*, X, col. 399, attributes the music of *Balbo e Dalisa* to him; the libretto of the opera with which these intermezzi were performed, Giuseppe Scarlatti's setting of [Apostolo Zeno], *Merope* (Rome, 1740), does not name their composer.

[28]The significance of *Il giocatore* in the history of opera would be even greater if, as [Jean Marie Bernard Clément and Joseph de La Porte], *Anecdotes dramatiques* (Paris, 1775), II, 411, suggest, its performance at Paris in 1752 and not that of *La serva padrona* provoked the *Querelle des Bouffons* (see O.G. Sonneck, "Il giocatore," *The Musical Antiquary*, IV [1912-13], 165-66). In any case, the piece seems to have enjoyed at least a *succès d'estime* on this occasion; according to [Jacques Durey de Noinville], *Histoire du théâtre de l'Académie Royale de Musique en France, depuis son établissement jusqu'à présent* (2nd. ed.; Paris, 1757), I, 279, "quoique la *Serva Padrona* ait eû un grand succès, les connoisseurs donnent la préférence à cette derniere Pièce [*Il giocatore*] ... qui a toujours passé pour le chef-d'oeuvre de l'Italie dans le goût de Musique comique."

[29]For a bibliography on this controversy, see Loewenberg, *Annals of Opera*, I, cols. 138-39.

[30]"Il giocatore," pp. 161-63. The anonymous manuscript (Brussels, Bibliothèque du Conservatoire Royale de Musique, No. 2372) that Sonneck attempted to attribute to Orlandini, and which he believed to be a contemporary score of the intermezzo, is, in fact, a nineteenth-century transcript. It differs from copies bearing Orlandini's name and the Venice, 1719, libretto mainly by the inclusion of an aria, "Con tanto stranutare," in part two that is lacking in the latter.

[31]See p. 49.

[32]Two other scores (Vienna, Oesterreichische Nationalbibliothek, MS 17.740, and Rostock, Universitätsbibliothek, MS Mus. XVIII:495), both bearing Orlandini's name as composer, preserve substantially the same music arranged, respectively, for alto and bass, and soprano and bass. At least two other singing teams must therefore have included Orlandini's setting of this intermezzo in their repertories. Still another pair of scores, virtually identical except for differences in clefs (Wolfenbüttel, Herzog-August-Bibliothek, Cod. Guelf., 257 and 258), have been cited as evidence for Leonardo Vinci's having composed *Il marito giocatore* by Georgy Calmus, "L. Vinci der Komponist von *Serpilla e Bacocco*," *Zeitschrift der Internationalen Musikgesellschaft*, XIV (1912-13), 114, 172-73. Vinci's name does, in fact, appear on the cover of one (No. 258), but his role could only have been that of arranger. The Wolfenbüttel scores, although differing in many details—particularly in the recitatives—from those attributed to Orlandini, are basically similar to them. To accept Vinci as composer of *Il marito giocatore*, one must believe that he was the first to set the libretto (if so it would antedate his earliest known composition by several months; see Helmuth Hucke, "Vinci," *MGG*, XIII, col. 1660), and that the three scores bearing Orlandini's name are later arrangements of the Neapolitan composer's music.

[33]"Catalogo purgatissimo," pp. 259, 261-62.

[34]October, 1752, p. 164. The same issue (p. 164) mentions that after a few performances the aria "Signor Giudite [*sic* Giudice], justitia" was substituted in the intermezzo's second part. Since this text belongs to Salvi's original libretto, its music may also have been by Orlandini.

[35]*Historisch-biographisches Lexicon der Tonkünstler* (Leipzig, 1790-92), II, col. 46.

[36]Orlandini's setting of *Ataulfo re de' Goti, ovvero La forza della virtù* received its first performance during the carnival of 1712 at the same theater as this intermezzo.

[37]*Der vollkommene Capellmeister* (Hamburg, 1739), p. 40.

[38]For a listing of these comic scenes, together with intermezzi and *scene buffe* by other composers performed in operas at Vienna between 1714 and 1728, see Robert Haas, "Die Musik in der Wiener deutschen Stegreifkomödie," *Studien zur Musikwissenschaft*, XII (1925), 7-8.

[39]See, for example, Gustav Friedrich Schmidt, *Chronologisches Verzeichnis der in Wolfenbüttel, Braunschweig, Salzthal, Bevern und Blankenburg aufgeführten Opern, Ballette und Schauspiele (Komödien) mit Musik bis zur Mitte des 18. Jahrhunderts* ("Neue Beiträge zur Geschichte der Musik und des Theaters am Herzoglichen Hofe zu Braunschweig-Wolfenbüttel," erste Folge [Munich, 1929]), pp. 12-14, 18. Conti's setting of Pariati's *Pimpinone* seems to have been the only one in which the female character was named Grilletta; therefore, he was probably responsible for the music of the anonymous revival of this intermezzo at Brunswick in 1731 recorded by Schmidt (p. 19).

[40]See Hellmuth Christian Wolff, *Die Barockoper in Hamburg (1678-1738)* (Wolfenbüttel, 1957), I, 116-17.

[41]See the intermezzi of Brunetta and Burlotto, Melissa and Serpillo, and Vespetta and Pimpinone listed in Appendix A.

[42]Published under the title *Pimpinone oder Die ungleiche Heirat*, ed. Theodor Georg Wilhelm Werner ("Das Erbe deutscher Musik," erste Reihe, Vol. VI [Mainz, 1936]). A comparison of this score with what appears to be Albinoni's original setting of *Pimpinone*, contained in the version of Antonio Orefici and Francesco Mancini's *L'Engelberta* performed at Naples in 1709 (Vienna, Oesterreichische Nationalbibliothek, MS 18.067, foll. 55-67', 131'-145', 170'-181) shows that Telemann's music for this intermezzo is original, and not, as some have conjectured (e.g., Loewenberg, *Annals of Opera*, col. 152), merely an arrangement of the Italian composer's work.

[43]See [Johann] Mattheson, *Der musicalische Patriot* (Hamburg, 1728), p. 193; and Th[eodor] Werner, "Zum Neudruck von G. Ph. Telemanns *Pimpinone* in den Reichsdenkmalen," *Archiv für Musikforschung*, I (1936), 361-65,

[44]See Florimo, IV, 14-25; and the following libretti: *La Salustia* (Naples, 1735), *Argene* (Naples, 1731), and Pietro Metastasio, *Il Demetrio* (Naples, 1732).

[45]"Porteranno con se Mustacchi, Bordoni, Tamburri, e qualunque altro Arnese opportuno per il loro Uffitio per non aggravar (oltre l'Onorario abbondante) l'Impresario di *maggior spesa.*" *Il teatro alla moda....* ([Venice, *ca.* 1720]), p. 54.

[46]".... forse il primo, e l'ultimo, che con faceta decenza, tutte le Passioni di que' rappresentati, Caratteri, quanto al vivo mai si possa, esprimer e nel Canto e nel Gesto sapeva." *De' poetici componimenti....* (Venice, 1761), p. 356.

[47]See Alberto Cametti, *Il teatro Tordinona poi di Apollo* (Tivoli, 1938), II, 362, 364; and Florimo, IV, 6-11. In Neapolitan libretti before 1700 he is described as "Virtuoso del Serenissimo di Montova" [Ferdinando Carlo Gonzaga]; according to Quadrio, III, ii, 531, he was also at some unspecified time in the service of the Marchese di Cravena.

[48]See Taddeo Wiel, *I teatri musicali veneziani del settecento* (Venice, 1897), pp. 11-20.

[49]See the libretti of *Melissa* (Bologna, 1708); and intermezzi of Vespetta and Lesbo contained in [Francesco di Lemene and Pier Jacopo Martello], *Lo scherno degli dei* (Bologna, [1708]).

[50]See the cast list of [Apostolo Zeno and Pietro Pariati], *Astarto* (Naples, 1709); and intermezzi contained in [Apostolo Zeno and Pietro Pariati], *L'Engleberta, o sia La forza dell'innocenza* (Naples, 1709).

[51]Florimo, IV, 12-21.

[52]Libretti for these intermezzi are contained in [Jacques] Pradon, *L'Attilio Regolo*, trans. Girolamo Gigli (Siena, n.d.); and *La costanza in amore vince l'inganno* (Rome, n.d.).

[53]See [Francesco Silvani], *La fede tradita, e vendicata* (Rome, 1712), [Antonio Salvi?], *Il Tartaro nella Cina* (Reggio, 1715); and *cf. Il Fernando* (Modena, 1717) and *La preziosa ridicola* (Modena, 1717). Due to the prohibition of women singers on Roman stages, Cavana's partners there were all castrati, including Annibale Fabbri (1711), Giacinto

Fontano "detto Farfallino" (1712), Domenico Genovesi (1713), Giovanni Battista Perugini (1719), Girolamo Bartoluzzi "detto il Reggiano" (1720-21), Tommaso Ferrarini (1721), Domenico Ricci (1724), and Biagio Erminii (1726). Vienna was the only other city where castrati were regularly employed to play the female role in intermezzi; the name of Giovanni Vincenzi frequently appears in cast lists of libretti and scores between 1715 and 1724 in this connection. But women singers also played female roles in Viennese intermezzi; the most notable was the young Faustina Bordoni (later the wife of Johann Adolph Hasse), who sang in Conti's intermezzi of Grilletta [Vespetta] and Pimpinone in 1717. (See also Haas, *Studien zur Musikwissenschaft*, XII, 8.) Castrati seem never to have sung male roles in intermezzi anywhere.

[54]Evidence for his presence in these cities is contained, respectively, in *Peribea in Salamina* (Padua, 1712); Domenico Lalli and Angiolo Birini, *Il Gran Mogol* (Naples, 1713); [Pietro Pariati], *Intermezzi di Vespetta, e Pimpinone* (Parma, [1714]); [Belisario Valeriani], *La caccia in Etolia* (Ferrara, 1715); [Apostolo Zeno and Pietro Pariati], *Sesostri rè di Egitto* (Milan, [1716]); *Tomiri amante inimica* (Brescia, [1716]); [Apostolo Zeno], *Il Venceslao* (Genoa, 1717); and Domenico Lalli, *L'amor tirannico* (Pesaro, 1722).

[55]Quadrio, III, ii, 538.

[56]See, for example, the libretto for *Intermezzi di Vespetta, e Pimpinone* (Parma, [1714]), in which Angelo Cantelli sang the male role.

[57]His vocal range is identified by Palmieri Pandolfini, "Notizia de tutte l'opere che si sono recitate in Firenze nel teatro di via della Pergola dall'anno 1718 in poi," Florence, Biblioteca Nazionale Centrale, MS II-97, No. 3, [fol. 181'].

[58]Wiel, p. 5.

[59]Florimo, IV, 35.

[60]Wiel, pp. 18-20.

[61]Beginning about 1720, they are regularly described in libretti as "Virtuosi del Sereniss. Principe d'Armstatt [sic]. The latter is not to be identified as the Landgraf Ernst Ludwig von Hessen-Darmstadt (1667-1739), composer and supporter of music at the Darmstadt court, but his less famous brother Philipp, Hapsburg governor of Mantua, who is named as their patron in the libretto for Giuseppe Maria Orlandini's setting of Benedetto Pasqualigo, *Antigona* (Venice, 1721). The singers' extensive travels must have left them little time for duties at Mantua; they did not, for example, appear in the intermezzi mentioned in the libretto for Orazio Pollaroli's setting of [Grazio Braccioli], *Orlando furioso* (Mantua, n.d.), performed at that city's Teatro Arciducale during the carnival of 1725. Perhaps the title was an honorary one.

[62]"Faranno per ogni Paese gl'*Intermezzi* medesimi,... " *Il teatro alla moda*, p. 54.

[63]"Adi 15 Luglio *1725* Nel nostro Teatro questa sera alle ore Venti quattro e tre quartj si è dato Principio alle tre opere.... e la comedia non e piaciuta p che lanno Troncata p fare che sia Breve e non vi si e trouato di Buono se non che due Partj che sono Dottore Viuarellj e Dottore Batachio li qualj erano i più Brauj che fosero nella detta

compagnia.... Lintermedj poj sono riesciutj un portento di natura che dà che Pistoia e
Pistoia non ne verrà maj più e sono la sig^{ra} Rosa Ungherellj, e il sig^{re} Antonio
Ristorinj Florentino e la sig^{ra} Rosa e Bologniese e li anno dato scrudi cento cinquanta
p loro onorario e scudi cinquanta p viaggio e vitto p la strada e questj vi si
comprende ancora il Ritorno e anno speso poj ottanta scudi nellj abitj solamente p i
due musicj che a dirla giusta erano un Incanto che uno abito era da Bacchettona e
laltra da Pellegrina tutti di ermisino di seta ma veramente erano Bellissimj p il sig^{re}
Antonio li anno fatto un abito da giocatore che ancora questo era Bene Inteso
lintermedio concerneua che Figuraua un giocatore che aueua perso tutto il suo alla
Bassetta, e la Donna Moglie lo Gridaua p che aueua perso tutto il suo e li trouo le
carte adosso e doppo auerlo Gridato piu volte seguitaua a far peggio e lo voleua
chiamare al Giudice, e cosj finj il Primo atto il secondo Intermezzo esce forj di scena
vestito da Giudice pro tribunalj sedentj e lej comparisce e querela il suo marito che lo
condannj alla Galera e li fa azionj che auerebbe mosso una Pietra e Luj dice che li
auerebbe fatto la Grazia se lej fosse stata sua cicisbea e doppo varie Preghiere risolue
di essere sua cicisbea, e li dà là mano quando lej li a dato la mano egli si caua la
Barba dal viso si spoglia e lej lo riconosce p suo marito e lej si scusa e luj dice questo
e la Bacchettona *ona* ona *ona ona* la Bella e Buona e li finisca alla fine del Terzo atto
compariua vestita a Pellegrina scaciata dal marito con Bellissimo abito chiedendo la
lemosina, e vestita come o detto da Pellegrina con fagotto, et il suo marito tira mano
alla spada p amazzarla et egli li piglia il fagotto e la scaccia et ella sempre
racomandosj dicendolj ammazamj ricordati de Primj amorj e con parole che auerebbero
liquefatto i Bronzi alla fine Luj la ripiglia e dice che si scorda dell Passato Le azionj
le finezze che lej fà all suo marito non si possono descriuerle solo dirò che i Gestj e il
modo che tiene nel Palco e una cosa che non si pò maj credere se non chi là vista a
segnio tale che io li posj nome ammazza luomo e la ragione se uno auesse moglie e li
stesse Intorno come sta sul palco rifinirebbe ognj omo e cosj non potrebbe durare e se
durasse morirebbe e p questo io la Chiamo Ammazza luomo, e veramente lej non e
Bella che se le fusse Dio ne guardj" "[Memorie di] cose [pistojesi] notate e
minutamente osservate.... per suo diuertimento [dal gennaio 1724 al 31 aprile 1728],"
Florence, Biblioteca Nazionale Centrale, Coll. Rossi-Cassigoli, No. 192, foll. 211'-12;
printed in Alberto Chiappelli, *Storia del teatro in Pistoia dalle origini alla fine del sec.
XVIII* (Pistoia, 1913), p. 195.

[64]"Adi 29: Agosto *1725* Questo Giorno alle ore 19: 1/2 e Partita da questa Città La
sig^{ra} Rosa Ungherellj col sig^{re} Antonio Ristorinj, e se ne sono andatj a Firenze p poj
Andare a Bolognia, a doue sono di Permanenza fino a Tanto che non verrà il Tempo
di Andare a Turino a doue li và a Recitare p la quinta volta sono Andatj moltissimj
Cav^{ri} a Farlj le visite e certo che e una donna Franca solo Basta dire che la sua
professione di Cantatrice che non sono minchione, e questa Donna In Pistoia vi, à
auto fortuna e ve la Incontrata Tanto Lej che il sig^{re} Antonio ma non e gran cosa p
che quj In Pistoia non vene sono maj state a mio Tempo di queste Donne Franche
come questa, vene sono state, mà non erano come questa Basta solo ci a fatto Calare
gente che non velo Crederestj maj ma a Regalj mangiativj p che a nostrj tempi de
denarj ci e Pochj che ne possino dare e La Donna era Brutta che se fosse stata Bella
Dio: ne guardi p che aueua una maniera Innarriuabile, e aueua una mozzione di
affetto che dir non poteua di più il piu che fosse il fauorito era Il sig^{re} Dottore
Giuseppe Biagio Desidirj che era uno dellj Impresarj ma à Donato forte e regalj di

Considerazione e La Acompagniata fino a Firenza e la regalata, e questo sig[re] e una migniella ma In questa Donna ve si sarebbe spiantato" Rossi-Melocchi, fol. 237'; Chiappelli, p. 201.

[65]See Schmidt, p. 12; Moritz Furstenau, *Zur Geschichte der Musik und des Theaters am Hofe zu Dresden* (Dresden, 1861-62), II, 115; Oscar Teuber, *Geschichte des Prages Theaters* (Prague, 1883-88), I, 116-17; Friedrich Walter, *Geschichte des Theaters und der Musik am kurpfälzischen Hofe* ("Forschungen zur Geschichte Mannheims und der Pfalz," Vol. I [Leipzig, 1898]), pp. 83-84; and Hans Heinrich Borcherdt, "Geschichte der italienischen Oper in Breslau," *Zeitschrift des Vereins für Geschichte Schlesiens*, XLIV (1910), 31, 48.

[66]Fürstenau, II, 160.

[67]See Alessandro Gandini et al., *Cronistoria dei teatri di Modena dal 1539 al 1871* (Modena, 1873), I, 55-56; intermezzi of Lisetta and Astrobolo ([Bologna, 1719]); *La preziosa ridicola, ed il cuoco del Marchese del Bosco* (Macerata, 1720); and casts for intermezzi mentioned but not printed in the following libretti: [Silvio Stampiglia], *La Partenope* (Modena, 1720); Apostolo Zeno, *Temistocle* (Padua, 1721); [Girolamo Gigli], *La fede ne' tradimenti* (Faenza, 1723); and Francesco Silvani, *Il Tolomeo re d'Egitto* (Venice, [1724]).

[68]Italian *opere serie* were not introduced in that country until 1736; see R[obert]-Aloys Mooser, *Annales de la musique et des musiciens en Russie au XVIIIme siècle* (Geneva, 1948-51), I, 52-53, 65ff., *et passim* for details of the Erminis' Moscow season.

[69]See Emilio Cotarelo y Mori, *Orígenes y establecimiento de la ópera en España hasta 1800* (Madrid, 1917), pp. 87-88, 119-20, 131-32.

[70]See Sesto Fassini, *Il melodramma italiano a Londra nella prima metà del settecento* (Turin, 1914), pp. 15-18. The text of this "intermede" seems to be a much-altered translation of the first comic scene between Blesa and Floro in Silvio Stampiglia, *Mario fuggitivo* (Vienna, 1708), pp. 17-20.

[71]The two had appeared together in intermezzi as early as 1730; see Chiappelli, p. 122, and the intermezzi mentioned in Pietro Metastasio, *Catone in Utica* (Livorno, 1730). They performed two pieces of their London season during the autumn of 1735 in Lucca; see Almachilde Pellegrini, *Spettacoli lucchesi nei secoli XVII-XIX* ("Memorie e documenti per servire alla storia di Lucca," Vol. XIV, Pt. 1 [Lucca, 1914]), pp. 403-404.

[72]See intermezzi of Dorina and Nibbio, Grilletta and Porsugnacco, Larinda and Vanesio, Moschetta and Grullo, and Serpilla and Bacocco listed in Appendix A.

[73]*General History of Music*, IV, 412.

[74]*Ibid.*, p. 459.

[75]Erich H. Müller, *Angelo und Pietro Mingotti: Ein Beitrag zur Geschichte der Oper im XVIII. Jahrhundert* (Dresden, 1917), *passim.*

[76] *Ibid., Anhang* II.

[77]See Wiel, pp. 93, 105, 106, 107, 110, 134, 137. Gaggiotti seems to have been the most experienced of the Mingottis' intermezzo singers; before 1737, when he joined their troupe, his name appears in libretti for intermezzo performances in S. Giovanni in Persiceto (1725 and 1729), Cento (1725 and 1726), Bologna (1728), Vicenza (1728), Venice (1729 and 1731), Mantua (1732), Genoa (1734), and Pisa (1737).

[78]See Müller, *Anhang* II, Nos. 89, 65, 127-28, 119-22, 107.

[79]Müller, p. 102.

[80]Müller, pp. 104-109; Th[omas] Overskou, *Den danske skueplads, i dens hisorie, fra de første spor af danske skuespil indtil vor tid* (Copenhagen, 1854-76), I, 156-57, 169-71, 184-86, 203-205.

[81]Libretti for the troupe's intermezzo performances in Vienna, Leipzig, and Brunswick are recorded by Oscar George Theodore Sonneck, *Catalogue of Opera Librettos Printed before 1800* (Washington, D.C., 1914), I, 224, 399, 615, 690-91, 995, 1108; and Robert Haas, "Beitrag zur Geschichte der Oper in Prag und Dresden," *Neues Archiv für Sächsische Geschichte und Altertumskunde,* XXXVII (1916), 78.

[82]E[lisabeth] Mentzel, *Geschichte der Schauspielkunst in Frankfurt a.M. von ihren Anfängen bis zum Eröffnung des städtischen Komödienhauses: Ein Beitrag zur deutschen kultur- und Theatergeschichte* ("Archiv für Frankfurts Geschichte und Kunst," New Series, Vol. IX [Frankfurt a.M., 1882]), p. 197.

[83]See Hubertus Bolongaro-Crevenna, *L'arpa festante: Die münchner Oper 1651-1825 von den Anfängen bis zum "Freyschützen"* (Munich, 1963), p. 232; Harald Kunz, "Höfisches Theater in Wien zur Zeit der Maria Teresa," *Jahrbuch der Gesellschaft für Wiener Theaterforschung,* 1953-54 (1958), 77-78; Teuber, I, 191-93; Arnold Schering, *Johann Sebastian Bach und das Musikleben Leipzigs im 18. Jahrhundert* ("Musikgeschichte Leipzigs," Vol. III [Leipzig, 1941]), pp. 280-81; Müller, p. 89; and Fürstenau, II, 260.

[84]Erich Rosendahl, *Geschichte der Hoftheater in Hannover und Braunschweig* ("Niedersächsische Hausbücherei," Vol. I [Hannover, 1927]), p. 18.

[85]"... elle a été très applaudie, par l'execution précise & vive, malgré le peu de convenance qu'on y trouve avec nos Opera ordinaires." June, 1729, p. 1223. On this occasion, the intermezzo itself furnished the *pièce de résistance*; each of its three parts was followed by a typically French entertainment composed of ballet, choruses, solo singing, and instrumental music that, in the words of the *Mercure* (p. 1224), "sert d'Intermede." [!]

[86]*Mercure de France,* June, 1729, p. 1403.

[87]*Mercure de France,* October, 1746, pp. 160-62.

[88]See J[ob] F[ranz] Lobstein, *Beiträge zur Geschichte der Musik im Elsass und besonders in Strassburg, von der ältesten bis auf die neueste Zeit* (Strasbourg, 1840), p. 132.

[89]For details of the Bambini troupe's repertory and performances in Paris, see articles in the *Mercure de France* between September, 1752, and April, 1754; Durey de Noinville, I, 273-320; J[acques]-G[abriel] Prod'homme, "La Musique à Paris, de 1753 à 1757, d'après un manuscrit de la bibliothèque de Munich." *Sammelbände der Internationalen Musikgesellschaft,* VI (1904-1905), 570-75; and Lionel de La Laurencie, "La Grande saison italienne de 1752: Les Bouffons," *S. I. M. revue musicale,* VIII (1912), No. 6, 18-33; No. 7, 13-22.

[90]See, for example, L[ionel] de la Laurencie, "Deux imitateurs français des Bouffons: Blavet et Dauvergne," *L'Année musicale,* II (1912), 65-125.

[91]See his *Drammaturgia.... accresciuta e continuata fino all'anno MDCCLV* (Venice, 1755), coll. 594, 600, 831; and Quadrio, III, ii, 506.

[92]"Grande si è moltissimo volte la sollecitudine," che s'impiega, in congiunture di recite d'Opere, per la scelta degl'Intermedj, che si frappongono, pel necessario interrompimento de la troppa serietà degli Argomenti, che si producono ne le Scene. A fine dunque di facilitare l'uso de' medesimi, ho giudicato bene, di farne una raccolta assai copiosa, con avere a tal' effetto uniti moltissimi manuscritti, eziandio forestieri, ed aver procurato il restante, di cui sia venuta la notizia, d'aver' ottenuto piu grido ne le Città principali d'Italia, ne' Teatri de le quali con applauso universale furono quelli rappresentati." [Foll. 2-2'.]

[93]See his *Comedie, e rime in lingua milanese* (Milan, 1701), I, 149-249, 250-394.

[94]See his *Nvova aggivnta di varie poesie.... sì in lingua milanese, come eroiche* (Venice, 1701), pp. 63-73.

[95]See his *Poesie miscellanee* (Milan, 1729), II, 117-221.

[96]*La gallina perduta,* identified by Quadrio, III, ii, 505, as the work of Francesco Ercolani belongs to this category, as do all the other intermezzi of the collection in which more than two characters figure, with the exception of those of Carissimo, Dirindina, and Liscione, written for—if not performed with—Domenico Scarlatti's *Ambleto* at Rome's Teatro Capranica during the carnival of 1715; See Ralph Kirkpatrick, *Domenico Scarlatti* (Princeton, N.J., 1953), pp. 63-64; and below, p. 196, note 49.

[97]Use of the word "foreign," of course, may be in reference to Amsterdam, the professed city of publication.

[98]See, for example, *La rinovata Camilla regina de' Volsci* (Rome, 1698), *Il trionfo di Cammilla regina de' Volsci* (Parma, 1698), *Il trionfo di Cammilla regina de Volsci* (Ferrara, 1699), *Li* [sic] *trionfo di Camilla regina de' Volsci* (Lucca, 1702), *Amore per amore* (Bologna, 1709), and *Le fede in cimento, ò sia La Camilla regina de' Volsci* (Bologna, 1719).

[99]See Appendix A.

CHAPTER III

[1]"Per dar tempo alle operazioni, e mutazioni dell'apparenze, e per maggiormente compiacerti, si sono aggiunte dopo l'impressione, le seguenti arie, e le Scene facete di Serpillo, Paggiotto di Corte." P. 75. An additional scene, between the characters Vespina and Zelto "per la scena ultima," [p. 80] is similar to the fourth comic episode of Lesbina and Adolfo added to Zeno's *Odoardo* for its performance at Naples in 1700 with music of Alessandro Scarlatti.

[2]His *Dramatick Works* (London, 1743), p. 247.

[3]"Quì si deve rappresentare l'ultimo Intermezzo per dar tempo all'azione di Aldrico." P. 52.

[4]"Il fine dell'Autore fù di formare una Tragedia in Musica col fine veramente Tragico (novità non più veduta, almeno sulle Scene d'Italia) e di avere il preggio d'essere il primo a farti sortir dal Teatro con le lagrime,...

Vi è stato in altro Teatro in qualche parte variato i fine, per non renderlo totalmente funesto; come ancora in questo con non poca pena di chì l'hà diretto.... come altresì vi sono dovute ponere le parti Buffe, mà in modo, che nõ interrompino il Drama, mà solo minorino la mestizia con un poco di allegria." (Naples, 1718), pp. 5-6.

[5]"Prelude," *Harvard Dictionary of Music* (Cambridge, Mass., 1953), p. 597.

[6]"Se ritroverai il presente Drama in qualche parte diverso dal suo primo Originale, rappresentato nel passato Autunno in Venezia, non l'attribuire ad ardire di chi ebbe la cura di guidarlo; ma solo al genio della Città, in cui si rappresenta, essendo stato necessario l'intricarvi le Parte Buffe, e rendere quelle in qualche parte necessarie per l'intrico del Drama,... per renderlo secondo il costume di questa Città." [Fol. 3'].

[7]"Intermezzo," *Grove's Dictionary of Music and Musicians* (5th ed.; London, 1954), IV, 516.

[8]One of the first Neapolitan libretti to employ this terminology was Silvio Stampiglia, *Partenope* (Naples, 1722), containing "intermezzi" of Eurilla and Beltramme.

[9]See Carl de Palma, *L'Orismene overo Dalli sdegni l'amore* (Naples, 1726).

[10]See, for example, *Achille in Sciro* (Prague, [1727]), [Apostolo Zeno], *Lucio Vero* (Macerata, 1728), and [Girolamo Gigli], *La fede ne' tradimenti* (Bologna, [1732]).

[11]".... non hanno mai avuto connessione veruna col Drama, a cui furono accoppiati, potendosi or tralasciare, or ripigliare a piacere,... tanto più che si sono sempre stampati a parte, e che possono a qual sia soggetto addattarsi." *Le glorie della poesia, e della musica contenute nell'esatta notitia de teatri della città di Venezia* (Venice, [1730?]), pp. 149-50. (But see above, p. 38.)

[12](Princeton University Dissertation, 1967), I, v.

[13]See his *L'Epulone: Opera melo-dramatica esposta, con le prose morali-critiche* (Venice, 1675), p. 186.

[14]In *La bellezza della volgar poesia* (Rome, 1700); for a translation of the relevant passage, see Freeman, I, 21-22.

[15]See the intermezzi of Dorisbe and Lido included in [Apostolo Zeno], *L'Engelberta* (Milan, [1708]), pp. 69-75; those of Vespetta and Lesbo printed with [Francesco di Lemene and Pier Jacopo Martello], *Lo scherno degli dei* (Bologna, [1708]), pp. 19-22, 33-36, 42-46; *Pimpinone, e Vespetta*, bound with [Francesco Silvani], *La fede tradita, e vendicata* (Ferrara, [1711]); and an untitled version of the latter intermezzi contained in *La costanza in amor vince l'inganno* (Rome, [1711]), pp. 21-24, 41-44, 65-68. Performances of unconnected intermezzi at Vienna began in 1714 with those of Dorimena and Tuberone, published with Apostolo Zeno, *L'Atenaide* (Vienna, n.d.), pp. 35-39, 63-68; the same text, reprinted at Hamburg in 1719, was the first independent Italian intermezzo performed in that city (see Hellmuth Christian Wolff, *Die Barockoper in Hamburg* [Wolfenbüttel, 1957], I, 116).

[16]"Quest'Opera, che tante volte è comparsa in diversi Teatri d'Italia, si fa vedere adesso in Roma con qualche piccola mutazione, e giunta di Ariette colle quali ha stimato di ravvivarla, e meglio adattarla all'uso d'oggidì il suo medesimo primo Autore. Egli, per comandamento del Generoso Personaggio, che la fa rappresentare,... ci ha tramezzate due Parti ridicole affatto sciolte dal nodo del Dramma (siccome oggi si pratica nelle Scene di Venezia, ed altrove) colle quali s'intrecciano gli stessi intermedj, di piacevoli invenzioni di danze, e comparse, al maggior divertimento composti." Pp. 3-4.

[17]The text is printed together with that of *Astarto* (Rome, 1715), pp. 31-35, 57-60; but the characters of the intermezzo do not appear in the opera itself.

[18]See Lione Allacci, *Drammaturgia.... accresciuta e continuata fino all'anno MDCCLV* (Venice, 1755), coll. 151, 470. The opera libretto contains an imprimatur dated May, 1715.

[19]"Questi trè Intermezzi sone stati ricavati da varie Scene dell'Abdolomino Dramma rappresentato in Napoli." *Ircano innamorato* (Ferrara, 1715), [fol. A1ʳ].

[20]*Drammaturgia*, col. 470.

[21]Unfortunately, libretti for some of these performances seem not to have been preserved, or perhaps were not printed at all. Data in Table 7 from sources other than libretti are enclosed in brackets and their source identified.

[22]But see p. 38.

[23]"Ora come sì fatti Intermedj in musica si sogliono alla maniera distendere, e rappresentare, che far si suole de' Melodrammi, sarebbe qui un gittar l'opera, se noi volessimo in altre parole allargarci. Basterà qui brevemente avvertire, che quanto allo stile, ed a versi le stesse regole in questi camminano, che nell'altre poesie per Musica.

Quanto alla divisione de' medesimi Intermedj in Atti, o in Parte, o in Iscene, ciascuno fino al presente ha fatto ciò, che gli è caduto in capriccio di fare. Non sarebbe, se non da lodare, se a questi pure si procurasse di dare proporzionevole e giusta forma." *Dalla storia e ragione d'ogni poesia* (Bologna and Milan, 1739-52), III, 505-506.

[24] According to Antonio Groppo, "Catalogo purgatissimo di tutti li drammi per musica recitatisi ne' teatri di Venezia dall'anno MDCXXXVII sin oggi [1767].... accresciuto di tutti gli scenarj, varie edizioni, aggiunte a drammi, e intermedi con la notizia di alcuni drammi nuovamente scoperti, e di altre rare particolarità," Venice, Biblioteca Marciana, MS Cl. VII, No. 2326, p. 162, where the date of the opera itself is incorrectly stated to be 1709.

[25] Freeman, I, 154.

[26] See above, Table 5.

[27] See Pietro Toldo, *L'OEuvre de Molière et sa fortune en Italie* (Turin, 1910) pp. 431-32, for a description of the alterations effected to shorten the text for these later editions.

[28] "Catalogo purgatissimo," pp. 259, 263.

[29] See Alessandro Gandini *et al.*, *Cronistoria dei teatri di Modena dal 1539 al 1871* (Modena, 1873), I, 51-53; and Taddeo Wiel, *I teatri musicali veneziani del settecento* (Venice, 1897), p. 58.

[30] See [Pietro Metastasio], *Siface* (Naples, 1734), pp. 58-72.

[31] *Cola mal maritato* (Venice, 1721); reprinted in *Raccolta copiosa d'intermedj* ([Milan], 1723), I, 103.

[32] See, for example, the intermezzi based upon comedies of Molière discussed below.

[33] *Raccolta copiosa d'intermedj*, I, 312.

[34] (Venice, [1724]), p. 7.

[35] See his *Della tragedia antica e moderna* (Rome, 1715), p. 85.

[36] See the intermezzi of Melinda and Tiburzio printed in the *Raccolta copiosa d'intermedj*, I, 86-102.

[37] The comparative brevity of "Amor prepara" is probably explained by the fact that it is a parody (or quotation) of a contemporary cantata aria.

[38] *Cf.* specimens of *dialogo laconico* in Andrea Perrucci, *Dell'arte rappresentativa premeditata, ed all'improviso* (Naples, 1699), pp. 228-36; reprinted in Enzo Petraccone, *La commedia dell'arte: Storia, tecnica, scenari* (Naples, 1927), pp. 96-105.

[39] *Grullo and Moschetta* (London, 1737), p. 10.

[40] *Le Bourgeois gentil-homme* (London, 1737), p. 2. Contemporary translations such as this, and those on the following pages are generally free and frequently even inaccurate, but they capture the spirit of the original better than a modern English rendering.

[41] *Pourceaugnac and Grilletta* (London, 1737), p. 16.

[42]See Toldo, pp. 202-206.

[43]*Les Précieuses ridicules* I.x.

[44]For a study of Molière's indebtedness to Italian improvised comedy, see Louis Moland, *Molière et la comédie italienne* (2nd ed.; Paris 1867).

[45]*Cf.* K[athleen] M[arguerite] Lea, *Italian Popular Comedy: A Study of the commedia dell'arte, 1560-1620 with Special Reference to the English Stage* (Oxford, 1934), I, 187.

[46]*L'Ulderica* (Naples, 1729), p. 62.

[47]First published with his *Il pescatore fortunato principe d'Ischia* (Bologna, [1716]), pp. 22-24, 34-36.

[48]Printed with [Apostolo Zeno and Pietro Pariati], *Costantino* (Vienna, [1716]), pp. [79]-96.

[49]A notice for an intermezzo with these characters appears in the libretto for Domenico Scarlatti's setting of [Apostolo Zeno and Pietro Pariati], *Ambleto* (Rome, 1715), but the intermezzo itself seems not to have been printed; instead, a pair of *Intermedj pastorali da rappresentarsi nella sala de' sig.*[ri] *Capranica nel drama dell'Ambleto* (Elpina and Silvano) were apparently substituted on this occasion. Ralph Kirkpatrick, *Domenico Scarlatti* (Princeton, N.J., 1953), pp. 63-64, speculates that the Roman censor may have insisted on the substitution, a reasonable assumption in view of the story's off-color humor; however, according to a libretto in the Collezione Carvalhaes of the Biblioteca Musicale S. Cecilia the piece *was* performed in Rome during the carnival of 1729 at the Teatro Valle with the play *Il Ruggiero rè di Sicilia*. Other editions of the text were published under the titles *La Dirindina* (Lucca, 1715), and *Il maestro di musica geloso* (Milan, 1732); a note in the former states that "la Musica eccellente di questa Farsetta è del Signor Domenico Scarlatti, che a tutti volentieri ne farà comodo."

[50]Concerning boasts of fecundity by dramatic poets about this time, see Marcello, p. 7— and the prefaces to many of their own libretti.

[51]*The Master of the Opera* (London, 1737), pp. 10-13.

[52]Both of these similes—together with some even more outrageous ones—are listed in Marcello's satire (see p. 10).

[53]*The Master of the Opera*, pp. 24-25.

[54]*Raccolta copiosa d'intermedj*, I, 31.

[55]*Ibid*, pp. 404-405.

[56]*Melinda, e Tiburzio* (Venice, 1721), part 1.

[57]*La preziosa ridicola*, part 3.

[58]See the second of their two intermezzi printed with Apostolo Zeno, *L'Atenaide* (Vienna, [1714]).

[59]*Raccolta copiosa d'intermedj,* I, 85.

[60]".... le parole della prima aria di Zaffira, nella Scena ultima dell'Atto Secondo, e proprio quella, che dice *Ogni Donna è pazza, e stolta, &c.,* sono d'un Degnissimo Autore, e vi si son poste per compiacere à chi le canta." [Vincenzo Grimani] *et al., Agrippina* (Naples, 1713), [p. 6]. The singer, Santa Marchesini, apparently exercised good judgment. This verse is included in at least two later editions of the text, although several other arias of the Neapolitan original were replaced in these versions; *cf. Intermezzi comici musicali* [of Zaffira and Lesbo] (Florence, 1717) and the intermezzi contained in [Francesco Silvani *et al.*], *La fede tradita, e vendicata* (Turin, [1719]), pp. 24-28, 48-52, 67-72.

[61]The *Raccolta copiosa d'intermedj* preserves the text of an edition printed before 1723 that apparently has been lost.

[62]In the Table, "X" denotes inclusion of the text in essentially unaltered form; "O" indicates considerable alteration.

[63]See untitled editions of the intermezzi between Pollastrella and Parpagnacco (Bologna, 1724), (Parma, 1733), and [Stuttgart, 1737]; intermezzi of Tilla and Pancrazio published as *Il vecchio pazzo in amore* (Venice, 1731) and *Il vecchio capricioso in amore* (Venice, 1732); and *Il giocatore* (Potsdam, [1748]).

[64]*Cf.* [Antonio Salvi], *Berenice regina di Egitto, o vero Le gare di amore, e di politica* (Rome, 1718), p. 65.

[65]See, for example, the editions of Bologna, [1739]; Venice, [1740]; Modena, [1741]; Venice, [1741]; Gorizia, 1741; Venice, [1742?]; Bologna, [1743]; Padua, [1747]; Venice, 1748; Potsdam, 1748; and Bassano, n.d. It might be argued that substitution of this text was incidental to the borrowing of Pergolesi's *music* for it; all preserved scores of *La serva padrona* containing the subsitute duet do, in fact, employ Pergolesi's setting. Yet Groppo, "Catalogo purgatissimo," p. 254, records that for this intermezzo's performance at Venice in 1740 the music of "Per te ho io nel core" was by Vinci.

[66]It is also possible, of course, that the intermezzo's arranger borrowed the music of Pergolesi's aria and altered its text slightly, perhaps with parodistic intent.

CHAPTER IV

[1]Edward Downes, "The Operas of Johann Christian Bach as a Reflection of the Dominant Trends in Opera Seria 1750-1780" (Harvard dissertation, 1958), Vol. I, has been an invaluable guide in this undertaking.

[2]*Some Observations Made in Travelling through France, Italy, &c. in the Years 1720, 1721, and 1722* (London, 1730), I, 85.

[3]"Ces bouffons pleurent, rient à gorge déployée, se démènent, font toutes sortes de pantomimes, sans jamais s'écarter de la mesure d'un demi-quart de seconde." *Lettres familières sur l'Italie* (Paris, 1931), II, 363.

[4]"Da kann man hören, Sieger schlagen, Enten schnarren, Frösche quacken, und bald wird man auch darinnen die Flöhe niesen und das Gras wachsen hören." *Historish-kritische Beyträge zur Aufnahme der Musik* (Berlin, 1754-62), I, 532-33.

[5]See, for example, the second comic scene between Stellina and Nesso in Apostolo Zeno, *L'Eumene* (Palermo, 1706), and [Bernardo Saddumene], *La contadina* (Parma, [1734]).

[6]See the intermezzi of Slapina and Barilotto in Antonio Salvi, *Lucio Papirio* (Rome, 1714), pp. 73-74.

[7][Vincenzo Grimani et. al.], *Agrippina* (Naples, 1713), p. 63; see also the third comic scene of Domenico Sarri, "Lucio Vero," Naples, Biblioteca del Conservatorio S. Pietro a Majella, MS I.6.25, foll. 154-55', in which Quinzio "da don[n]a" sings an aria "da falzetto."

[8]*Italian Popular Comedy: A Study in the commedia dell'arte, 1560-1620 with Special Reference to the English Stage* (Oxford, 1934), I, 194-95.

[9]"Replichi quanto vuole, sino à mostrar d'affogarsi." Naples, Biblioteca del Conservatorio S. Pietro a Majella, MS 31.3.33 [fol. 183'].

[10]See, for example, Manfred Bukofzer, *Music in the Baroque Era* (New York, 1947), p. 245.

[11]"The Operas of Johann Christian Bach," I, 204.

[12]See, for example, the aria "Consiglio a noi consiglio," quoted above, p. 78.

[13]*Raccolta copiosa d'intermedj* ([Milan], 1723), I, 403.

[14]Quoted above, pp. 84-85.

[15]"*Incalzeranno, e lenteranno* il Tempo, e ciò particolarmente ne *Duetti* a motivo de *Lazi*,..." *Il teatro alla moda* [Venice, ca. 1720], p. 54.

[16]For a description of some of these formulas see Edward Downes, "*Secco* Recitative in Early Classical Opera Seria (1720-80)," *Journal of the American Musicological Society*, XIV (1961), 60-61; see also Sven Hostrup Hansell, "The Cadence in 18th-Century Recitative," *The Musical Quarterly*, LIV (1968), 228-48.

[17]"Opera without Drama: Currents of Change in Italian Opera, 1675 to 1725, and the Roles Played Therein by Zeno, Caldara, and Others" (Princeton University Dissertation, 1967), I, 196-200, 204.

[18]See Max Schneider, "Die Begleitung des Secco-Rezitativs um 1750," *Gluck Jahrbuch*, III (1917), 90-91.

[19]*L'armonico pratico al cimbalo* (Venice, 1708), p. 91; trans. Frank S. Stillings, *The Practical Harmonist at the Harpsichord* ("Music Theory Translation Series," Vol. I [New Haven, 1963]), p. 79.

[20]See "The Operas of Johann Christian Bach," III, 90. The majority of non da capo arias found in both intermezzi and *opere serie* are cast in binary form, *i.e.*, they are da capo arias without a second part.

[21]"Sino a tanto si fa *il Ritornello* dell'*Arie* si ritirerà il VIRTUOSO *verso le Scene*, *prenderà Tabacco, dirà agli amici, che non è in voce, ch'è raffredato, &c....*" *Il teatro alla moda*, p. 24.

[22]See Freeman, "Opera without Drama," I, 215-22, for summaries of various eighteenth-century aria categorizations and proof that for Antonio Caldara, at least, specific categories of texts did not imply specific musical settings.

[23]"PArti Buffe pretenderanno l'*Onorario* eguale alle *prime Parti serie*, e tanto più se nel cantare si servisero *d'Intonazione, Passi, Trilli, Cadenze, &c. da Parte seria.*" *Il teatro alla moda*, p. 54.

[24]As in the case of arias, binary form accounts for the majority of non da capo types.

[25]"The Operas of Johann Christian Bach," I, 427-28, 430.

[26]*The Gamester* (London, 1736), pp. 8-9.

[27]*Ibid.*, pp. 22-23.

[28]*A General History of Music from the Earliest Ages to the Present Period* (London, 1776-89), IV, 277.

[29]*Ibid.*

[30]*A General History of Music*, IV, 224.

[31]It is, of course, impossible to generalize about the *size* of the operatic orchestra over so long a period. Information from secondary sources, moreover, is virtually nonexistent to formulate such a generalization for Italian theaters. The 91 orchestras whose constitution and strength are tabulated in Adam Carse, *The Orchestra in the XVIIIth Century* (Cambridge, 1940), pp. 18-27, are predominately German court ensembles; and Ulisse Prota-Giurleo, *La grande orchestra del Teatro S. Carlo nel settecento* (Naples, 1927), the only major study of Italian archival material, is unfortunately devoted to one of the few important opera houses operating during the first half of the eighteenth century in which intermezzi were never performed.

[32]Freeman, "Opera without Drama," I, 246-47.

[33]*Der Operntypus Johann Adolf Hasses und seine textlichen Grundlagen* ("Berliner Beiträge zur Musikwissenschaft," Vol. II [Leipzig, 1925]), p. 29.

[34]See the duet "Che caldo mi viene" from his intermezzi of Larinda and Vanesio.

[35]See above, p. 102.

[36]See, for example, Monteverdi's directions for the execution of pizzicato in his *Il combattimento di Tancredi e di Clorinda* of 1624.

[37]See, for example, the arias "Esser vile, e far da bravo" from intermezzi of Palandrana and Zamberlucco, Bologna, Biblioteca universitaria, MS 646 (Vol. IV), foll. 175-76; and "Ic bin lipaber" [*sic*] from Alessandro Scarlatti's comic scenes for *Tigrane*, Naples, Biblioteca del Conservatorio S. Pietro a Majella, MS 31.3.33, [foll. 132-33$'$].

[38]See Frank Walker, "Two Centuries of Pergolesi Forgeries and Misattributions, *Music and Letters*, XXX (1949), 313-15; and C[harles] L. Cudworth, "Notes on the Instrumental Works Attributed to Pergolesi," *Music and Letters*, XXX (1949), 321-22.

[39]At the performance of *La serva padrona* by the *Bouffons* at Paris in 1752 with the pantomime ballet *Acis et Galathée*, for example, Pergolesi's intermezzo was prefaced by an overture of Telemann; see the *Mercure de France*, September, 1752, p. 169.

[40]*Cf.*, for example, the versions of Hasse's *La serva scaltra overo La moglie a forza* (Dorilla and Balanzone) contained in Monte Cassino, Biblioteca dell'Abbazia, MS 124-G-29; and Rome, Biblioteca Casanatense, MS 2506 (0.II.104).

[41]See, for example, the final comic scene of Rosicca and Morano in Francesco Feo, *Siface*, Naples, Biblioteca del Conservatorio S. Pietro a Majella, MS 32.3.27, [fol. 123].

[42]MS 2507 (0.II.105), foll. 84-85$'$.

CONCLUSION

[1]*Some Observations Made in Travelling through France, Italy, &c. in the Years 1720, 1721, and 1722* (London, 1730), I, 85.

[2]" ... ce mêlange monstreueux de sérieux & de comique outré ... révolte la raison. Figurez-vous voir représenter la mort de César & Pourceaugnac, dont on donneroit un Acte de chacun alternativement." *Lettre sur le mechanisme de l'opéra italian* (Paris, 1756), p. 48.

[3]" ... si déplacé dans le milieu d'une action tragique, que les deux Pièces se nuisoient mutuellement, & que l'une des deux ne pouvoit jamais intéresser qu'aux depens de l'autre." *Dictionnaire de musique* (Paris, 1768), p. 351.

[4]".... tosto inoltrandosi la corruttela, gli accessorj divennero l'azion principale, si moltiplicarono gli intermedj senza modo nè regola, e lo spettacolo divenne un mostro." (Venice, 1785), I, 330.

[5]See above, p. 3.

[6]See Ulisse Prota-Giurleo, *Il teatro di corte del Palazzo Reale di Napoli* (Naples, 1952), p. 106.

[7]"…. balli speciosissimi, giammai in questa capitale osservati." Quoted in Benedetto Croce, *I teatri di Napoli: Secolo XV-XVIII* (Naples, 1891), p. 320.

[8]See Corrado Ricci, *I teatri di Bologna nei secoli XVII e XVIII* (Bologna, 1888), pp. 460-63.

[9]*Tavola cronologica di tutti li drammi o sia opere in musica recitate alli teatri detti del Falcone, e da S. Agostino da cento anni in addietro* (Genoa, 1771), p. 26.

[10]See Taddeo Wiel, *I teatri musicali veneziani del settecento* (Venice, 1897), pp. 172 ff.

[11]"… les avant-coureurs des Opéras Comiques Italiens." (Paris, 1787), I, 211.

[12]"Indubbiamente, l'opera buffa non è che un intermezzo ampliato." "Origini dell'opera comica," *Rivista musicale italiana*, IV (1897), 421.

[13]"…. la nostra opera buffa non fu che uno sviluppo, un ampliamento degli intermezzi per musica,…" *La scuola musicale di Napoli e i suoi conservatorii* (Naples, 1880-82), IV, 584; nowhere in his *Storia letteraria dell'opera buffa napolitana dalle origini al principio del secolo XIX* (Naples, 1883) does Scherillo make this assertion.

[14]*Music in the Baroque Era* (New York, 1947), p. 244.

[15]*L'opera comica italiana nel '700* (Bari, 1923), I, 27.

[16]See, for example, Homer Ulrich and Paul A. Pisk, *A History of Music and Musical Style* (New York, 1963), pp. 340, 221-22.

[17]Florimo, IV, 34 ff.; for a correction of Florimo's dating of *La Cilla* and notes on some other early Neapolitan *opere buffe*, see Claudio Sartori, "Gli Scarlatti a Napoli: Nuovi contributi," *Rivista musicale italiana, XLVI (1942), 380-90.*

[18]See Wiel, pp. 1-146; and Werner Bollert, *Die Buffoopern Baldassare Galuppis* (Bottrop, 1935), pp. 20-22.

[19]"Ensembles and Finales in 18th Century Italian Opera," *Sammelbände der Internationalen Musikgesellschaft*, XII (1910-11), 112-14.

[20]See Ricci, p. 429.

[21]Buini's name does not appear in the libretto, but [Alessandro Macchiavelli], *Serie cronologica dei drammi recitati sù de' pubblici teatri di Bologna* (Bologna, 1737), p. 74, attributes both text and music of the opera to the Bolognese composer and poet.

[22]*The Master of the Opera* (London, 1737), p. 6.

[23]For a translation see above, pp. 84-85.

[24]See Oscar Sonneck, *Catalogue of Opera Librettos Printed before 1800* (Washington, D.C., 1914), I, 968.

[25]In a version entitled *L'odio vinto dalla costanza*, partly rewritten by Bartolomeo Vitturi; see Lione Allacci, *Drammaturgia.... accresciuta e continuata fino all'anno MDCCLV* (Venice, 1755), col. 569.

[26]Unfortunately, neither the arranger of *Melinda's* text nor its composer are mentioned in the libretto (Venice, 1731), a copy of which is preserved in the Biblioteca Marciana at Venice.

[27]To complete a bibliographer's confusion, the name of Lisetta, heroine of Buini's *opera buffa* is assigned to Melinda's maid, a mute character in the intermezzo.

[28]Much of *Melinda's* dialogue and no fewer than three of its aria texts are, in fact, identical to those of the *opera buffa*, a circumstance that in other dramatic music of the period argues for musical borrowing as well.

[29]The *Urtext* of this duet is Nibbio's aria "Risolva, e le prometto" from the first part of Metastasio's *L'impresario delle Canarie*.

[30]*A Short History of Opera* (2d ed.; New York, 1965), I, 250.

[31]See the cast lists reprinted in Wiel, pp. 166 ff.

[32]For discussion of Galuppi's ensemble finales see Marianne Fuchs, "Die Entwicklung des Finales in der italienischen Opera Buffa vor Mozart" (Vienna Dissertation, 1932), pp. 76-83; and Bollert, pp. 104-109.

[33]Bollert, p. 107.

[34]"Ensembles and Finales in 18th Century Italian Opera," *Sammelbände der Internationalen Musikgesellschaft*, XI (1909-10), 545-46.

APPENDIX

[1]According to Lione Allacci, *Drammaturgia.... accresciuta e continuata fino all'anno MDCCLV* (Venice, 1755), col. 164, this was the title of both the 1708 and 1725 Venetian libretti. Only one, undated libretto with this title seems to have been printed; a copy is preserved in the Collezione Rossi of the Biblioteca Marciana, Venice.

[2]Allacci, col. 290; Antonio Groppo, "Catalogo purgatissimo di tutti li drammi per musica recitatisi ne' teatri di Venezia dall'anno MDCXXXVII sin oggi [1767].... accresciuto di tutti gli scenarj, varie edizioni, aggiunte a drammi, e intermedi con la notizia di alcuni drammi nuovamente scoperti, e di altre rare particolarità," Venice, Biblioteca Marciana, MS Cl. VII, No. 2326, p. 162.

[3]See above, pp. 41-42.

[4]Although Sarri is not named specifically as composer of the intermezzi in the Neapolitan libretto with which they were printed ([Antonio Salvi], *Ginevra principessa di Scozia* [Naples, 1720]), nor in the score of this opera (Naples, Biblioteca del Conservatorio S. Pietro a Majella, MS 32.2.22), another, similar score of the intermezzi alone (Dresden, Sächsische Landesbibliothek, MS. Mus. 2356/F/1) bears Sarri's name.

[5]R[obert]-Aloys Mooser, *Annales de la musique et des musiciens en Russie au XVIIIme siècle* (Geneva, 1948-51), I, 113, 115, 386.

[6]Erich H. Müller, *Angelo und Pietro Mingotti: Ein Beitrag zur Geschichte der Oper im XVIII. Jahrhundert* (Dresden, 1917), pp. 106-107.

[7]Identified in the Vienna, 1747, libretto.

[8]Remo Giazotto, *La musica a Genova* (Genoa, 1951), p. 331.   This intermezzo is *not* listed in the *Tavola cronologica* (Genoa, 1771), as Giazotto claims.

[9]Groppo, p. 230.

[10]Mooser, I, 87, 113, 114, 386.

[11]Almachilde Pellegrini, *Spettacoli lucchesi nei secoli XVII-XIX* ("Memorie e documenti per servire alla storia di Lucca," Vol. XIV, Pt. 1 [Lucca, 1914]), p. 404.

[12]Emilio Cotarelo y Mori, *Orígenes y establecimiento de la opera en España* (Madrid, 1917), p. 135.

[13]Müller, *Mingotti*, p. XXXIII.

[14]*Ibid.*, pp. 104-108.

[15]*Ca.* 1750-60; see Friedrich Walter, *Geschichte des Theaters und der Musik am kurpfälzischen Hofe* ("Forschungen zur Geschichte Mannheims und der Pfalz," Vol. I [Leipzig, 1898]), pp. 146, 365.

[16]Identified in the libretto for Leonardo Leo's setting of *Emira* (Naples, 1735).

[17]See Naples, Biblioteca del Conservatorio S. Pietro a Majella, MS. 28.4.20 and Benedetto Croce, *I teatri di Napoli: Secolo XV-XVIII* (Naples, 1891), p. 309.   The text of these intermezzi is also printed (under the title *La vedova ingegnosa*) in the libretto of Leo's *Emira,* performed at the Teatro San Bartolomeo to celebrate the return of Charles III from Sicily in the summer of 1735, but their composer is not named there.   According to Ulisse Prota-Giurleo, *Il teatro di corte del Palazzo Reale di Napoli* (Naples, 1952), p. 106, Ignazio Prota furnished the intermezzo's music on this occasion, but it seems unlikely that another composer would have reset Mariani's text so soon after its first appearance at the same theater.   Unfortunately, the music of *La vedova ingegnosa* is lacking in the score of Leo's *Emira* at the Naples Conservatory (MS 28.4.21), making comparison with Sellitti's setting impossible.   Francesco Caffarelli has confused the problem of authorship further by publishing (Rome, [1963?]) an

anonymous manuscript in the Copenhagen Royal Library that contains elements of Sellitti's music for this intermezzo as the work of Giovanni Battista Pergolesi.

[18]Oscar Teuber, *Geschichte des Prager Theaters von den Anfängen des Schauspielwesens bis auf die neueste Zeit* (Prague, 1883-88), I, 191-92.

[19]Arnold Schering, *Johann Sebastian Bach und das Musikleben Leipzigs im 18. Jahrhundert* ("Musikgeschichte Leipzigs," Vol. III [Leipzig, 1941]), p 281; Robert Haas, "Beitrag zur Geschichte der Oper in Prag und Dresden," *Neues Archiv für Sächsische Geschichte und Altertumskunde*, XXXVII (1916), 78.

[20]Haas, p. 78.

[21]Müller, *Mingotti*, pp. 104-108.

[22]*Ca.* 1750-60; see Walter, pp. 145-46, 365.

[23]Haas, p. 78.

[24]See above, pp. 41-42.

[25]Pietro Toldo, *L'OEuvre de Molière et sa fortune en Italie* (Turin, 1910), p. 431.

[26]With the characters named Lisetta and Bordigone.

[27]Alberto Chiappelli, *Storia del teatro in Pistoia dalle origini alla fine del sec. XVIII* (Pistoia, 1913), pp. 119-20.

[28]Walter, pp. 83-84.

[29]Giazotto, p. 332.

[30]Mooser, I, 113, 115, 386.

[31]Only the characters' names and cast are mentioned in the libretto of the opera with which the intermezzo was performed; see Pietro Metastasio *et al.*, *L'Issipile* (n.p., [1749]).

[32]Allacci, col. 129.

[33]See "Vecchio avaro, intermezzi alla verità in cimento di Vivaldi" [Venice, 1720], Monte Cassino, Biblioteca dell'Abbazia, MS 124-I-4.

[34]C. Cinelli, *Memorie cronistoriche del teatro di Pesaro dall'anno 1637 al 1897* (Pesaro, 1898), p. 23.

[35]Pellegrini, p. 341.

[36]Mooser, I, 113, 114, 386.

[37]Ascension.

[38]Summer.

[39]Fall.

[40]Chiappelli, pp. 122, 210.

[41]Between 1733 and 1735; see Mooser, I, 112, 113, 116, 387.

[42]Pellegrini, p. 404.

[43]Groppo, p. 263.

[44]Erich H. Müller, "Zum Repertoir der hamburger Oper von 1718 bis 1750" *Archiv für Musikwissenschaft,* VII (1925), 332.

[45]Müller, *Mingotti,* p. 72; Haas, p. 78.

[46]Haas, p. 78.

[47]Müller, *Mingotti,* p. 124.

[48]Walter, pp. 145, 365.

[49]Müller, *Mingotti,* pp. XXXIV, XXXVI.

[50]*Ibid.,* pp. 104-108.

[51]Haas, p. 78.

[52]Allacci, col. 121.

[53]Although not specifically attributed to this composer in the libretto of the opera with which it was printed (Hasse's setting of [Apostolo Zeno and Pietro Pariati], *L'Astarto* [Naples, 1726]), the intermezzo's music was also likely by Hasse.

[54]Giuseppe Sorge, *I teatri di Palermo nei secoli XVI-XVIII-XVIII: Saggio storico* (Palermo, 1926), p. 345.

[55]Mooser, I, 113, 115, 386.

[56]See Allacci, col. 470; and above pp. 68-69.

[57]Groppo, p. 208.

[58]Allacci, col. 470; [Allessandro Macchiavelli], *Serie cronologica dei drammi recitati sù de' pubblici teatri di Bologna dall'anno di nostra salute 1600 sino al corrente 1737* (Bologna, 1737), p. 77.

[59]Groppo, pp. 221, 224.

[60] *Ibid.*, p. 225

[61] Mooser, I, 53, 76, 368.

[62] Identified in the score, "Intermedi dell'opera seconda di S. Casciano," Rome, Biblioteca Apostolica Vaticana, Codex Barb. lat. 4231, foll. 151-86'.

[63] In an expanded version of the text divided into 3 *azioni* of 3 intermezzi each.

[64] Alfred Loewenberg, *Annals of Opera: 1597-1940* (2nd ed; Geneva, 1955), col. 181.

[65] *Ibid.*

[66] Groppo, p. 258.

[67] Frank Walker, "Goldoni and Pergolesi," *Monthly Musical Record*, LXXX (1950), 204.

[68] Müller, *Mingotti*, p. VIII.

[69] Haas, pp. 78-79.

[70] Teuber, I, 191-92.

[71] Cotarelo y Mori, p. 131.

[72] Friedrich Walter, *Das Archiv und Bibliothek des Grossh. Hof- und Nationaltheaters in Mannheim* (Leipzig, 1899), II, 214.

[73] Giuseppe Radiciotti, *G. B. Pergolesi: Vita, opere ed influenza su l'arte* (Rome, 1910), p. 205.

[74] Schering, p. 281.

[75] Haas, p. 79.

[76] Oscar George Theodore Sonneck, *Catalogue of Opera Librettos Printed before 1800* (Washington, D.C., 1914), I, 691.

[77] Mooser, I, 238, 239, 246.

[78] Cotarelo y Mori, p. 225.

[79] Walter, *Geschichte des Theaters*, pp. 145, 365.

[80] Müller, *Mingotti*, pp. 107-108.

[81] Although not specifically named as composer of these intermezzi in the libretto for his setting of *Ezio*, with which they were printed on this occasion, it is reasonably certain that Hasse was responsible for their music from the fact that the text of subsequent editions bearing his name is virtually identical to that of the first.

[82]With the female character called Dorilla.

[83]Identified in the Hamburg, 1746, libretto.

[84]Mooser, I, 53, 77, 371.

[85]Cinelli, p. 30.

[86]With the female character named Madama Giandini.

[87]Mooser, I, 238, 239, 245.

[88]*Ibid.*, 255.

[89]Müller, *Mingotti*, pp. 106-107.

[90]José Subirá, *El teatro del Real Palacio* ("Monografías del Instituto Espagñol de Musicología," Vol. IV [Madrid, 1950]), p. 43.

[91]This text was originally published (Venice, 1707) as the first of three *azioni* collectively entitled *Melissa;* the *azioni* consisted of three intermezzi each, and bore the subtitles *Melissa schernita, Melissa vendicata* and *Melissa contenta.* All three *azioni* were revived at Bologna in 1708, the second was heard at Verona in 1712, and a two-part pasticcio version consisting of the third intermezzi of *Melissa schernita* and *Melissa contenta* was performed at Bologna in 1716. The first *azione,* however, seems to have enjoyed many more revivals than the others of the set; the latter are distinguished from *Melissa schernita* by the presence of a second female character (Grilletta), sung by the interpreter of *Melissa* (the two women never appear onstage together).

[92]Identified in Dresden, Sächsische Landesbibliothek, MS I/F/71 (now lost).

[93]Teuber, pp. 116-117.

[94]Performed in a German version adapted from all three *azioni* of the Italian original (with the third greatly altered) by Ulrich von König as a *Lustige Nach-Spiel* with a prologue entitled *Das neubeglüchte Sachsen;* see Hellmuth Christian Wolff, *Die Barockoper in Hamburg (1678-1738)* (Wolfenbüttel, 1957), I, 120-22.

[95]See Hubertus Bolongaro-Crevenna, *L'arpa festante; Die Münchner Oper 1651-1825 von den Anfängen bis zum "Freyschützen"* (Munich, 1963), p. 90.

[96]His name appears in the libretto of *Siroe rè di Persia* after notice of the intermezzo, but without specific reference to it.

[97]Groppo, p. 229.

[98]Pellegrini, p. 429.

[99]Only the roles are given in the libretto of the opera with which the intermezzo was performed ([Girolamo Gigli], *La fede ne' tradimenti* [Florence, n.d.]).

[100]The libretto is dated 1745; see [Friedrich] Chr[ysander], "Mattheson's Verzeichniss Hamburgischer Opern von 1678 bis 1728, gedruckt im *Musikalischen Patrioten,* mit seinen handschriftlichen Fortsetzungen bis 1751, nebst Ausätzen und Berichtigungen," *Allgemeine musikalische Zeitung* XII (1877), col. 280; and Müller, *Mingotti,* p. XXI.

[101]Composer of a "maggior parte" of the music.

[102]Müller, *Mingotti,* pp. XXVIII, XXIX.

[103]*Ibid.,* p. 56.

[104]*Ibid.,* pp. 106-108.

[105]Allacci, col. 646; Groppo, p. 163.

[106]See above, pp. 41-42.

[107]Allacci, col. 594.

[108]Allacci, col. 290; Groppo, p. 162.

[109]See above, pp. 41-42.

[110]Gustav Friedrich Schmidt, *Chronologisches Verzeichnis der in Wolfenbüttel, Braunschweig, Salzthal, Bevern und Blankenburg aufgeführten Opern, Ballette und Schauspiele (Komödien) mit Musik bis zur Mitte des 18. Jahrhunderts* ("Neue Beiträge zur Geschichte der Musik und des Theaters am Herzoglichen Hofe zu Braunschweig-Wolfenbüttel," Erste Folge, [Munich, 1929]), p. 12.

[111]Lodovico Frati, "Musicisti e cantanti bolognesi del settecento: Notizie e lettere," *Rivista musicale italiana,* XXI (1914), 201; Allacci, col. 600.

[112]Macchiavelli, p. 73.

[113]Mooser, I, 53, 79, 377.

[114]Haas, p. 83.

[115]These intermezzi must have received their first setting prior to 1723, since this text appears in the *Raccolta copiosa d'intermedj* (see above, pp. 57-61.)

[116]Groppo, p. 226.

[117]Macchiavelli, p. 78.

[118]Pellegrini, pp. 403-404.

[119]See Frank Walker, "Two Centuries of Pergolesi Forgeries and Misattributions," *Music and Letters,* XXX (1949), 311-12.

[120]Although Hasse is not identified as composer of these intermezzi in the libretto of Scarlatti's opera, their text as printed there is similar to that of at least one score that bears Hasse's name (Dresden, Sächsische Landesbibliothek, MS Mus. 2477/F/100).

[121]Groppo, pp. 227-28; Allacci, col. 212.

[122]Carl Mennicke, *Hasse und die Brüder Graun als Symphoniker* (Leipzig, 1906), p. 508.

[123]Mooser, I, 113, 115.

[124]Mennicke, p. 508.

[125]Cotarelo y Mori, p. 88.

[126]Müller, "Repertoir," p. 330.

[127]Mennicke, p. 508.

[128]*Ibid*; Haas, p. 77.

[129]Groppo, p. 279.

[130]Mennicke, p. 508; L[ouis] Schneider, *Geschichte der Oper und des königlichen Opernhauses in Berlin* (Berlin, 1852), p. 125.

[131]Schneider, p. 133.

[132]Teuber, I, 205-206; Haas, p. 71.

[133]Müller, *Mingotti,* p. 106.

[134]Mennicke, p. 508; Haas, p. 83.

[135]Mennicke, p. 508.

[136]Subirá, p. 44.

[137]Allacci, col. 133.

[138]*Ibid.*

[139]Groppo, p. 191.

[140]Frati, p. 201.

[141]Pellegrini, pp. 340-41.

[142]Chiappelli, pp. 119-20.

[143]Sorge, p. 256.

[144]Hans Heinrich Borcherdt, "Geschichte der italienischen Oper in Breslau," *Zeitschrift des Vereins für Geschichte Schlesiens,* XLIV (1910), 48.

[145]Allacci, col. 507.

[146]Mooser, I, 53, 75, 368.

[147]Groppo, p. 230.

[148]Loewenberg, col. 137.

[149]Mooser, I, 113, 115, 386.

[150]Loewenberg, col. 137.

[151]Paul Alfred Merbach, "Das Repertoire der Hamburger Oper von 1718 bis 1750," *Archiv für Musikwissenschaft,* VI (1924), 372.

[152]Pellegrini, p. 437.

[153]Groppo, p. 259.

[154]*Ibid.,* p. 262.

[155]Chrysander, col. 281.

[156]Müller, *Mingotti,* p. 55; Haas, p. 77.

[157]Loewenberg, col. 138.

[158]Schneider, p. 136.

[159]Müller, *Mingotti,* p. XXXV.

[160]*Ibid.,* p. 105.

[161]Mooser, I, 264.

[162]Müller, *Mingotti,* p. 107.

[163]Loewenberg, col. 138.

[164]Due to the difficulty of distinguishing between the rash of parodies generated by the performance at Paris in 1752 and versions of Federico's original text, only revivals before 1753 are listed.

[165]Loewenberg, col. 173.

[166]Paolo-Emilio Ferrari, *Spettacoli drammatico-musicali e coreografici in Parma dall'anno 1628 all'anno 1883* (Parma, 1884), p. 32.

[167]Corrado Ricci, *I teatri di Bologna nei secoli XVII e XVIII: Storia aneddotica* (Bologna, 1888), p. 449.

[168]Pellegrini, p. 429.

[169]"Musica del Pergolesi Napolitano, a riserva dell'ultimo dueto il quale fu del Vinci..." Groppo, p. 254.

[170]*Ibid.*, p. 258.

[171]*Ibid.*, p. 275.

[172]Müller, *Mingotti*, pp. X, XVII, XIX, XX.

[173]*Ibid.*, p. XXIV.

[174]Loewenberg, col. 173.

[175]Müller, *Mingotti*, pp. XXVIII, XXIX.

[176]Schering, p. 281.

[177]Radiciotti, p. 205.

[178]Charles Burney, *A General History of Music from the Earliest Ages to the Present Period* (London, 1776-89), IV, 459.

[179]Cotarelo y Mori, p. 216.

[180]Loewenberg, col. 174.

[181]*Ibid.*

[182]Müller, *Mingotti*, pp. XXXI, XXXII, XXXIII, XXXIV.

[183]Walter, *Geschichte des Theaters*, pp. 145, 365.

[184]Identified in the Vienna, 1717, libretto.

[185]See above, pp. 41-42.

[186]Alessandro Gandini et al., *Cronistoria dei teatri di Modena dal 1539 al 1871* (Modena, 1873), I, 51.

[187]With the female character named Grilletta.

[188]Schmidt, p. 13.

[189]Cinelli, p. 23.

[190]Pellegrini, p. 340.

[191][Johann] Mattheson, *Der musicalische Patriot* (Hamburg, 1728), p. 193.

[192]Borcherdt, p. 48.

[193]Wolff, I, 117.

[194]Schmidt, p. 19.

[195]Mooser, I, 53, 73, 74, 76, 368.

BIBLIOGRAPHY

Manuscript Scores

The following pages list scores of operatic comic scenes and intermezzi consulted during preparation of the present study (see also Table 2, pp. 23-24). They are arranged alphabetically by dramatis personae (female role first), a method that proved to be the only rational means of ordering pieces that usually lack a title and are frequently anonymous. Information in brackets is supplied from libretti, except in some cases where composers have been ascribed by comparison of anonymous manuscripts with attributed copies. Words of titles in parentheses are those present in scores but lacking in their corresponding libretti. The spelling of composers' names has been standardized, following, wherever possible, the forms used in *Baker's Biographical Dictionary of Music and Musicians* (5th ed., 1958); thus "Giovanni Adolfo Hasse" is here rendered "Johann Adolph Hasse," "Domenico Sarro" becomes "Domenico Sarri," etc.

Bibliographical data and information concerning performances for the music of comic scenes and intermezzi interspersed throughout or bound at the end of scores for the *opere serie* with which they were presented are given in the following order:

> DRAMATIS PERSONAE Title (No. of scenes or intermezzi) Composer
> City and date of performance
> Title of *opera seria*
> Composer of *opera seria*
> Library sigla, shelf No., inclusive folio or page Nos.

In the absence of indications to the contrary, intermezzi contained in a Neapolitan or Viennese manuscript *opera seria* seem generally to be the work of the opera's composer, but no attributions have been made on this basis alone.

A list of library sigla will be found on p. xiii.

ALISCA AND BLESO (2) Antonio Caldara
  Gratz, 1728
  La forza dell'amicizia, ovvero Pilade ed Oreste
  Johann Georg Reutter Jr. (I) and Antonio Caldara (II and III)
  A:Wn, 17.112, I, [foll. 113-24$'$]; II, [foll. 70$'$-84].

ARMILLA AND BLESO (4)
[Naples, 1716]
Carlo rè d'Alemagna
Alessandro Scarlatti
I:Bu, 646 (Vol. V), foll. 57$'$-67$'$, 79-82$'$, 109$'$-118$'$, 153-62$'$.

ARMILLA AND PLANCO (4)
[Naples, 1708]
L'Agrippina
Nicola Porpora
I:Nc, 32.2.19, [foll. 65-79, 106$'$-118, 136$'$-38$'$, 197$'$-212$'$].

BAGATELLA, MAMALUCCA AND PATTATOCCO (2)
[Vienna,] 1715
Ciro
Francesco Conti
A:Wn, 18.087, I, [foll. 93-135]; II, [foll. 76-99$'$].

BRUNETTA AND BURLOTTO (3) [Domenico Sarri]
[Naples,] 1720
(La) Ginevra [principessa di Scozia]
Domenico Sarri
I:Nc, 32.2.22, [foll. 48$'$-60$'$, 96$'$-106$'$, 139-49].

BRUNETTA AND BURLOTTO (3) Domenico Sarri
D:Dl, Mus. 2356/F/1.

CARLOTTA AND PANTALEON (1)
1731
GB:Lbm, Add. 14235, foll. 58-83.

COLOMBINA AND PERNICONE (3)
[Naples, 1723]
[Trajano]
[Francesco Mancini]
I:Nc, 32.2.1, foll. 56-69, 127-38$'$, 186-97.

CORIMBA AND MILONE (2)
[Naples, 1706]
Le gare generose trà Cesare, e Pompeo [Pompeo, e Cesare]
Domenico Sarri
I:Nc, 32.2.21, [foll. 27-33, 125$'$-31$'$].

DELINA AND BALBO Con la burla da dovero (3) Ignazio Fiorillo
D:WR, Mus. IIIb:7.

DORILLA AND BALANZONE   La serva scaltra ouvero La moglie a forza (3) Johann
    Adolph Hasse
        I:MC, 124-G-29.

DORILLA AND BALANZONE   La serva scaltra overo La moglie a forza (3) Johann
    Adolph Hasse
        I:Rc, 2506 (0.II.104).

DORILLA AND ORCONE (3)
        Naples, 1715
        (II) Tigrane[, overo: L'egual impegno d'amore, e di fede]
        Alessandro Scarlatti
        I:Nc, 31.3.33, [foll. 68-76', 130'-44, 179'-90'].

DORIMENA AND TUBERONE (2) Francesco Conti
        [Vienna,] 1714
        L'Atenaide
        Marc' Antonio Ziani (I), Antonio Negri (II), and Antonio Caldara (III)
        A:Wn, 17.192, I, [foll. 78-109]; II, [foll. 99-119].

DORINA AND NIBBIO (2) [Domenico Sarri]
        [Naples, 1724]
        Didone ab(b)andonata
        Domenico Sarri
        I:Nc, 31.3.12, foll. 66-76', 127-43'.

DORINA AND NIBBIO (1 [= No. 1 of preceding]) Domenico Sarri
        [Naples, 1724]
        Didone ab(b)andonata
        Domenico Sarri
        I:Nc, I.6.25, foll. 1-11'.

DRA[GONTANA] AND POL[ICRONE] Intermedij rappresentati nel teatro di S. Cassano
    nell'opera d'Achille placato (4) Antonio Lotti
        [Venice, 1707]
        B:Br, Coll. Fétis, No. 2567

DRUSILLA AND STRABONE (2) Giuseppe Sellitti
        [Naples, 1735]
        Demofoonte
        [Domenico Sarri (I), Francesco Mancini (II), and Leonardo Leo (III)]
        I:Nc, 28.4.20, foll. 69-92', 148-69.

DRUSILLA AND STRAMBONE   Die schlaue Wittwe (2)
        D:WR, Mus, IIa:77.

ELISA AND TULLO (3)
[Naples, 1725]
Zenobia in Palmira
Leonard Leo
I:Nc, 28.4.24, foll, 47'-59', 110-23', 150-55.

ERIGHETTA AND DON CHILONE (3)
Vienna, 1725
Griselda
Francesco Conti
A:Wn, 17.238, I. [foll. 106'-135']; II, [foll. 125-72']; III, [foll. 62'-95].

ERIGHETTA AND DON CHILONE (3)
[Naples, 1726]
L'Ernelinda
Leonardo Vinci
I:Nc, 32.2.39, foll. 81-93, 172-84', 205-210.

EURILLA AND BELTRAMME (2)
[Naples, 1722]
(La) Partenope
Domenico Sarri
I:Nc, 31.3.13, [foll. 63-70', 110'-22, 163-73'].

FARFALLETTA, LIRONE AND TERREMOTO (3)
Vienna, 1718
Astarto
Francesco Conti
A:Wn, 17.242, I, [foll. 94-132]; II, [foll. 68-86]; III, [foll. 87-115].

FIAMMETTA AND PANCRAZIO Il vecchio avaro (3) Francesco Gasparini
I:MC, 124-I-4.

GALANTINA AND PAMPALUGO (2)
[Vienna,] 1715
Teseo in Creta
Francesco Conti
A:Wn, 17.196, I, [foll. 69'-90']; II, [foll. 95'-112].

LARINDA AND VANESIO (3) Johann Adolph Hasse
I:Rc, 2507 (O.II.105), foll. 1-40'.

LARINDA AND VANESIO L'artigiano gentiluomo (2) [Johann Adolph Hasse]
D:D1, Mus, 2477/F/99.

LESBINA AND MILO (3) [Giuseppe Vignola]
[Naples, 1707]
La fede tradita e vendicata
Francesco Gasparini [and Giuseppe Vignola]
I:Nc, 32.3.30, foll. 20-25′, 56-61′, 85′-87′.

LESBINA AND SEMPRONIO La franchezza delle donne (2) Guiseppe Sellitti
Naples, 1734
Siface
[Giuseppe Sellitti]
I:Nc, 32.4.12, [foll. 197-241].

LIDIA AND SERGIO (3)
Naples, 1719
Cambise
Alessandro Scarlatti
I:Nc, 31.3.29, I, [foll. 64′-74′]; II, [foll. 74′-85]; III, [foll. 45′-58′].

LISETTA AND ASTROBOLO Intermedi dell'opera seconda di S: Casciano (4)
Fran[ces]co Gasparini
1707
I:Rvat, Cod. Barb. lat. 4231, foll. 151-86′.

LISETTA AND ASTROBOLO (3)
Vienna, 1717
La verità nell'inganno
Antonio Caldara
A:Wn, 18.095, I, [foll. 81-93′]; II, [foll. 78-89′]; III, [foll. 60-72].

LIVIETTA AND TRACOLLO (2) Giovanni Battista Pergolesi
I:Nc, 32.2.9.

LIVIETTA AND TRACOLLO (2) [Giovanni Battista] Pergolesi
[Naples,] 1734
I:MC, 125-G-26.

LIVIETTA AND TRACOLLO (2) [Giovanni Battista Pergolesi]
I:Fc, D.278.

LIVIETTA AND TRACOLLO Tracollo, il finto pazzo (2) Giovanni Battista Pergolesi
D:W, Mus. IIa:80[a,b].

LUCILLA AND PANDOLFO Il tutore (2) Johann Adolph Hasse
I:MC, 124-G-26.

LUCILLA AND PANDOLFO Il tutore (2) Johann Adolph Hasse
    [Dresden,] 1738
    D:Dl, Mus. 2477/F/101.

LUCILLA AND PANDOLFO Il tutore e la pupilla (2) [Johann Adolph Hasse]
    D:WR, Mus. IIa:94.

LUCILLA AND PANDOLFO Intermezzi del tutore (2) Johann Adolph Hasse
    D:Mbs, Mus. 196.

MADAMA AND CUOCO (2)
    A:Wn, 17.634. 2 vols.

MERLINA AND CAPITAN GALOPPO La fantesca (3) Johann Adolph Hasse
    I:MC, 124-G-28.

MERILLA AND MORANTE (3) Domenico Sarri
    [Naples, 1718]
    (L') Arsace
    Domenico Sarri
    I:Nc, I.6.23, [foll. 50$'$-58, 104-112$'$, 132-42].

MIRENA AND FLORO Nana francese, e Armena (3) Franc[esc]o Gasparini (1 and 3)
    and Giovanni Bononcini (2)
        [Dresden, 1718]
        (L'Ascanio) [Gl'odj delusi dal sangue]
        [Antonio Lotti]
        D:Dl, Mus 2159/F/5, I, 141-59; II, 105-127; III, 67-84.

MOSCHETTA AND GRULLO (2)
    [Naples, 1727]
    Siroe rè di Persia
    Domenico Sarri
    I:Nc, 32.2.24 [foll. 75-89$'$, 154-71].

PALANDRANA AND ZAMBERLUCCO Intermezzi trà Palandrana vecchia vedova e
    Zamberlucco giouine da bravo (3)
        [Naples, 1716]
        Carlo rè d'Alemagna
        Alessandro Scarlatti
        I:Bu, 646 (Vol. V), foll. 171-97.

PERICCA AND VARRONE (5)
    [Naples, 1714]
    (Il) Scipione nelle Spagne
    Alessandro Scarlatti
    I:Bu, 646 (Vol. IV), foll. 26-31, 49-56, 72-77, 102$'$-109$'$, 123$'$-31$'$.

PIMPINELLA AND MARCANTONIO (1) Johann Adolph Hasse
  [Dresden, 1743]
  Numa
  Johann Adolph Hasse
  D:D1, Mus. 2477/F/28, III, 80-118.

PIPA AND BARLAFUSO (3) Antonio Caldara
  Vienna, 1716
  Costantino
  Antonia Lotti, [J.J. Fux (overture), and Antonio Caldara (licenza)]
  A;Wn, 17.993, I, [fol. 92-106$'$]; II, [foll. 78-105]; IV, [foll. 57-70$'$].

PLAUTILLA AND ALBINO (3)
  [Naples, 1723]
  Silla dittatore
  Leonardo Vinci
  I:Nc, 32.4.13, foll. 63-66$'$, 110-20, 145-57.

POLLASTRELLA AND PARPAGNACCO (arias and duets only)
  D:ROu, Mus. saec. XVIII.70^{24a-f}.

RODISBE AND ARISTONE (3)
  [Naples,] 1705
  L'incoronatione di Dario
  Giuseppe Aldrovandini
  I:Nc, I.II.17, [foll. 34-36, 49$'$-50, 88-95].

ROSETTA AND MALORCO (4) Carmine Giordano
  Naples, 1712
  La vittoria d'amor conjugale
  [Antonio Lotti?] and Carmine Giordano
  I:Nc, 27.5.26, foll. 59$'$-64, 78$'$-87$'$, 120-26, 143$'$-50.

ROSICCA AND MORANO (2)
  [Naples,] 1723
  Siface (re di Numidia)
  Francesco Feo
  I:Nc, 32.3.27, [foll. 53-67$'$, 111-23].

ROSINA AND LESBO (2)
  Vienna, 1721
  Meride, e Selinunte
  Giuseppe Porsile
  A:Wn, 18.023, II, [foll. 69$'$-94$'$]; IV, [foll. 50-78$'$].

RUBINA AND PINCONE (3)
[Naples, 1713]
(L')amor tirann[ic]o (ossia Zenobia)
Francesco Feo
I:Nc. 32.3.28, foll. 59-64$'$, 104$'$-110, 144-53$'$.

SCINTILLA AND DON TABARANO D. Tabarano, e Scintilla (2) Johann Adolph Hasse
I:Rc, 2507 (0.II.105), foll. 48-85$'$.

SCINTILLA AND DON TABARANO (2) [Johann Adolph Hasse]
I:MC, 124-G-27.

SCINTILLA AND DON TABARANO (2) Johann Adolph Hasse and G. B. Pergolesi
I:Fc, B.355.

SCINTILLA AND DON TABARANO (2) [Johann Adolph Hasse]
D:D1, Mus. 2477/F/100.

SCINTILLA AND DON TABARANO (2) Johann Adolph Hasse
D:SW, 2478^{a-b}.

SERPILLA AND BACOCCO Il giocatore (3) Giuseppe Maria Orlandini
I:Fc, D.239.

SERPILLA AND BACOCCO (3) [Giuseppe Maria Orlandini]
B:Bc, 2372.

SERPILLA AND BACOCCO Il giocatore (3) [Giuseppe Maria] Orlandini
D:ROu, Mus. saec. XVIII:49^5.

SERPILLA AND BACOCCO Bacocco è Serpilla (3) [Giuseppe Maria] Orlandini
A:Wn, 17.740.

SERPINA AND UBERTO La serva padrona (2) Giovanni Battista Pergolesi
I:Nc, 34.2.29. 2 vols.

SERPINA AND UBERTO La serva padrona (2) Giovanni Battista Pergolesi
I:Nc, 6.4.42.

SERPINA AND UBERTO La serva padrona (2) Giovanni Battista Pergolesi
I:Nc, 30.4.20.

SERPINA AND UBERTO La serva padrona (2) Giovanni Battista Pergolesi
I:Fc, D.279.

SERVILIA AND FLACCO (3)
[Naples, 1727]
La caduta de['] Decemviri
Leonardo Vinci
I:Nc, 32.4.10, [foll. 81-90, 158-71, 225-30.]

SESTILIA AND QUINZIO (3)
[Naples, 1722]
Lucio Vero
Domenico Sarri
I:Nc, I.6.25, foll. 51-62, 115-27', 154-65'.

SOFIA AND BARLACCO La furba, e lo sciocco (2)
[Naples, 1731]
Artemisia
Domenico Sarri
I:Nc, 31.3.10, [foll. 72-94', 175-93'].

VESPETTA AND PIMPINONE (3)
[Naples, 1709]
L'Engelberta
Antonio Orefici and Francesco Mancini
A:Wn, 18.057, foll. 55-67', 131'-45', 170'-81.

VESPETTA AND PIMPINONE (3)
Vienna, 1717
Sesostri rè di Egitto
Francesco Conti
A:Wn, 17.210, I, [foll. 94-121']; II, [foll. 78'-95']; III, [foll. 41-68'].

Books and Articles

Abert, Anna Amalie. *Claudio Monteverdi und das musikalische Drama.* Lippstadt, 1954.

Abert, Hermann. *Niccolo Jommelli als Opernkomponist.* Halle, a.S., 1908.

Ademollo, Alessandro. *Bibliografia della cronistoria teatrale italiana.* Milan, 1888.

_____. *I teatri di Roma nel secolo decimosettimo.* Rome, 1888.

Allacci, Lione. *Drammaturgia... accresciuta e continuata fino all'anno MDCCLV.* Venice, 1755.

Arteaga, Stefano. *Le rivoluzioni del teatro musicale italiano dalla sua origine fino al presente.* 2nd ed. 3 vols. Venice, 1785.

Bacher, Otto. *Die Geschichte der frankfurter Oper im achtzehnten Jahrhundert.*
("Veröffentlichungen der deutschen Musikgesellschaft, Ortsgruppe Frankfurt a.M.,"
Vol. I.) Frankfurt a.M., 1926.

_____. "Zur Geschichte der Oper auf frankfurter Boden im 18. Jahrhundert,"
Zeitschrift für Musikwissenschaft, VIII (1925-26), 93-102.

Bellucci-la Salandra, Mario. "Domenico Sarri: Saggio cronologico delle sue opere,"
Musica d'oggi, XVII (1935), 93-98, 133-37.

Bernardi, G[ian] G[iuseppe].   "Contributo allo studio dell'elemento comico nell'opera
seria veneziana del secolo XVII," *Musica d'oggi,* XII (1935), 53-61.

Bollert, Werner. *Die Buffoopern Baldassare Galuppis: Ein Beitrag zur Geschichte der
italienischen komischen Oper im 18. Jahrhundert.* Bottrop, 1935.

Bolongaro-Crevenna, Hubertus. *L'arpa festante: Die münchner Oper 1651-1825 von den
Anfängen bis zum "Freyschützen."* Munich, 1963.

[Bonlini, Gian Carlo.] *Le glorie della poesia, e della musica contenute nell'esatta notitia
de teatri della città di Venezia, e nel catalogo purgatissimo de drami musicali quiui
sin hora rapresentati con gl'auttori della poesia, e della musica, e con le annotationi
a suoi luoghi proprij.* Venice, [1730?].

Borcherdt, Hans Heinrich.   "Geschichte der italienishchen Oper in Breslau," *Zeitschrift
des Vereins für Geschichte Schlesiens,* XLIV (1910), 18-51.

Breggi, Paolo. *Serie degli spettacoli rappresentati al Teatro Regio di Torino dal 1688 al
presente coi nomi dei poeti, dei maestri compositori, dei coreografi e degli artisti.*
Turin, 1872.

Brosses, Charles de. *Lettres familières sur l'Italie,* ed. Yvonne Bezard. 2 vols. Paris, 1931.

Brunelli, Bruno. *I teatri di Padova dalle origini alla fine del secolo XIX.* Padua, 1921.

Bukofzer, Manfred F. *Music in the Baroque Era.* New York, 1947.

Burney, Charles. *A General History of Music from the Earliest Ages to the Present
Period.* 4 vols. London, 1776-89.

Burt, Nathaniel. "Opera in Arcadia," *The Musical Quarterly,* XLI (1955), 145-70.

Bustico, Guido. *Bibliografia delle storie e delle cronistorie de' teatri d'Italia.* Milan, 1929.

Calmus, Georgy.   "L. Vinci der Komponist von *Serpilla e Bacocco,*" *Zeitschrift der
Internationalen Musikgesellschaft,* XIV (1912-13), 114, 172-73.

Cametti, Alberto. *Il teatro di Tordinona poi di Apollo.* 2 vols. Tivoli, 1938.

Carey, Henry. *Dramatick Works.* London, 1743.

Carmena y Millán, Luis. *Crónica de la ópera italiana en Madrid desde el año 1738 hasta nuestros días.* Madrid, 1878.

Carse, Adam. *The Orchestra in the XVIIIth Century.* Cambridge, 1940.

"Cattalogo di tutti li drami rappresentati in musica in Venezia dall'anno 1637 fino al presente [1790?] col nome de' compositori della poesia, e della musica e coll'indicazione de' teatri, ove furono rappresentati illustrato con particolari annotazioni." 2 vols. Venice, Biblioteca Marciana, MS Cl. VII, Nos. 1613-14 (9035-36).

Chiappelli, Alberto. *Storia del teatro in Pistoia dalle origini alla fine del sec. XVIII.* Pistoia. 1913.

Chrysander, Friedrich. "Geschichte der braunschweig-wolfenbüttelschen Capelle und Oper vom sechzehnten bis zum achtzehnten Jahrhundert," *Jahrbücher für musikalische Wissenschaft,* I (1863), 147-286.

_____. "Mattheson's Verzeichniss hamburgischer Opern von 1678 bis 1728, gedruckt im *Musikalischen Patrioten,* mit seinen handschriftlichen Fortsetzungen bis 1751, nebst Zusätzen und Berichtigungen," *Allgemeine musikalische Zeitung,* XII (1877), cols. 198-200, 215-20, 234-36, 245-51, 261-66, 280-82.

Cinelli, C. *Memorie cronistoriche del teatro di Pesaro dall'anno 1637 al 1897.* Pesaro, 1898.

[Clément, Jean Marie Bernard and Joseph de la Porte.] *Anecdotes dramatiques.* 3 vols. Paris, 1775.

Cosentino, Giuseppe. *Il teatro Marsigli-Rossi.* Bologna, 1900.

Cotarelo y Mori, Emilio. *Origenes y establecimiento de la ópera en España hasta 1800.* Madrid, 1917.

Croce, Benedetto. *I teatri di Napoli: Secolo XV-XVIII.* Naples 1891.

_____. *I teatri di Napoli dal rinascimento alla fine del secolo decimottavo.* 3rd ed. Bari, 1926.

Cudworth, C[harles] L. "Notes on the Instrumental Works Attributed to Pergolesi," *Music and Letters,* (1949), 321-28.

Curiel, Carlo L. *Il teatro S. Pietro di Trieste: 1690-1801.* Milan, 1937.

D'Arienzo, N[icola]. "Origini dell'opera comica," *Rivista musicale italiana*, II (1895), 597-628; IV (1897), 421-59; VI (1899), 473-95; VII (1900), 1-33.

De Angelis, Alberto. *Nella Roma papale: Il teatro Alibert o delle Dame (1717-1863)*. Tivoli, 1951.

De Dominicis, Giulia. "I teatri di Roma nell'età di Pio VI," *Archivio della R. Società Romana di Storia Patria*, XLVI (1923), 48-243.

Della Corte, Andrea. "Intermezzo scenico," *Enciclopedia italiana di scienze, lettere ed arti*, XIX (1933), 393-94.

_____. *L'opera comica italiana nel '700: Studi ed appunti*. 2 vols. Bari, 1923.

_____. "Tragico e comico nell'opera veneziana della seconda parte del seicento," *La rassegna musicale*, XI (1938), 325-33.

Dent, Edward J. *Alessandro Scarlatti: His Life and Works*. New impression with preface and additional notes by Frank Walker. London, 1960.

_____. "Ensembles and Finales in 18th Century Italian Opera," *Sammelbände der Internationalen Musikgesellschaft*, XI (1909-1910), 543-69; XII (1910-11), 112-38.

Dotto, Paolo. "Teatri antichi di Palermo: Il teatro 'Santa Cecilia'," *Musica d'oggi*, XIII (1931), 65-73.

Downes, Edward O. D. "The Operas of Johann Christian Bach as a Reflection of the Dominant Trends in Opera Seria 1750-1780." 2 vols. Harvard Dissertation, 1958.

_____. "The Neapolitan Tradition in Opera," *International Musicological Society: Report of the Eighth Congress, New York 1961*, I (Kassel, 1961), 277-84.

_____. "*Secco* Recitative in Early Classical Opera Seria (1720-80)," *Journal of the American Musicological Society*, XIV (1961), 50-69.

Duchartre, Pierre-Louis. *La commedia dell'arte et ses enfants*. Paris, 1955.

[Durey de Noinville, Jacques Bernard.] *Histoire du théâtre de l'Académie Royale de Musique en France, depuis son établissement jusqu'à présent*. 2 parts. 2nd ed. Paris, 1757.

Enciclopedia dello spettacolo. 9 vols. Rome, 1954-62.

Fassini, Sesto. *Il melodramma italiano a Londra nella prima metà del settecento*. Turin, 1914.

Fehr, Max. *Apostolo Zeno (1668-1750) und seine Reform des Operntextes*. Zurich, 1912.

Ferrari, Paolo-Emilio. *Spettacoli drammatico-musicali e coreografici in Parma dall'anno 1628 all'anno 1883.* Parma, 1884.

Fischer, Wilhelm. "Zur Entwicklungsgeschichte des wiener klassischen Stils," *Studien zur Musikwissenschaft,* III (1915), 24-28.

Florimo, Francesco. *La scuola musicale di Napoli e i suoi conservatorii.* 4 vols. Naples, 1880-82.

Frati, Lodovico. "Musicisti e cantanti bolognese del settecento: Notizie e lettere," *Rivista musicale italiana,* XXI (1914), 189-202.

Freeman, Robert Schofield. "Opera without Drama: Currents of Change in Italian Opera, 1675 to 1725, and the Roles Played Therein by Zeno, Caldara, and Others." 2 vols. Princeton University Dissertation, 1967.

Fuchs, Marianne. "Die Entwicklung des Finales in der italienischen Opera Buffa vor Mozart." Vienna Dissertation, 1932.

Fürstenau, Moritz. *Zur Geschichte der Musik und des Theaters am Hofe zu Dresden.* 2 vols. Dresden, 1861-62.

Gandini, Alessandro, Luigi Francesco Valdrighi, and Giorgio Ferrari-Moreni. *Cronistoria dei teatri di Modena dal 1539 al 1871.* 3 vols. Modena, 1873.

Gandolfi, Riccardo. "La cappella musicale della corte di Toscana (1539-1859)," *Rivista musicale italiana,* XVI (1909), 506-530.

Gasparini, Francesco. *L'armonico pratico al cimbalo.* Venice, 1708.

Gerber, Ernst Ludwig. *Historisch-biographisches Lexicon der Tonkünstler. . . .* 2 vols. Leipzig, 1790-92.

Gerber, Rudolf. *Der Operntypus Johann Adolf Hasses und seine textlichen Grundlagen.* ("Berliner Beiträge zur Musikwissenschaft," Vol. II.) Leipzig, 1925.

Giazotto, Remo. *Il melodramma a Genova nei secoli XVII e XVIII con gli elenchi completi dei titoli, dei musicisti, dei poeti e degli attori di quei componimenti rappresentati tra il 1652 e il 1771 ai teatri detti "del Falcone" e "da S. Agostino."* Genoa, 1941.

_____. *La musica a Genova nella vita pubblica e privata dal XIII al XVIII secolo.* Genoa, 1951.

Goldoni, Carlo. *Delle commedie....* 17 vols. Venice, 1761-78.

_____. *Memoires ... pour servir à l'histoire de sa vie, et à celle de son théâtre.* 3 vols. Paris, 1787.

Goldschmidt, Hugo. *Studien zur Geschichte der italienischen Oper im 17. Jahrhundert.* 2 vols. Leipzig, 1901-1904.

Groppo, Antonio. *Catalogo di tutti i drammi per musica recitati ne' teatri di Venezia dall'anno 1637 in cui ebbero principio le pubbliche rappresentazioni de' medesimi sin all'anno presente 1745.* Venice, [1745?].

_____. "Catalogo purgatissimo di tutti li drammi per musica recitatisi ne' teatri di Venezia dall'anno MDCXXXVII sin oggi [1767].... accresciuto di tutti gli scenarj, varie edizioni, aggiunte a drammi, e intermedi con la notizia di alcuni drammi nuovamente scoperti, e di altre rare particolarità." Venice, Biblioteca Marciani, MS Cl. VII, No. 2326 (8263).

Grout, Donald Jay. *A Short History of Opera.* 2nd ed. New York, 1965.

Haas, Robert. "Beitrag zur Geschichte der Oper in Prag und Dresden," *Neues Archiv für sächsische Geschichte und Altertumskunde,* XXXVII (1916), 68-96.

_____. *Die Musik des Barocks.* Wildpark-Potsdam, [1929].

_____. "Die Musik in der wiener deutschen Stegreifkomödie," *Studien zur Musikwissenschaft,* XII (1925), 3-64.

_____. "Die Oper im 18. Jahrhundert," *Handbuch der Musikgeschichte,* ed. Guido Adler. 2nd. ed. Berlin, 1930.

Hadamowsky, Franz. "Barocktheater am wiener Kaiserhof: Mit einem Spielpan (1625-1740)," *Jahrbuch der Gesellschaft für wiener Theaterforschung,* 1951-52 (1955), 7-117.

Hansell, Sven Hostrup. "The Cadence in 18th-Century Recitative," *The Musical Quarterly,* LIV (1968), 228-48.

Hucke, Helmuth. "Die neapolitanische Tradition in der Oper," *International Musicological Society: Report of the Eighth Congress, New York 1961,* I (Kassel, 1961), 253-77.

Jahn, Otto. *W.A. Mozart.* 2nd ed. 2 vols. Leipzig, 1867.

Jander, Owen Hughes. "Alessandro Stradella and his Minor Dramatic Works." 2 vols. Harvard University Dissertation, 1962.

Kirkpatrick, Ralph. *Domenico Scarlatti.* Princeton, N.J., 1953.

Kunz, Harald. "Höfisches Theater in Wien zur Zeit der Maria Theresa," *Jahrbuch der Gesellschaft für wiener Theaterforschung.* 1953-54 (1958), 3-113.

[Laborde, Jean Benjamin de.] *Essai sur la musique ancienne et moderne.* 4 vols. Paris, 1780.

La Laurencie, L[ionel] de. "Deux imitateurs français des bouffons: Blavet et Dauvergne," *L'année musicale,* II (1912), 65-125.

_____. "La Grande saison italienne de 1752:   Les bouffons," *S. I. M. revue musicale,* VIII (1912), No. 6, 18-33; No. 7, 13-22.

La Vallière, Louis César de La baume Le Blanc.] *Ballets, opera, et autres ouvrages lyriques, par ordre chronologique depuis leur origine.* ... Paris, 1760.

Lea, K[athleen] M[arguerite]. *Italian Popular Comedy: A Study in the commedia dell'arte, 1560-1620 with Special Reference to the English Stage.* 2 vols. Oxford, 1934.

Lenotti, Tullio. *I teatri di Verona.* (Edizioni di "Vita Veronese," No. 2.) Verona, 1949.

Liebrecht, Henri. *Histoire du théâtre français à Bruxelles au XVIIe et au XVIIIe siècle.* ("Bibliothèque de La Revue de littérature comparée," Vol. XI.) Paris, 1923.

Lobstein, J[ob] F[ranz]. *Beiträge zur Geschichte der Musik im Elsass und besonders in Strassburg, von der ältesten bis auf die neueste Zeit.* Strasbourg, 1840.

Loewenberg, Alfred. *Annals of Opera: 1597-1940.* 2 vols. 2nd ed. Geneva, 1955.

Lorenz, Alfred. *Alessandro Scarlatti's Jugendoper: Ein Beitrag zur Geschichte der italienischen Oper.* 2 vols. Augsburg, 1927.

Luin, E. J. *Fortuna e influenza della musica di Pergolesi in Europa.* ("Quaderni dell'Accademia Chigiana," Vol. VI.) Siena, 1943.

Lustig, Renzo. "Per la cronistoria dell'antico teatro musical: Il teatro della Villa Medicea di Pratolino," *Rivista musicale italiana,* XXXVI (1929), 259-66.

[Macchiavelli, Alessandro.] *Serie cronologica dei drammi recitati sù de' pubblici teatri di Bologna dall'anno di nostra salute 1600 sino al corrente 1737.* Bologna, 1737.

Maggi, Carlo Maria. *Comedie, e rime in lingua milanese.* 2 vols. Milan, 1701.

_____. *Nvova aggivnta di varie poesie.... sì in lingua milanese, come eroiche.* Venice, 1701.

_____. *Poesie miscellanee....* 2 vols. Milan, 1729.

Manferrari, Umberto. *Dizionario universale delle opere melodrammatiche.* 3 vols. Florence, 1954-55.

[Marcello, Benedetto.] *Il teatro alla moda o sia Metodo sicuro, e facile per ben comporre, & esequire l'opere italiane in musica all'uso moderno,...* [Venice, ca. 1720].

Margadonna, Michele. *Pergolesi.* Milan, 1961.

Marpurg, Friedrich Wilhelm. *Historisch-kritische Beyträge zur Aufnahme der Musik.* 5 vols. Berlin, 1754-62.

Marques, Joaquim José. *Cronologia da ópera em Portugal.* Lisbon, 1947.

Martello, Pier Jacopo. *Della tragedia antica e moderna.* Rome, 1715.

Mattheson, [Johann]. *Der musicalische Patriot.* Hamburg, 1728.

————. *Der vollkommene Capellmeister.* Hamburg, 1739.

McClure, Theron Reading. "A Reconstruction of Theatrical and Musical Practice in the Production of Italian Opera in the Eighteenth Century." Ohio State University Dissertation, 1956.

Mengelberg, Curt Rudolf. *Giovanni Alberto Ristori: Ein Beitrag zur Geschichte italienischer Kunstherrschaft in Deutschland im 18. Jahrhundert.* Leipzig, 1916.

Mennicke, Carl. *Hasse und die Brüder Graun als Symphoniker nebst biographien und thematischen Katalogen.* Leipzig, 1906.

Mentzel, E[lisabeth]. *Geschichte der Schauspielkunst in Frankfurt a.M. von ihren Anfängen bis zur Eröffnung des städtischen Komödienhauses: Ein Beitrag zur deutschen kultur- und Theatergeschichte.* ("Archiv für Frankfurts Geschichte und Kunst," New Series, Vol. IX.) Frankfurt a.M., 1882.

Merbach, Paul Alfred. "Das Repertoire der Hamburger Oper von 1718 bis 1750," *Archiv für Musikwissenschaft,* VI (1924), 354-72.

Mic, Constant. *La commedia dell'arte.* Paris, 1927.

Metastasio, Pietro. *Tutte le opere,* ed. Bruno Brunelli. 5 vols. Milan, 1943-54.

Mocenigo, Giovanni juniore. *I teatri moderni di Vicenza dal 1650 al 1800 o Dei due distrutti teatri di Piazza e delle Grazie.* Bassano, 1894.

Moland, Louis. *Molière et la comédie italienne.* 2nd ed. Paris, 1867.

Molière, J[ean] B[aptiste] P[oquelin]. *Le opere....* Italian translation by Nic. di Castelli. 4 vols. Leipzig, 1698.

Mooser, R[obert]-Aloys. *Annales de la musique et des musiciens en Russie au XVIIIme siècle.* 3 vols. Geneva, 1948-51.

_____. *Opéras, intermezzos, ballets, cantates, oratorios joués en Russie durant le XVIIIe siècle.* 2nd ed. Geneva, 1955.

Morini, Ugo. *La R. Accademia degli Immobili ed il suo teatro "La Pergola" (1649-1925).* Pisa, 1926.

Müller, Erich H. *Angelo und Pietro Mingotti: Ein Beitrag zur Geschichte der Oper im XVIII. Jahrhundert.* Dresden, 1917.

_____. *Die Mingottischen Opernunternehmungen: 1732-1756.* Dresden, 1915.

_____. "Zum Repertoir der hamburger Oper von 1718 bis 1750," *Archiv für Musikwissenschaft,* VII (1925), 329-33.

Die Musik in Geschichte und Gegenwart, ed. Friedrich Blume. 14 vols. and Supplement. Kassel, 1949-.

Nietan, Hanns. "Die Buffoszenen der spätvenezianischen Oper 1680-1710: Ein Beitrag zur Geschichte der komischen Oper." Halle University Dissertation, 1924.

Noack, Elisabeth. *Musikgeschichte Darmstadts vom Mittelalter bis zur Goethezeit.* ("Beiträge zur mittelrheinischen Musikgeschichte," No. 8.) Mainz, 1967.

Oliver, A. Richard. "Molière's Contribution to the Lyric Stage," *The Musical Quarterly,* XXXIII (1947), 350-64.

Overskou, Th[omas]. *Den danske skueplads, i dens hisorie, fra de første spor af danske skuespil indtil vor tid.* 7 vols. Copenhagen, 1854-76.

Paglicci-Brozzi, Antonio. "Il Regio Ducal Teatro di Milano nel secolo XVIII: Notizie aneddotiche," *Gazzetta musicale di Milano,* XLVIII (1893), 808, 811-12, 824-28, 845-47, 860-62; XLIX (1894), 25-27, 33-36, 49-50, 65-66, 81-82, 97-100, 113-15, 129-30, 145-46.

Pandolfini, Palmieri. "Notizia di tutte l'opere che si sono recitate in Firenze nel teatro di via della Pergola dall'anno 1718 in poi." Florence, Biblioteca Nazionale Centrale, MS II-97, No. 3, [foll. 181-206'].

Pastore, Giuseppe A. *Leonardo Leo.* Galatina, 1957.

Pauly, Reinhard G. "Benedetto Marcello's Satire on Early 18th-Century Opera," *The Musical Quarterly*, XXXIV (1948), 222-33.

Pavan, Giuseppe. "Saggio di cronistoria del teatro musicale romano: Il teatro Capranica (Catalogo cronologico delle opere rappresentate nel secolo XVIII)," *Rivista musicale italiana*, XXIX (1922), 425-44.

_____. *Saggio di cronistoria teatrale fiorentina: Serie cronologica delle opere rappresentate al teatro degli Immobili in via della Pergola nei secoli XVII e XVIII.* Milan, [1901].

Pellegrini, Almachilde. *Spettacoli lucchesi nei secoli XVII-XIX.* ("Memorie e documenti per servire alla storia di Lucca," Vol. XIV, Pt. 1.) Lucca, 1914.

Peretts, V[ladimir] N[ikolaevich], ed. *Italianskiia komediĭ i intermediĭ predstarlenniia pri dvorie imperatritsy Anny Ivannovny v 1733-1735 gg.* Petrograd, 1917.

Perrucci, Andrea. *Dell'arte rappresentativa premeditata, ed all'improviso.* Naples, 1699.

Petraccone, Enzo. *La commedia dell'arte: Storia, tecnica, scenari. Naples, 1927.*

Piovano, Francesco. "A propos d'une récente biographie de Léonard Leo," *Sammelbände der Internationalen Musikgesellschaft,* VIII (1906-1907), 70-95.

Pirrotta, Nino. "Commedia dell'arte and Opera," *The Musical Quarterly,* XLI (1955), 305-324.

_____. *Li due Orfei da Poliziano a Monteverdi, con un saggio critico sulla scenografia di Elena Povoledo.* Turin, 1969.

Powers, Harold S. "Il Serse trasformato," *The Musical Quarterly,* XLVII (1961), 481-92; XLVIII (1962), 73-92.

Prod'homme, J[acques]-G[abriel]. "La Musique à Paris, de 1753 à 1757, d'après un manuscrit de la bibliothèque de Munich," *Sammelbände der Internationalen Musikgesellschaft,* VI (1904-1905), 568-87.

Prölss, Robert. *Geschichte des Hoftheaters zu Dresden von seinen Anfängen bis zum Jahre 1862.* Dresden, 1878.

Prota-Giurleo, Ulisse. *Il teatro di corte del Palazzo Reale di Napoli.* Naples, 1952.

Prunières, Henry. "I libretti dell'opera veneziana nel secolo XVII," *La rassegna musicale,* III (1930), 441-48.

Pulver, Jeffrey. "The Intermezzi of the Opera," *Proceedings of the Musical Association,* XLIII (1916-17), 139-63.

Quadrio, Francesco Saverio. *Della storia e della ragione d'ogni poesia.* 4 vols. in 6 pts. and Index. Bologna and Milan, 1739-52.

Raccolta copiosa d'intermedj, parte da rappresentarsi col canto, alcuni senza musica, con altri in fine in lingua milanese. 2 vols. Amsterdam [Milan], 1723.

Radiciotti, Giuseppe. *G.B. Pergolesi: Vita, opere ed influenza su l'arte.* Rome, 1910.

_____. *Pergolesi.* Milan, 1935.

_____. *Giovanni Battista Pergolesi: Leben und Werk.* Translated, enlarged, and revised by Antoine-E[lisée] Cherbuliez. Zurich, 1954.

_____. *Teatro musica e musicisti in Recanati.* Recanati, 1904.

_____. *Teatro musica e musicisti in Sinigaglia: Notizie e documenti.* Milan, 1893.

Rava, Arnaldo. *I teatri di Roma.* Rome, 1953.

Renieu, Lionel. *Histoire des théâtres de Bruxelles depuis leur origine jusqu'à ce jour.* 2 vols. Paris, 1928.

Riccoboni, Luigi. *Réflexions historiques et critiques sur les differens théâtres de l'Europe.* Amsterdam, 1740.

Reichenburg, Louisette. *Contribution à l'historie de la "Querelle des Bouffons."* Philadelphia, 1937.

Ricci, Corrado. *I teatri di Bologna nei secoli XVII e XVIII: Storia aneddotica.* Bologna, 1888.

Rolandi, Ulderico. *Il libretto per musica attraverso i tempi.* Rome, 1951.

Rolli, Paolo [Antonio]. *De' poetici componimenti...* Venice, 1761.

Rosendahl, Erich. *Geschichte der Hoftheater in Hannover und Braunschweig.* ("Niedersächsische Hausbücherei," Vol. I.) Hannover, 1927.

Rossi[-Melocchi], Gio[vanni] Cosimo. "[Memorie di] cose [pistojesi] notate e minutamente osservate.... per suo mero diuertimento [dal gennaio 1724 al 31 aprile 1728]." Florence, Biblioteca Nazionale Centrale, Coll. Rossi-Cassigoli, No. 192.

Rousseau, J[ean]-J[acques]. *Dictionnaire de musique.* Paris, 1768.

Rudhart, Fr[anz] M[ichael]. *Die italiänische Oper von 1654-1787.* ("Geschichte der Oper am Hofe zu München," Pt. 1.) Freising, 1865.

Sacerdote, Giacomo. *Teatro Regio di Torino: Cenni storici intorno al teatro e cronologia degli spettacoli rappresentati dal 1662 al 1890.* Turin, 1892.

[Salvioli, Giovanni.] *I teatri musicali di Venezio nel secolo XVII (1637-1700): Memorie storiche e bibliografiche.* Milan, [1879].

Sandberger, Adolf. "Zur Geschichte der Oper in Nürnberg in der zweiten Hälfte des 17. und zu Anfang des 18. Jahrhunderts," *Archiv für Musikwissenschaft, I (1918-19), 84-107.*

Sartori, Claudio. "Gli Scarlatti a Napoli: Nuovi contributi," *Rivista musicale italiana,* XLVI (1942), 374-90.

Schaal, Richard. "Die vor 1801 gedruckten Libretti des Theatermuseums München," *Die Musikforschung,* X (1957), 388-96, 487-97, XI (1958), 54-69, 168-77, 321-36, 462-77; XII (1959), 60-75, 161-77, 299-306, 454-61; XIII (1960), 38-46, 164-72, 299-306, 441-48; XIV (1961), 36-43, 166-83.

Scherillo, Michele. *L'opera buffa napoletana durante il settecento: Storia letteraria.* 2nd ed. [Milan, 1917].

————. *Storia letteraria dell'opera buffa napolitana dalle origini al principio del secolo XIX.* Naples, 1883.

Schering, Arnold. *Johann Sebastian Bach und das Musikleben Leipzigs im 18. Jahrhundert.* ("Musikgeschichte Leipzigs," Vol. III.) Leipzig, 1941.

Schmidt, Gustav Friedrich. *Cronologisches Verzeichnis der in Wolfenbüttel, Braunschweig, Salzthal, Bevern und Blankenburg aufgeführten Opern, Ballette und Schauspiele (Komödien) mit Musik bis zur Mitte des 18. Jahrhunderts nach den vorhandenen Textbüchern, Partituren und nach anderen gedruckten und handschriftlichen Quellenurkunden.* ("Neue Beiträge zur Geschichte der Musik und des Theaters am Herzoglichen Hofe zu Braunschweig-Wolfenbüttel," Erste Folge.) Munich, 1929.

————. *Die frühdeutsche Oper und die musikdramatische Kunst Georg Caspar Schürmann's.* 2 vols. Regensburg, 1933-34.

————. "Zur Geschichte, Dramaturgie und Statistik der frühdeutschen Oper (1627-1750)," *Zeitschrift für Musikwissenschaft,* V (1922-23), 582-97, 642-65; VI (1923-24), 129-57, 496-530.

Schneider, L[ouis]. *Geschichte der Oper und des königlichen Opernhauses in Berlin.* Berlin, 1852.

Schneider, Max. "Die Begleitung des Secco-Rezitativs um 1750," *Gluck Jahrbuch,* III (1917), 88-107.

Sesini, Ugo. *Libretti d'opera in musica.* ("Catalogo della biblioteca del Liceo Musicale di Bologna," Vol. V.) Bologna, 1943.

Sittard, Josef. *Zur Geschichte der Musik und des Theaters am württembergischen Hofe.* 2 vols. Stuttgart, 1890-91.

Sonneck, Oscar George Theodore. *Catalogue of Opera Librettos Printed before 1800.* 2 vols. Washington, D.C., 1914.

_____. "Il giocatore," *The Musical Antiquary,* IV (1912-13), 160-74.

Sorge, Giuseppe. *I teatri di Palermo nei secoli XVI-XVII-XVIII: Saggio storico.* Palermo, 1926.

Spitz, Charlotte. *Antonio Lotti in seiner Bedeutung als Opernkomponist.* Borna-Leipzig. 1918.

Subirá, José. *El teatro del Real Palacio (1849-1851) con un bosquejo preliminar sobre la música palatina desde Felipe V hasta Isabel II.* ("Monografías del Instituto Español de Musicología," Vol. IV.) Madrid, 1950.

Tardini, V[incenzo]. *I teatri di Modena: Contributo alla storia del teatro in Italia.* 3 vols. Modena. 1899-1902.

Travola cronologica di tutti li drammi o sia opere in musica recitate alli teatri detti del Falcone, e da S. Agostino da cento anni in addietro, cioè dall'anno 1670 in 1771 inclusive, con li nomi de' più celebri, e famosi musici attori, che hanno recitato con applauso in Genova in detti teatri, e quelli delle noblissime dame, cavalieri, e personaggi riguardevoli, a' quali sono state consecrate. Genoa, 1771.

Teuber, Oscar. *Geschichte des Prager Theaters von den Anfängen des Schauspielwesens bis auf die neueste Zeit.* 3 vols. Prague, 1883-88.

Toldo, Pietro. *L'OEuvre de Molière et sa fortune en Italie.* Turin, 1910.

Villars, F[ranz] de. *La serva padrona: Son apparition à Paris en 1752, son influence, son analyse, querelle des bouffons.* Paris, 1863.

[Villeneuve, Josse de]. *Lettre sur le mechanisme de l'opéra italien.* Paris, 1756.

Walker, Frank. "Goldoni and Pergolesi," *Monthly Musical Record,* LXXX (1950), 200-205.

_____. "Two Centuries of Pergolesi Forgeries and Misattributions," *Music and Letters,* XXX (1949), 297-320.

Walter, Friedrich. *Das Archiv und Bibliothek des Grossh. Hof- und Nationaltheaters in Mannheim.* 2 vols. Leipzig, 1899.

_____. *Geschichte des Theaters und der Musik am kurpfälzischen Hofe.*
("Forschungen zur Geschichte Mannheims und der Pfaltz," Vol. I.) Leipzig, 1898.

Weilen, Alexander von. *Zur wiener Theatergeschichte: Die vom Jahre 1629 bis zum
Jahre 1740 am wiener Hofe zur Aufführung gelangten Werke theatralischen
Charakters und Oratorien.* Vienna, 1901.

Werner, Th[eodor] W[ilhelm]. "Zum Neudruck von G. Ph. Telemanns *Pimpinone* in den
Reichsdenkmalen," *Archiv für Musikforschung,* I (1936), 361-65.

Wiel, Taddeo. *I teatri musicali veneziani del settecento: Catalogo delle opere in musica
rappresentate nel secolo XVIII in Venezia (1701-1800) con prefazione dell'autore.*
Venice, 1897.

Wolff, Hellmuth Christian. *Die Barockoper in Hamburg (1678-1738).* 2 vols. Wolfenbüttel,
1957.

_____. *Die venezianische Oper in der zweiten Hälfte des 17. Jahrhunderts.* ("Theater
und Drama," Vol. VII.) Berlin, 1937.

Worsthorne, Simon Towneley. *Venetian Opera in the Seventeenth Century.* Oxford, 1954.

Wotquenne, Alfred. *Libretti d'opéras et d'oratorios italiens du xviie siècle.* ("Catalogue
de la Bibliothèque du Conservatoire Royal de Musique de Bruxelles," Annexe I.)
Brussels, 1901.

Wright, Edward. *Some Observations Made in Travelling through France, Italy, &c. in the
Years 1720, 1721, and 1722.* 2 vols. London, 1730.

Zeller, Bernhard. *Das Recitativo accompagnato in den Opern Johann Adolf Hasses.*
Halle a.S., 1911.

INDEX

Included are titles, dramatis personae (female role first), composers, librettists, and singers of operatic intermezzi and comic scenes.